Dear Reader,

I don't know anyone who wasn't heartbroken upon learning of the 18-year ordeal that Jaycee Dugard survived after being abducted at the age of 11 near her home in South LakeTahoe, California. When she and her two young daughters revealed themselves to authorities in 2009, their courage won the hearts of millions.

Like so many others, I've read countless articles and watched numerous shows about beautiful Jaycee and her frightening abductor, Phillip Garrido. I thought I had a good understanding of their story. Then I read the book you are holding in your hands—and my eyes were opened to facts and insights that brought the story into a more vivid and more compelling focus.

Award-winning investigative reporter Robert Scott, the author of over a dozen widely praised nonfiction books, has uncovered aspects of this gripping case that will amaze, outrage, surprise, and move you.

As bestselling author and former prosecutor Robert K. Tanenbaum said:

"Robert Scott shows that the Jaycee Dugard story is more compelling and more shocking than the news previously reported. SHATTERED INNOCENCE is a fascinating account of a young girl's abduction by a monster who should never have been free to walk the streets. This is a ground-breaking book."

I invite you to share my sense of discovery by reading through this copy of SHATTERED INNOCENCE.

Michaela Hamilton

Michaela Hamilton
Executive Editor
Kensington Publishing Corp.

D0190981

Also by Robert Scott

SHATTERED INNOCENCE

ROBERT SCOTT

PINNACLE BOOKS
Kensington Publishing Corp.
http:///www.kensingtonbooks.com

Some names have been changed to protect the privacy of individuals connected to this story.

PINNACLE BOOKS are published by

Kensington Publishing Corp.
119 West 40th Street
New York, NY 10018

All Kensington Titles, Imprints, and Distributed Lines are available at special quantity discounts for bulk purchases for sales promotions, premiums, fund-raising, and educational or institutional use. Special book excerpts or customized printings can also be created to fit specific needs. For details, write or phone the office of the Kensington special sales manager: Kensington Publishing Corp., 119 West 40th Street, New York, NY 10018, attn: Special Sales Department, Phone: 1-800-221-2647.

Pinnacle and the P logo Reg. U.S. Pat. & TM Off.

ISBN-13: 978-0-7860-2411-7
ISBN-10: 0-7860-2411-9

First printing: September 2011

10 9 8 7 6 5 4 3 2 1

Printed in the United States of America

ACKNOWLEDGMENTS

I'd like to thank my great editors at Kensington, Richard Ember and Michaela Hamilton, for all their help on this book. Thanks also to the staff at the El Dorado County Court and Contra Costa County Court.

Children should never go to a bus stop alone. They're no match for an adult.

—Phillip Garrido

The innocence of the town was basically taken away that day.

—South Lake Tahoe mayor Jerry Birdwell

If you are alive after eighteen years, you did the right thing. I don't care what you did, it was the right thing.

—Ken Lanning

I'm so happy to be back!

—Jaycee Lee Dugard

I

BEYOND BELIEF

CHAPTER 1

ROBOT CLONES

August 24, 2009

Forty-year-old Lisa Campbell slowly walked into her office on the University of California (UC) campus at Berkeley after lunch. It was just another warm pleasant afternoon during summer break, but things would become more lively soon with incoming students for the fall semester. Lisa was the special events manager with the University of California Police Department (UCPD). A native of Chicago, she had been in police work for four years in Cook County, Illinois, and then eight years as an officer for the city of Chicago. Lisa eventually moved to California and, by 2009, had taken on many different tasks in her law enforcement career in San Diego and Los Angeles. One of those tasks had been working with issues about abused and neglected children.

Shortly after 1:00 P.M. on Monday, August 24, Lisa received a phone call from a records technician that there was a man in the lobby of Sproul Hall who wanted to meet with her about an upcoming event. The man said that he wanted to conduct some type of demonstration or lecture on campus. This was not an uncommon occurrence, and even though Lisa was busy, she told the records technician to send the man down to her office and she would schedule an appointment for him.

A short time later, a middle-aged man came into Lisa's office and he had two young girls who followed slowly behind him. One of the girls was in her mid-teens, and the other one looked to be about ten years old. Almost immediately, the man started telling Lisa about his organization in a very agitated voice. Much of what he was saying didn't make any sense to Lisa, and he rambled on and on in a disjointed manner, never really getting to the point. Finally Lisa interrupted him and said, "What can we do for you? How does this relate to the UC campus?"

The man took a breath and tried explaining himself, but he was still having a hard time conveying what he wanted Lisa to do for him. Lisa recalled later, "He wasn't consistent. His thoughts were all over the place. At one point, he did say, 'This is going to be really big! It has something to do with the government and the FBI.' He wanted UC Berkeley involved, because whatever was going to happen, was going to happen on campus."

Lisa told the man she had to schedule him for another appointment because she had so many other things to attend to that day. She asked him if she could schedule him for 2:00 P.M. on Tuesday, August 25, and he replied, "Yeah, that's great! Excellent! I look forward to sitting down with you. You're really going to love this! It's going to change the world! I'll see you tomorrow at two o'clock."

Lisa asked the man his name so that she could put it down on her calendar. He said his name was Phillip Garrido. When Lisa asked the man what the nature of the event was, Garrido responded, "It's called 'God's Desire.'"

Once the strange man and the two girls departed, Lisa was left with an uneasy feeling about the whole situation. She later said, "My initial impression of him was that he was clearly unstable. The girls were very quiet. They were very subdued. They were nonresponsive and didn't show the energy that children their age would normally do. They weren't in school, and that caught my attention. School had already started in the area. And the man—he was very animated, unlike the girls. The older girl stared straight up at the ceiling the whole time. She didn't make any eye contact at all."

Once the man and the girls left, Lisa was so uneasy about what had just occurred, she went to her captain in the UCPD and said, "This guy who came in was a little peculiar. There were things that just didn't settle right with me. I've scheduled an appointment for him to come back tomorrow at two o'clock, but I have some concerns about the kids he brought with him. I want to get a better assessment about them."

One reason Lisa had concerns was that she, in her police officer duties in Chicago, had often dealt with domestic violence and child welfare issues. She had seen her share of abused and molested children and knew how to read the nonverbal signs of such children. Many times they had furtive looks, the way the children whom Phillip Garrido had brought with him had. The two girls hadn't said anything negative to her while they were there, but as Lisa had told her police captain, something just didn't "settle right" with her about them.

* * *

On August 25, after lunch, Lisa contacted Allison "Ally" Jacobs, who was an officer with UCPD, to come in and "size up" the man who had been there on the previous day. Lisa told Ally, "There are some things about him and the kids that are alarming. I'd like you to be another trained eye on this. You might see something I don't."

Ally asked if Lisa had the man's name, and Lisa said that it was Phillip Garrido. Ally replied, "Well, let's run him [through the computer system]. We need to see why you're so concerned."

Ally went to the dispatch center and ran a routine records check on Phillip Garrido. What she found did indeed alarm her. Phillip Craig Garrido was listed as a federal parolee who had been convicted of kidnapping and rape in 1976. He was also a registered sex offender within the state of California. The fact that there had been two young girls with him the previous day really concerned Ally. She said later, "It sent up red flags right away." Ally wondered who those two girls were and what their relationship was to the man.

Ally recalled, "Lisa had mentioned that the two young kids didn't seem right. I thought this could be something a little more than we bargained for. I went back to Lisa and told her about what I'd just found out about Garrido. Then I asked her, 'What do you want me to do?'"

Lisa replied that she wanted Ally to sit in with her when Garrido came back to her office at two o'clock. If they were lucky, he would bring the girls with him once more. Lisa said, "Can you just watch this guy and see if there is something wrong? I'm not a sworn police officer here, but you are. Maybe there is something a police officer might have to deal with at the time."

Ally agreed to sit with Lisa, after briefly telling her sergeant about the matter. The sergeant agreed it was something worth doing, and told Ally to go ahead and sit in with Lisa and make her own observations about the man. Obviously there was something not quite right with the situation, since most registered sex offenders cannot have children accompany them. But at that point, none of the officers knew what the problem might be.

Around 2:30 P.M. on August 25, Phillip Garrido and the two girls walked back into the UCPD building on campus. Ally recalled, "Lisa and I walked into her office, with Phillip Garrido right behind us, and then the girls. There was an empty desk in Lisa's office and I made like it was my desk. We didn't want to alert him to anything. We didn't really know what we were dealing with. We wanted to just keep it really mellow and see what was going on here.

"As we walked in, I introduced myself as Officer Jacobs, and told him, 'This is my desk, and that's Lisa's desk.' We all sat down and Lisa asked, 'How can I help you?' His youngest daughter sat down in a chair directly across from me, about five feet away. The older daughter stood next to her, directly between her and Phillip. And he was standing right in front of Lisa's desk.

"He put down his attaché case, opened it, and pulled out a book about 'Schizophrenia and the FBI.' When I say a book, it was more like a bunch of typed pages in book form. He opened it up and just started talking about it. It was really hard to understand what he was talking about, and Lisa kept saying, 'How can we help you, sir? How can special events help you?' She was trying to get him back on track."

Phillip Garrido was too wound up, however, to settle down and keep on track. He told Lisa and Ally that this project was going to be "Huge! It was God's Desire." And then suddenly out of nowhere, he stated, "Years ago, I was arrested for kidnapping and rape."

Ally recounted, "I already knew that, but I didn't think he would say something like that in front of those two girls." Ally looked for some kind of reaction on the girls' faces to Garrido's comment. There wasn't any reaction at all, however, which was strange in it own right.

Phillip then stated, "I've learned differently now." And he started expounding about his relationship with God and Jesus and how they had changed his life. Whatever he was trying to explain concerned his "book" and the event had something to do with this revelation, but he was not making himself clear to either Lisa or Ally.

Ally recalled, "I was having a really hard time following his thoughts. So I focused my attention on the two girls. At first they really blended into the background. I didn't understand why they were really there at all. And I said to Mr. Garrido, 'Sorry to interrupt you, but who are these two young ladies?'"

Phillip answered, "Oh, these are my daughters," and he introduced them to Ally and Lisa as Angel and Starlit. (Sometimes also spelled as Starlet or Starlite.)

Ally turned to the girls and asked, "How old are you?"

The younger one said she was eleven, and the older one fifteen.

Ally asked, "Do you go to school?"

In quick response, they both answered as if on cue, "We're homeschooled."

Ally recalled, "One of the first things I noticed right away was the coloring of the girls. They were extremely pale in comparison to Phillip. They both had bright blue eyes, just like his—penetrating blue eyes. But they were so pale. I just got a weird, uneasy feeling about them.

"I was looking at the younger girl, who was sitting directly in front of me. It was almost as if she was looking into my soul. That's how her eyes were so penetrating. And she had a smirk on her face. The older daughter, her eyes would dart up at the ceiling. Then she would look at her dad, as if she worshipped him.

"When we asked questions, the younger daughter would focus her attention on us. She would give eye contact and answer our questions. The older one, not so much. Her eyes were just all over the place around the room. I kind of got the feeling the kids were like robots."

Ally noticed that the younger daughter had a bump near one eye. It was covered over somewhat by her hair, and Ally stated when she saw that, "I kind of went into police mode to investigate if abuse had happened. While I was talking to her, Lisa was talking to Phillip Garrido. I asked the girl what had happened to her eye. She immediately replied, with a very rehearsed response, 'It's a birth defect. It's inoperable. I'll have it for the rest of my life.'

"I was taken aback by that response. Because if I was a little girl and somebody asked me about this thing on my face, I would probably be a little embarrassed. But she didn't seem embarrassed at all. She just wouldn't stop smiling.

"It was then that my police mode turned into my mother mode. I have two young sons, and I think that was a key factor, what with police intuition and a mother's intuition. I wasn't focused on Garrido, because I'm used to the rantings and ravings of people because of the job I do. I focused more on the girls."

Lisa was very aware of the strange situation as well. She later said, "All while Ally was focused on the girls,

Phillip had pulled out his book. He was showing me pages and trying to tell us more about his program and what he'd written in his book. He wasn't clear and he wasn't concise. He just couldn't stay focused. He jumped all over the place and was very animated. But he was very persistent about what he was talking about, which created a distraction for Ally to talk to the girls. When he looked over at her, I would try to engage him, and Ally and I kind of played off each other.

"If he looked at Ally, it was an opportunity for me to look at the girls. The older one at one point had eye contact with me. Immediately she looked back up at the ceiling. The younger one had a kind of smirk on her face, but she engaged us a little bit more. During the whole time, Phillip never stopped talking."

Ally noted the girls were very drab in appearance, and recalled, "They were dressed in a monotone fashion. It was almost like *Little House on the Prairie* meets robot clones. They were sitting and standing like robots. The younger one didn't move and she had an eerie smile on her face the whole time. And the older one had rehearsed answers. She really didn't like talking to us.

"At one point, I focused my attention on the home-schooling aspect. I wanted to know a little bit more about the family's life. By now, I was back in police mode. I was thinking, 'What kind of crimes do I have here?' I asked about their homeschooling and I asked Mr. Garrido if he taught them. Did his wife teach? He said, 'My wife teaches, and I help with that.'

"Then the younger girl said, 'We have an older sister that lives with us, too. She's twenty-eight.'

"Immediately the older girl said, without missing a beat, 'She's twenty-nine.' And she looked right up at her dad. She seemed bothered that this was mentioned."

At the time, Ally didn't think much about the comment concerning the older sister. She just noted that there was another young woman in the Garrido household that was either twenty-eight or twenty-nine years old and sister to these two others. Ally was mainly focusing on whether there was a crime involved with this situation, and tried to figure out if there was something upon which she could detain Phillip Garrido. She wondered if she needed to call Child Protective Services (CPS) or the Berkeley Mental Health Services to come in.

Ally noted, "Phillip was clearly disturbed. I didn't know if he took medication or not. All of this was going through my head as I sat there. My training was kicking in, and I was thinking, 'What do I have here? What can I do?'

"All of this happened within a matter of minutes. I think the whole meeting from beginning to end was less than fifteen minutes long. So while Lisa was talking to him, I was in cop mode, thinking, 'What can I do?' Basically, I couldn't come up with anything at the moment. I was searching the younger daughter's face for any kind of sign from her. I was just looking at her to see if she would give me a sign—'Help me!' Any kind of sign if she couldn't talk. But I wasn't reading anything from those kids.

"Knowing that I probably couldn't pull them away from their dad to talk to them, I decided what I was doing was all I could do at present. Just listen, send them on their way, and maybe contact the parole officer."

At the end of the meeting, Ally spoke up and said to Phillip, "Sir, what would you like for us to do for you? Would you like to forward me that book, and I hand it on to my supervisor? Would that make you happy?"

Phillip answered enthusiastically, "Yes, would you, please!"

Garrido gave Lisa and Ally a copy of the book as

well. Ally noticed that he had been shaking a lot during his conversation with Lisa, and without warning, he now grabbed his oldest daughter and unexpectedly said, "I'm so proud of my girls! They don't know any curse words. They don't know anything bad about the world."

Ally recalled at that moment, "I felt so horrible for those girls. I knew there was something wrong. But I just said to him, 'Well, you should be proud. You have two lovely daughters.'"

At that point, Phillip and the girls went on their way; and for a moment, Ally and Lisa just looked at each other. The whole meeting had been bizarre and surreal in the extreme. Ally recalled, "Lisa and I turned toward each other, and I heaved a big sigh. I said to her, 'What do we do now?' I told Lisa my thoughts and said, 'We can't call CPS. We can't call Berkeley Health. I don't know what to do. There's no real crime here. I can't prove anything.' We were just talking and saying there was something up with those girls, but we didn't know what. We didn't know what kind of activities were happening at their home. We didn't have any proof. As a cop, you want to have proof before you act. I was very frustrated.

"I told Lisa the only thing I can do right now is call Phillip Garrido's parole officer and talk to him. Maybe this is Phillip's normal behavior and they're already aware of it, and maybe I was just taking all of this out of context."

Deciding that calling the parole officer was the only viable course of action, Ally phoned Phillip Garrido's officer, who was not in his office at the time. She left a message on the answering machine and described her concerns. She described how disturbed Phillip Garrido seemed and all the strange material he brought to the UC office. Ally also said that he had brought his two young daughters with him and they seemed out of touch with reality and very robotic. Ally stated that she'd like the parole officer to call her back and perhaps they could set up a meeting where she could go into further details about her concerns.

As Ally noted, "I thought that was going to be the end of it. But the parole officer called me back the next day. He said, 'Can you please tell me the situation again?' So I described the situation to him. And he stopped me when I said that Phillip Garrido brought his two daughters to campus. He said, 'He doesn't have any daughters!'

"My stomach just sank. I said, 'Well, he had two daughters with him that day. They had his blue eyes. They looked like him. They were calling him 'Daddy.' I had no reason to believe they weren't his daughters. And they even referenced an elder sister at home.'

"The parole officer replied, 'Well, I think he had some granddaughters. I'm not sure. Let me double-check on that. What I'll do, I'll call him into the office and I'll meet with him. I'll just tell him that because of parole he's not allowed to come back to your campus.'"

Ally said later, "I thought, 'Great. That's fine with me. My job is done.'"

Ally Jacobs and Lisa Campbell's job on the matter might have been over for the moment, but within hours, their lives and many other lives around them would never be the same. By late afternoon on Wednesday, August 26, 2009, the San Francisco Bay Area and the whole world would know what had occurred in their office on the UC Berkeley campus. And like everyone else, both Ally and Lisa would be absolutely stunned by what was revealed.

CHAPTER 2

A YOUNG WOMAN NAMED "ALYSSA"

Edward Santos was a parole agent working out of the Fairfield, California, office in 2009. If there was any one constant with parole agents in that office, it was that they all had very heavy case loads. In Contra Costa County alone, where Phillip Garrido lived near the city of Antioch, there were hundreds of registered sex offenders whose cases had to be attended to.

Santos already knew that Phillip Garrido, age fifty-eight, lived with his wife Nancy, fifty-four, east of Antioch, on semirural Walnut Avenue. Walnut Avenue was a collection of modest homes, with large backyards and lots of trees. In the background, across the railroad tracks, were the remains of the paper mills that had once dominated the area. The paper mills had been closed for years by 2009, but a handful of other industries were still scattered along the south shore of the San Joaquin River. A few small grape vineyards were also located near Walnut Avenue, and an extensive Catholic cemetery was three blocks from the Garrido home.

Most of the people who lived in the Garrido neighborhood were either working-class or retired. Some of them knew that he was a registered sex offender and was on parole. Many others had no clue that he was a sex offender. Most didn't know a great deal about him, other than he sometimes acted strangely and would come up to them talking about his religious beliefs. And they knew that he sometimes wandered down the street, singing as he walked along. Most of the songs were religious in nature, although he would mix in old rock tunes on occasion.

Phillip, who generally went by the name Phil, was six feet four inches tall, weighed two hundred pounds, and had thinning hair. Only recently, within the last year, he had been required by state law to wear a GPS monitoring device around one of his ankles. All of this stemmed from the kidnapping and rape of a woman in the Lake Tahoe region in 1976. Phil had taken the woman across state lines from California to Nevada, and because of that reason, he had served his time in federal prison. But since 1989, Phil had been out of prison and on parole. Eventually the federal government relinquished parole on Phil, but the state of Nevada did not, concerning its case against him. And in essence, California parole agents were "watching over Phil" on Nevada's case. As it turned out, "watching" was very loosely enforced when it came to Phil Garrido.

On the afternoon of August 25, 2009, Parole Agent Santos received a phone call on his answering machine from UCPD officer Ally Jacobs. Officer Jacobs, of course, had left a message about her meeting with

Phil Garrido and his two daughters at the UC Berkeley campus. When Santos phoned Jacobs back, she was already gone from work for the day. But because of the disturbing information that she had left on his answering machine, Santos decided to take a trip out to Garrido's residence on Walnut Avenue.

At around 6:00 P.M., Santos and Agent LaGrassa contacted Phil at his home, and Phil answered the door. Not quite knowing what was going on, the agents placed handcuffs on Phil's wrists to be on the safe side, and they escorted him outside the house. Agent La-Grassa stayed outside with Phil, while Santos went back into the house, where he contacted Phil's wife, Nancy, and Phil's elderly mother, Patricia, often known as Pat. It was quite obvious that Phil's mother suffered from memory loss. Santos searched the entire house, but found no one else there. Nonetheless, because of Officer Ally Jacobs's message, the parole agents took Phil to the Concord Parole Office, about twenty-five miles west of Walnut Avenue, for questioning about the two girls whom he had called his daughters.

All the way there, Phil was adamant that he hadn't done anything wrong. He kept saying that the kids Jacobs had seen were actually those of his brother, and Officer Jacobs misunderstood him when he said they were his daughters. Phil added that one of the girls' parents had come and picked them up from Walnut Avenue when he returned home from Berkeley. He also said that the parents had given him permission to take the girls to UC Berkeley.

When Phil and the agents reached the Concord Parole Office, Santos checked Phil Garrido's file. Then Santos contacted his supervisior, G. Sims, at the Fairfield Parole Office, and discussed the file on Garrido with Sims. Even though Garrido had a "no contact with minors" clause in the file, it was discovered there was no "nexus" as to why that was there. In parole agent terms, this was an SCOP (special condition of parole). There was one new amendment in the file dating back to July 2009, prohibiting Phil from being in the presence of minors. But on August 25, 2009, the parole agent and supervisor decided that the condition didn't apply to Phil at the moment because Phil had no current or prior convictions involving minors. His kidnapping and rape conviction from 1976 had concerned an adult female. Not knowing what to do about all of this, Agents Santos and LaGrassa took Phil Garrido back home and told him to report to the Concord Parole Office again, at eight the following morning.

Phil Garrido, wife Nancy, the two girls who had been with Phil at UC Berkeley, and a young blond woman, who appeared to be in her late twenties, all trooped into the Concord Parole Office about 8:10 A.M. on August 26. They came in while Santos was on the phone with Officer Ally Jacobs. Phil signed in at the front desk, and Nancy, the young blond woman, and the two girls took seats in the lobby. As soon as Santos came back to the lobby, Phil Garrido waved for Nancy, the young woman, and the two girls to follow him, and they all started to make their way toward Santos's office.

Santos told Phil to wait alone outside the office, and he asked Nancy, the young woman, and the two girls to follow him to a conference room. When they all sat down, Santos introduced himself as Phil's parole agent. Then he asked the young blond woman and the two girls their names. The young woman said that her name was Alyssa Franzen. (At later times, her name would be spelled as Allissa, Alicia, and Alissa.) After Phil's mother, Patricia, divorced, she remarried and became Patricia Franzen. The oldest girl said her name was Angel, and the youngest one was named Starlit, or Starlet, or Starlite, depending on who was talking about her. Alyssa looked over at Nancy Garrido, while Santos said that he needed information on the parents of the two girls. Immediately Alyssa spoke up and said that she was their mother.

Santos said with astonishment, "You look too young to be their mother!"

Alyssa laughed and replied, "I get that all the time from people. They think I'm their sister."

Santos wanted to know how old Alyssa was, and she told him that she was twenty-nine. When Santos asked her for identification, Alyssa said that she had left it at home. Santos wanted to know the date of her birth, and she said that it was May 3, 1980. Asked to spell her full name, she hesitated for a moment, then spelled it out loud and slowly: Allissa Franzen. This, of course, was different from Alyssa, which would become the most common spelling of her name.

Asked where Alyssa and the girls lived, she said sometimes they stayed with relatives of Phil and Nancy Garrido; other times, they stayed with Phil and Nancy at Walnut Avenue. Santos noted, "While I tried to get further information about Alyssa and the girls, she became defensive and agitated. She wanted to know why she was being interrogated by me. Nancy quickly jumped into the conversation and said, 'Yes, Agent Santos, why are you interrogating us? We have done nothing wrong.'"

Santos explained to them that he was not interrogating them, but rather was looking into an incident that had occurred on the UC Berkeley campus with Phil and two young girls on the previous day. Alyssa spoke up and said that she was aware that Phil had taken the two young girls in question to UC on

August 25, and also acknowledged that she knew he was a registered sex offender and on parole. Alyssa declared that she had no problem with Phil taking the girls to the UC campus.

Santos asked Alyssa if she knew what crime Phil had committed. Alyssa responded that it was for kidnapping and rape of a woman many years previously. Then Alyssa added that he was a changed man and was a great person around her kids. "He has a gift!" she declared. After Alyssa said this, the two girls chimed in and spoke up in Phil Garrido's defense. They claimed he was a great person and had never done anything objectionable around them. In fact, the girls praised him to the realm of adoration.

Santos tried to get more personal information about Alyssa, but she dug in her heels and wouldn't answer his questions. She even asked if she needed a lawyer at that point. Santos tried to reassure her that any information she gave out about herself or the girls was going to stay in the file and not be made public. Once again, however, Alyssa became agitated and stated, "I haven't done anything wrong!"

Seeing that he was getting nowhere with them, Santos asked Nancy, Alyssa, and the two girls to go downstairs and wait, while he spoke with Phil Garrido alone. Once the women and girls had gone downstairs, they left the building and went out to the parking lot and sat in their vehicle. Santos then went back to the lobby and escorted Phil to his office.

Santos began by asking Phil what his relationship was to Alyssa and the two girls. Phil answered the question by posing a question of his own: "What do you mean?"

Not to be put off, Santos asked the same question again, and after thinking about it for a while, Phil answered, "They are all sisters." Phil then said that he thought Alyssa was twenty-eight or twenty-nine years old.

Santos asked who the girls' father was, and once again Phil thought for a while before saying, "A relative of mine." So Santos asked one more time, and Phil gave a very odd answer, "He's the son of my mother."

Santos replied in amazement, "So that makes him your brother?"

Santos noted, "He looked at me with astonishment and said, 'Yes.'"

Then Phil added that the girls' parents were divorced and that they sometimes lived with his brother, Ron, and sometimes with their mother. At other times, the girls lived with himself and Nancy. Asked where Ron lived, Phil said that he didn't know the address or phone number, but that he lived somewhere in Oakley, California, about five miles from the Garrido home. Asked about the girls' mother, Phil said her name was Janice and that she lived in Brentwood, California. He also said that he didn't know her address or phone number.

At the end of this conversation, Santos escorted Phil to a different office and had a parole agent stay there with him. Because of all the inconsistent information he was getting, Santos contacted Agent Lovan, and they went to talk to Nancy, Alyssa, and the two girls in the parking lot. Santos took Alyssa back into a room separately from the others, and asked her why she had lied to him previously. Alyssa asked, "What do you mean?" Santos replied, "Phil just told me that you are those girls' older sister and not their mother."

To this, Alyssa looked confused and finally said that she was the guardian of the two girls, so she considered herself to be their mother. Santos wasn't having any of this double-talk and told Alyssa if she continued to refuse to cooperate, he would contact Child Protective

Services and the local police department. Faced with that prospect, Alyssa admitted, "I'm their biological mother."

Trying to get any more information out of Alyssa by this point was like trying to pull nails. Santos insisted that she give him some identification or an address and phone number of relatives of the girls. To this, Alyssa replied that she had learned a long time ago not to carry any personal information around or to give that information to strangers. Santos asked her to explain herself, and Alyssa kept repeating that she didn't know why she was being interrogated and that she might need a lawyer.

It's not apparent when Nancy Garrido joined Santos and Alyssa, but she was there at some point and started telling Alyssa that she needed a lawyer. Then suddenly Alyssa's demeanor seemed to change and she became more concerned about the girls' welfare than her own. Santos asked Alyssa why Phil had said the girls were her sisters. Alyssa replied, "He was just trying to protect me."

So Santos asked what Phil was trying to protect her from, but she wouldn't answer. And to all other questions about herself, Alyssa clammed up. Getting absolutely nowhere, at 9:17 A.M., Santos called 911 and had them contact the Concord Police Department (CPD). Santos requested an officer come over to his location and assist him in this matter.

While waiting for an officer to arrive, Alyssa continued saying, "I don't know what is going on! I've done nothing wrong!" Starlit spoke up and said that she needed to use the restroom immediately. Because Santos didn't want any of the females out of his sight by that point, and they were not supposed to use the restroom in the parole office, he escorted them to the adjacent Concord Public Library, which had restroom facilities. Once they got there, however, he discovered that the restroom was closed.

At that point, Alyssa said to Santos, "I'm sorry I lied to you." And then she added that she was from Minnesota and that she was hiding from an abusive husband. Alyssa declared that she had been on the run for five years and was terrified of being found by her ex-husband. Then she patted Santos's shoulder and said, "You can see why I learned a long time ago never to give out my personal information."

Santos reassured her again that none of the information she gave him would be made public, but Alyssa said she couldn't take that chance. Soon thereafter, Officer Mike Von Savoye arrived from the Concord Police Department and Santos briefed him on the situation. Officer Von Savoye tried getting information from Alyssa, but she was just as uncooperative with him as she had been with Santos. Even when another CPD officer came on scene, Officer Kaiser, Alyssa was just as adamant in her refusal to give personal information.

Meanwhile, Starlit was becoming more and more insistent that she needed to use a restroom. The parole officer finally agreed to let her use the restroom in the parole office complex, and Alyssa was separated once again from Nancy Garrido and the two girls. To Officer Kaiser's requests for information, Alyssa gave the story of being on the run from an abusive ex-husband. Not long thereafter, Phil Garrido was allowed into the room. Santos noted, "It appeared that Alyssa kept looking to him for answers. Garrido stated that she should get a lawyer."

At that point, Santos escorted Phil out of the room once more, back to his office. There Santos asked, "Why is she protecting you?"

"What do you mean?" Phil asked with surprise.

"She's trying to protect you from something."

To this, Phil only replied, "She needs a lawyer."

By now, the whole complex was filling up with policemen. CPD sergeant Hoffman arrived in Santos's office and said to Phil, "Tell us what the female's name is." Santos left the room to see if Alyssa had given out any more information to Officer Kaiser or Officer Savage. Shortly thereafter, while still in Santos's office, Sergeant Hoffman spoke to Santos and told him some very startling news. Phil Garrido had just admitted to Hoffman that he was the father of Angel and Starlit.

Santos's mind was practically spinning at this point. He returned to his own office and asked Phil, "Why have you made us go through all of this?"

Phil mumbled something to the effect that he wasn't sure why he had done so.

Santos asked Phil, "Did you do it because you didn't want Nancy to know?"

Phil immediately responded, "Oh, no! She knows and she forgave me a long time ago."

Santos countered, "This doesn't make any sense! There has to be another reason!"

Phil continued to evade answering Santos's questions, but Santos was persistent. Finally Phil said that if they brought Alyssa back into the room, he would tell Santos all about the confusion and double-talk. Santos replied, "I'll only let you do that if you first tell me what you're going to say to her. I don't want you dropping a bomb on her!" Then Santos asked Phil if Alyssa knew where her parents were located. Phil answered that she knew they lived somewhere in Los Angeles.

Santos's later reports would be confusing as to when certain events exactly happened. Part of that may have stemmed from the confusing nature of the varied stories he was getting from Phil, Nancy, and Alyssa. Whatever the exact timing, at some point, Phil Garrido spoke these words to Santos: "A long, long time ago, I kidnapped and raped Alyssa."

Santos exited the room with this information and gave it to Sergeant Hoffman. In the next moment, it wasn't Phillip Garrido who dropped a bombshell. It was Alyssa. After all the intransigence and double-talk, Alyssa indicted that she was Jaycee Dugard.

It was if a ghost had suddenly appeared in the room. Eleven-year-old Jaycee Lee Dugard had been kidnapped in South Lake Tahoe, California, on June 10, 1991. She had remained missing for eighteen years, and most people believed she was long dead. When Alyssa indicted that she was Jaycee Dugard, she set off seismic waves that were about to circle the entire planet.

CHAPTER 3

VANISHED

On May 3, 1980, Terry Dugard had a daughter whom she named Jaycee Lee. Terry was a single mother, and for the first ten years of Jaycee's life, the household belonged to only her and her mom. Then Terry met a forty-year-old man named Carl Probyn, and they were married. The new family moved into a house in a suburb of Los Angeles.

In 1989, a baby girl was born to the Probyns and they named her Shayna. The next summer, the entire family made what turned out to be a fateful trip to Lake Tahoe. Carl and Terry loved the area so much, they decided to move there. Pulling up stakes from Southern California, the Probyn family moved into a house on Washoan Boulevard, in the small town of Meyers, adjacent to the city of South Lake Tahoe. At 6,300 feet, Meyers was a vast change from the urban landscape they had been used to. Just south of the street, uninhabited forests stretched clear up to ten-thousand-foot Mount Freel, the highest peak in the region.

Jaycee Lee Dugard (Jaycee always using her mother's maiden name) initially had some problems with the new blended family. Jaycee was hesitant at first to accept her new stepfather into her life, because she had spent so many years alone with her mother. In fact, Jaycee never knew who her biological father was.

Once the move was made to Lake Tahoe, however, things seemed to be getting a lot better, as far as Jaycee accepting the new dynamics of her family. Carl later said of the move, "Things got a million percent better."

Jaycee was a quiet, shy girl, so she had a hard time making new friends at school. One girl at Meyers Elementary School who knew Jaycee was Nicole Sipes. Sipes later said, "She was a new kid. She was kind of soft-spoken and kept to herself a little bit."

But Meyers Elementary School principal Karen Gillis related that Jaycee was liked by the other students, even though she was shy. And Jaycee eventually joined the Girl Scouts and played on a soccer team.

Terry was a good mom and showered both of her daughters with love and affection. And as time went on, Jaycee began to accept, more and more, her life in Tahoe, with a new blended family, new friends, and a new school. In fact, Jaycee was so fond of school, she hated to see the school year end in June 1991. One thing Jaycee did look forward to in the summer was her hope that she would be able to work with horses during the school break. The Tahoe area was a wonderland of forests, meadows, mountains, and lakes, and the whole family, including Jaycee, loved the area. The prospect that she could work with horses over the summer months was more than just a pipe dream. There were several stables not far from where the Probyns lived.

On the evening of Sunday, June 9, 1991, Terry later related that Jaycee was still feeling some of the effects of the blended family life, and she said to Terry, "You never talk to me anymore, Mom!"

Terry recalled, "So we sat down and talked. Jaycee let me know that she wanted a dog and a set of fourteen-dollar markers for drawing." Terry made no promises about the dog, but she did promise to buy Jaycee the markers, as well as a new bathing suit. Then Terry added, "I gave her a big hug and a big kiss and scooted her off to bed."

Monday morning, June 10, 1991, seemed like any other Monday morning in the Probyn household, except for one thing. On that morning, Terry vowed that she would make it to work on time for a change. Terry always had problems of being late on Monday mornings to her job at a local printing shop, and she wanted to break that habit. Terry recalled, "That morning, I walked out the door without kissing Jaycee good-bye. I broke my routine."

After Terry left for work, Jaycee started up the road, at around 8:05 A.M., to the school bus stop on the Pioneer Trail. She was a real trouper, and had walked that route even in the depths of winter when the snow along the Tahoe roads could reach immense heights. It was a cool breezy June morning now, with just a hint of the coming summer. As Jaycee walked along Washoan Boulevard, the only sounds were the birds in the trees.

Carl was at work in his garage, and he happened to look down the road and noticed an older gray sedan slowly drive by Jaycee. Then according to Carl, "It drove up toward the house and then made an awkward U-turn back toward Jaycee."

Carl looked on in stunned surprise as the sedan, without any warning, pulled right in front of Jaycee and blocked her path. Then the passenger door opened and a dark-haired woman jumped out. In total disbelief, Carl watched as the woman grabbed Jaycee and pulled the screaming girl into the car.

Carl related, "I immediately jumped on my bike. I didn't have my car keys on me. I pedaled up hill as fast as I could toward the car." The car began to take off and Carl followed, pedaling for all he was worth. According to Carl, the hill was steep and the car was soon moving out of sight. Knowing that he would never catch it, Carl raced back home and called 911.

Within two minutes of the abduction, Carl was giving the dispatcher a description about the kidnapping and the car. Carl said that the woman who snatched Jaycee had long dark hair and a dark complexion. He thought she might have been of Middle Eastern ethnicity. It was an older model, two-tone sedan, and dark gray in color, with lighter gray trim. And as far as Jaycee Lee went, Carl said that she was eleven years old, weighed eighty pounds, and stood four feet six inches tall. She had blue eyes and long blond hair, tied up in a ponytail. She was wearing pink stretch pants, a white blouse, a pink sweater, a shiny pink windbreaker, and tennis shoes. She had been carrying a blue denim book bag.

Apparently, the first responder was a California Highway Patrol (CHP) officer who was the closest law enforcement officer in the area. Within a very short time, there were South Lake Tahoe Police Department (SLTPD) cars on the scene and El Dorado County Sheriff's Office (EDSO) vehicles as well. They fanned out looking for the two-tone gray sedan. Soon thereafter, more CHP officers were sent out, scouring the area for the sedan and the kidnapped girl. U.S. Forest Service personnel joined the hunt, as did a police helicopter. Even casino security guards across the state

line in Nevada began searching the casino parking lots
for the gray sedan.

There was a huge dragnet of officers all over the
area within an hour of the kidnapping. This was unusual, compared to a lot of child abduction cases,
where a child could go missing for hours or even days
without anyone being sure that she was more than just
a runaway. Often valuable time was lost before it could
be ascertained that the child had been kidnapped and
had not simply run away from home. With Jaycee Lee
Dugard, none of that precious time was wasted with
false assumptions.

Around 9:15 A.M., a police officer showed up at the
place where Terry Probyn worked. Terry said later,
"My first reaction when I saw the officer was that I had
a parking ticket or something to do with the IRS.
Then he said to me, 'Ma'am, we have reason to believe your daughter has been kidnapped.' I basically
lost my heart."

Because ex-husbands and ex-boyfriends were always
on the top of the list for child abductions, Terry was
asked about this situation. Terry told an officer that
she didn't even know where Jaycee Lee's biological
father lived now or how to get in touch with him. She
thought he might be living in Southern California.
When Jaycee's father was finally contacted, it came as
a complete surprise to him. He said later that he didn't
even know he had a daughter with Terry. Before long,
it became apparent to law enforcement officers that
this man had nothing to do with Jaycee's abduction.
A police spokesperson soon said, "This appears to be
a legitimate kidnapping. However, we have not received a ransom demand. There has been an airplane

and helicopter out there in the search. We've got everybody in the world out there looking for her."

It may not have been everybody in the world, but there were plenty of law enforcement personnel out looking for Jaycee, her kidnappers, and the vehicle they had been driving. Before long, there were also plenty of citizen volunteers in the area keeping an eye out for the car as well. Local radio stations KOWL, KRLT, and KTHO ran numerous announcements about the kidnapping and the details about the girl, the car, and the dark-haired woman kidnapper.

A kidnap hotline was set up by the El Dorado Sheriff's Office and posters of the missing girl began running off copy machines at an incredible rate. So were copies of a sketch of the kidnappers' vehicle and a rendering of the dark-haired woman. She was depicted in frontal view and in profile. She had shoulder-length hair, dark-colored eyes, and dark eyebrows. Some locals described her as "witchy-looking," and others wondered if she was a meth user. The sketch showed a woman with sunken cheeks, a common side effect of meth use.

Because Lake Tahoe was a tourist destination, a lot of visitors took posters with them before they returned home. Trish Williams, of Child Quest International, noted, "The visitors will be going back home and they'll be taking these pictures with them. The more widespread this information becomes, the better. There's a lot the public can do." Within two days of the abduction, there was also a $5,000 reward on the El Dorado County Secret Witness Tip Line for information leading to the arrest of the kidnapping suspects.

Although Williams spoke as if the kidnappers had secreted Jaycee out of the Tahoe Basin, the local sheriff's office was not so sure about that. Their main focus was still on the assumption that the kidnappers were locals, holed up somewhere in the area. It could be in a home, apartment, cabin, motor home, or even in a tent out in the woods somewhere. The city of South Lake Tahoe might have been urban, but the surrounding area was mountainous and heavily forested. There were a thousand and one places the kidnappers and Jaycee could be hidden, and not even a helicopter crew could spot them. A spokesman for the El Dorado County Sheriff's Office said of the situation, "We believe the kidnappers are still in the Tahoe Basin. That's our best shot. We haven't had a sighting elsewhere."

The kidnapping, of course, had sent a chill through the area, especially for parents whose children went to Meyers Elementary School. One of the Probyns' neighbors told a reporter, "The kids are always walking up here to the bus stop. I did see one on Monday morning, with blond hair and a white blouse. Had I known, I would have come out of the house."

Debra Walker, whose daughter sometimes walked to and from the school bus stop with Jaycee Lee, said, "There's a lot of kids who come to that bus stop. And there's usually two cars filled with parents that watch the children there." Whether or not there were any parents in cars watching that day, Walker didn't know. But she added, "Even if there were, I don't think it would have mattered. The kidnapping happened so quickly, I don't think it would have mattered."

Two days after Jaycee's abduction, Terry Probyn held a press conference attended by print reporters and television reporters. Clutching her young daughter, Shayna, and a stuffed pink bunny, Terry made an emotional plea to the kidnappers. "Please don't hurt her! She's a good girl. Just drop her off. No questions asked. You may like her, but we love her, too. And it's time for her to come home to her family! Her sissy's been asking for her."

Then Terry spoke directly to the cameras and to Jaycee. "If you're watching out there, you know I love you!"

One reporter asked Terry what she hoped for from the community. Terry answered, "Pray for my daughter."

The El Dorado County sheriff, who was also at the press conference, was asked why he thought Jaycee had been targeted. Sheriff Don McDonald replied that he didn't know, and surmised that the kidnapping might have been a random act. The kidnappers may have seen Jaycee walking down Washoan Boulevard and merely acted on impulse. Detective Jim Watson let it be known that there were canine units and horse units out searching the woods of the area.

Even then, there was a segment of media hysteria, which would be so present years later concerning Jaycee. One journalist who was there was a man named Mike Taugher, and he witnessed some disturbing behavior by certain reporters. Mike recalled, much later, for the Bay Area News Group, "At one point, a well-dressed woman at the back of the swarm of reporters yelled, 'What are you hiding in that house?'" Apparently, she was angry because law enforcement would not let her camera crew into the Probyn home. Taugher wrote, *I figured later she must have worked for a television tabloid show. All I knew at the time was that she was scum, and she looked like well-paid scum.*

By now, the reward for Jaycee had grown by a multiplier of six to $30,000. One wealthy couple from Marin County, California, had put up $10,000 of their own money to the reward fund. They weren't even related to Terry Probyn or Jaycee, nor had they ever known them. They had simply been touched by the Probyn family's plight and concern for the missing girl.

Law enforcement was receiving tips and possible sightings at the rate of one per every five minutes, and reports came in from as far away as Minneapolis, Minnesota, about the missing girl. Three days after the kidnapping, police scrambled in Vacaville, California, which was about one hundred miles west of Lake Tahoe, when a vehicle matching the kidnappers' sedan was spotted. It turned out to be a false alarm.

Even more promising was a report in South Lake Tahoe. A vehicle matching the police drawing was spotted in town, and pink pants were lying on the floorboard of the vehicle. The pink pants were said to be very similar to those that Jaycee had been wearing when last seen. Undersheriff James "Jim" Roth, however, later said, "The pants did not match the victim. It was a big zero."

There were lots of "big zeroes" as one reported sighting after another, which looked so promising for a while, were checked out and then dismissed. One very good lead came in about an incident involving a dark-haired woman who had acted strangely during the week before Jaycee's kidnapping. A mother had spotted the woman interacting with her young blond-haired daughter at a local motel. The dark-haired woman fled away in a pickup truck with gardening tools in the back when spotted. This had all happened in South Lake Tahoe seven days before Jaycee Lee was taken. In fact, it had occurred not that far away from Washoan Boulevard, where Jaycee lived.

Commenting on the array of supposed sightings and tips in the South Lake Tahoe area alone, Roth said, "There's literally been hundreds of them!" They were, in effect, swamping the investigators as the days went by, and many of the tips went unread simply because there were not enough officers to read them all and still have a large force out in the field.

Not that law enforcement was dismissing any of the tips or supposed sightings at present. All of the tips had to be looked at, no matter how far off-base they might seem. Special Agent Albert Robinson, the lead FBI agent on the case, asked the public to think back a week or two and try to remember any suspicious activity around their children. Robinson said, "Even though it may seem trivial, it may fit into the puzzle."

Hikers, backpackers, mountain bikers, and horsemen were all asked to keep an eye out as they traveled through the backcountry around Tahoe. And there was a lot of backcountry; some of it wilderness with no permanent human habitation at all. Even an older sedan could make it up many of the dirt roads that snaked off into the trees and mountains. And there were also hundreds, if not thousands, of summer cabins that were generally not occupied that early in the season. A cabin could easily be broken into by the kidnappers, and no one would know if they and the girl were there.

Four days after the abduction, another very promising lead surfaced. Someone near Fallen Leaf Lake, an area about ten miles northwest of South Lake Tahoe, remembered spotting a vehicle matching the kidnappers' car around 3:30 P.M. on June 10. The vehicle had been around Fallen Leaf Lake, an area with lots of summer cabins and a public campground. The sedan had been driven by a man, with a woman passenger, and there had been a young girl asleep on the backseat. The girl had blond hair and had been wearing pink clothing, according to the person who had spotted the vehicle.

The public campground was scoured by officers and so were the summer cabins. Later, there was a report that officers had entered one cabin with guns drawn. If so, that incident was just as fruitless as all the others. Neither Jaycee nor the car was discovered there.

America's Most Wanted filmed Carl Probyn in the garage of his house and then Jaycee's bedroom. Terry was in the bedroom surrounded by Jaycee's teddy bears and stuffed animals. There was also footage of Jaycee at her recent eleventh birthday party that depicted Jaycee blowing out the candles on her cake.

Carl told a *Daily Tahoe Tribune* reporter about the kidnapping: "My first reaction was to think somebody was playing a joke. When I saw the door fly open, I immediately jumped on the bike. It hasn't been fun." Carl, who was a veteran, added, "I think I'd rather be in Vietnam."

The *Tahoe Daily Tribune* noted that on Saturday, June 15, the focus had shifted in law enforcement. They were scaling back on roadblocks, house-to-house searches, and car searches; instead, they took to sitting at their desks and going through the immense piles of tips that had come in. By now, there were over one hundred officers from various agencies working on the case. Sheriff McDonald told the reporters that the investigators' focus now was getting the facts down on paper, organizing data, and "ensuring nothing has slipped through the cracks."

One very important fact noted by the *Tribune* that day was that law enforcement believed *there are no indications the kidnappers have left the Tahoe Basin and investigators believe their best chances of recovering the girl is by concentrating efforts locally.*

Then in one short sentence, the *Tribune* added

a caveat: *Still, the abductors may have escaped the area undetected.*

By now, more than ten thousand posters of the missing girl, dark-haired woman, and suspects' vehicle blanketed the area. Child Quest International director Trish Williams related that the posters were being distributed to gas stations, fast-food restaurants, convenience stores, rest areas, campgrounds, and bus stations. Trish added, "The kidnappers could have ditched their car and taken her someplace." Trish also said that Child Quest's responsibility was spreading the information out as far as possible, while law enforcement's focus was on all the leads and tips that had come in.

Trish added that her first duty had been to get to know Terry Probyn and the family. "I talk to Terry quietly, and get as much information as possible to aid the authorities in the search." And Trish related that one good thing was that Carl Probyn had seen the abduction vehicle and the woman kidnapper. Trish told a reporter for the *Reno Gazette-Journal*, "We've got a lot more to go on than in many cases, and that makes me hopeful."

Greg Mengell, of Sacramento's Interstate Association for Stolen Children, was also monitoring the situation in Lake Tahoe. Mengell said, "I think the family is really fortunate to have the FBI working on the case. I think there is a good chance we can find her and bring her back. We've found kids that have been gone a year, a year and a half; that were assumed to be victims of murder. She could be home tonight or be home a year from now. Or never."

The prospect of "never" was addressed by the *Reno Gazette-Journal*. It ran an article about Elizabeth Ackerman, whose ten-year-old son, Anthony, had been kidnapped while walking from a school bus stop to his home. This had happened in Lemmon Valley, Nevada, and Elizabeth hadn't seen Anthony in ten years.

When Elizabeth heard people declaring on the news, "I know how Terry Probyn feels," Elizabeth said, "No, they don't! Only a few can say that." Since Anthony's abduction, she had cared for his two dozen prized 4-H rabbits for years; then worn out by the task, she gave them all away to friends. Her husband became an alcoholic, and eventually he and Elizabeth divorced. She moved to rural Fallon, Nevada, about eighty miles east of Lake Tahoe, and started a ranch. Elizabeth spoke of starting over with a new life, with a horse, chickens, and geese. But still, the pain of her loss persisted. Elizabeth related, "Peace of mind? No, I have none. Not until I find his body or he walks back into my life. Tell Terry (Probyn) to push the authorities. Don't give up hope. Don't give up."

One of the best leads the detectives had so far on Jaycee Dugard's case turned out to be just another dead end. It was the tip about the dark-haired woman who had been in contact with a woman's young blond daughter a week before Jaycee's kidnapping. This woman turned out to be a Good Samaritan. Sheriff McDonald said that his office and the FBI determined that the dark-haired woman in that incident had seen the young blond girl alone outside the Beverly Lodge, near busy Highway 50, in early June. The woman on her own initiative took the child to the motel office, where she found the mother inside. After handing the child over to her mother, the woman quickly left. Detectives were able to determine that this dark-haired woman was in no way connected to the disappearance of Jaycee Lee Dugard.

On a different subject, FBI agent Robert Mahoney

told a reporter that hypnosis had been used on some individuals who had "witnessed" the kidnapping. This seemed to indicate Carl Probyn, but who else might have been hypnotized remained a mystery. Mahoney added that a few more bits of useful information were gathered by this technique. But none of it was important enough to crack the case wide open.

A short time later, Sheriff McDonald related that some self-proclaimed psychics were also contacting authorities. As to this, McDonald stated, "Law enforcement is taking these tips seriously when they are specific enough to be useful." Unfortunately, the amount of information from psychics that was not useful was staggering. And like all the tips, each bit of information took time to separate the wheat from the chaff.

By the end of the first week since the abduction, Sheriff McDonald spoke of the frustration surrounding the case. Even with a good description of the female abductor and the kidnappers' car, there were still no solid leads as to where they were or where Jaycee had been taken. And McDonald noted that the segment on *America's Most Wanted* had not brought in the amount of tips that were expected. He wondered if this was in light of the possibility that the kidnappers were still in the Lake Tahoe area. They couldn't exactly be sighted elsewhere if they had never left the Tahoe Basin.

Sheriff McDonald also said that sex offenders in the Tahoe area were being talked to, and their files reviewed. Then he added that detectives wanted one tipster in particular to call them back. This man had spoken so rapidly on the phone during his first call that he couldn't be understood. The man had even called in a second time, but his speech was just as rushed and incoherent. Why this particular man might have useful information was not divulged by McDonald.

Meanwhile, the FBI's Behavioral Science Unit was working up a profile of the abductors. FBI supervisory specialist George Vinson told reporters, "We've still got a full court press in place. It's turning into a complex investigation, because we lack new sightings and eyewitnesses." What he meant by that was, after the first good witnessing by Carl Probyn of the actual kidnapping of Jaycee Lee Dugard, there had not been one new sighting that was valid. It seemed that they were as far away from solving the case as they had been one hour after it had occurred.

Just how hard investigators had been working for a full week could be gauged by the work log of one El Dorado Sheriff's Office sergeant. In the last seven days, he had worked from twelve to sixteen hours every day on the case. Undersheriff Jim Roth related, "It's kind of like putting a puzzle together and trying to figure out just how the little pieces fit together, and not learning how the big picture looks."

After a week's duration, the community response in the Tahoe area was still extremely strong, and fifty thousand posters about the case had been run off copy machines and distributed, along with five thousand of them in Spanish. Local businesses raffled off goods and services to raise money for the Tip Line and to give to Jaycee's family. Radio station KRLT aired three hours of programming in relation to the raffle, trying to drum up even more business. The plight of the Probyns was on many people's minds in the region, and conversations about the missing girl filled restaurants, coffee shops, taverns, and casinos.

Consciousness about the missing girl spread out in other ways as well. The EDSO set up a location where parents could have their children fingerprinted for free. If the child was ever abducted, there would be prints on file to help in the search. Apparently, Jaycee Lee did not have her fingerprints on file.

On another front, school psychiatrist Dr. Dianne Salzenstein met with classmates of Jaycee to listen to their concerns. Dr. Salzenstein said that one of the main themes coming from the children was: "We thought Tahoe was a safe place." She tried to reassure the children that Jaycee's kidnapping was an isolated incident and that their parents would keep them safe. She also emphasized that if their parents went with them to a school bus stop, it didn't make them "babyish."

Dr. Salzenstein added, "For many of them, Jaycee was part of their daily lives. Her empty desk is still there. One student told me, 'We keep thinking she's going to show up.'"

Fourth grader Jordan Werley told a reporter, "Right now, we don't have any clues. If we got more clues, we can find Jaycee."

Another fourth grader, Lindsay Daugherty, related, "I'm kind of scared. I hope she's okay."

And one of Jaycee's fifth-grade classmates, Trevor Lewis, stated, "We're trying to make it the best we can now." In fact, Trevor and other boys had been making missing posters about Jaycee's disappearance even before the official missing posters came out.

In a show of solidarity and remembrance of Jaycee, schoolkids at Meyers Elementary School tied pink ribbons to a chain-link fence around the school grounds. Pink was Jaycee's favorite color. The schoolchildren also created handmade signs that expressed their hopes that Jaycee would soon be found, and tied pink ribbons to car antennas.

Adding a chill to the atmosphere in Lake Tahoe was a recent article in the *Daily Tribune* about a kidnapped nine-year-old girl in Chula Vista, California. The girl had been snatched right out of her front yard in broad daylight. A few days later, the girl's body was discovered in an industrial park. Although no one was saying **it** out loud, the thought in many people's minds was that Jaycee Lee Dugard might have suffered a similar fate.

CHAPTER 4

DWINDLING LEADS

In the second week after the abduction, EDSO undersheriff Jim Roth admitted something very important. He said, "Looking back [at the initial hours after the kidnapping], if we were to do it again, we might have done things differently. I'm sure we would."

He was addressing the fact that many people wondered why roadblocks had not been set up immediately on the main roads leading out of the Tahoe Basin. There were, after all, very few main roads that led out of the South Lake Tahoe area. Highway 50 went basically east and west, and Highway 89 went north and south.

Roth did go on to say that even though the main roads hadn't been sealed off immediately, there were patrol cars alongside the roads, with instructions to the officers to be on the lookout for the reported gray sedan. Roth added that roadblocks might have back-fired. He said, "It would have created such large traffic jams that it would have been easy for the abductors to turn around and avoid them." He stressed it was better for hidden patrol cars to monitor the traffic on the main roads, rather than having roadblocks.

On top of this, Roth noted that there were other smaller roads out of the basin as well. For instance, by using the Pioneer Trail eastward, a vehicle could use side streets around the casino area bottleneck and eventually make its way up over the Kingsbury Grade into Nevada. From there, a person could go any numbers of ways across Nevada or back into California. In fact, in the first vital minutes, the abductors might have already been past the areas where law enforcement vehicles were stationed.

The news spread across the country about the missing girl, and *People* magazine ran an article on the abduction. Much of it focused on Terry and Carl Probyn and how they were coping. In fact, in the first few days after the abduction, Terry had barely been coping at all. She admitted, "I went into a dark hole of drunkenness, tears, and heavy troubled sleep. I couldn't function. I was walking the floors, ranting and raving, thinking the worst."

It didn't help matters that often, irrationally, Terry lashed out at Carl, asking why he hadn't done more in the first few minutes after seeing the abduction occur. On one level, Terry knew that he had done all that he could have done by pedaling his bike after the sedan, and then calling 911 within two minutes of the kidnapping. But still, her emotions were running so strong, they overcame rational thought.

Making matters worse, the investigators were asking Carl many of the same questions, knowing the majority of kidnappings are family related. At one point, an investigator asked Carl, "Did you ever wish Jaycee wasn't here?" This question came during one of the two polygraph tests that Carl took and passed. Carl admitted later that he had replied to the investigator's question, "Sure, there were times I wished Jaycee wasn't in our life. I think every parent has wished that about their kids." And, of course, with Carl, part of it was that Jaycee took a protracted period of time in accepting him into the life she had shared alone with her mother for so long.

Eventually authorities agreed that Carl had nothing to do with Jaycee's abduction. EDSO sergeant Jim Watson said, "We're 99.9 percent sure this is not a family abduction."

Even Terry came around to the notion that she and Carl had to work together as a team if they were ever going to see Jaycee again. Terry told the reporter for *People,* "One Sunday I was by myself, and suddenly I just got this inner strength to quit crying and get on with it." The "getting on with it" included distributing thousands upon thousands of posters that detailed Jaycee, the car, and the dark-haired woman.

Possible sightings were still coming in from every point of the compass, and Terry let it be known that some of them were disturbing and frightening. She got multiple tips about Satanists who had kidnapped her daughter to use in horrifying rituals. Another tip was from a woman who "felt" that Jaycee was in a car trunk at one of the local casinos in Stateline. Terry and Carl went to the casino parking lots and pounded on the trunks of vehicles that even remotely matched the abductors' car.

One new lead swerved back to the fact that Carl had thought the woman abductor might have been of Middle Eastern descent. In the week before the abduction, the Probyns had been working at an art fair in the Tahoe area. Some people who had been at the art fair remembered a woman matching the description as being there. And Terry related to *People* that Jaycee Lee had been troubled on the night before she was taken. Now Terry wondered if Jaycee had wanted to talk about the dark-haired woman at the art fair and her concerns. Had the woman made Jaycee feel uneasy? Had the woman spoken with Jaycee there? These were just more questions that Terry could not answer.

In a strange way, the dark-haired woman at the art fair was somehow comforting to Terry. It raised the possibility that the dark-haired woman had lost a child at some point and had stolen Jaycee to replace her own child. If that was the case, it might mean that Jaycee had not been taken to be sexually exploited and then murdered. Terry said, "Maybe she (the dark-haired woman) took Jaycee because of her grief. If that's true, all I can say is, 'Please let my child go!'"

While talking to the reporter for *People*, Terry sat in Jaycee's room. The walls were covered with family photos, and there were stuffed animals everywhere. Terry admitted that she often looked out the window, up toward the bus stop on the Pioneer Trail. She day-dreamed that Jaycee would come walking down the road from the bus stop, and all of this was a nightmare that would end.

On the six-month anniversary of Jaycee's kidnap-ping, there was a candlelight vigil in South Lake Tahoe. This was attended by Carl and Terry Probyn, friends of the family, and many people who had worked on the case. *America's Most Wanted* was back for the occasion and did an update on the case. But even with this new exposure, no concrete leads came in about the kidnapping.

As time went on, leads and tips began to diminish. Reporter Mike Taugher, who worked in the Tahoe area, recalled, however, that journalists still contacted the Probyns and that their calls were always returned by Terry and Carl. One day, Taugher followed a photographer and Terry into Jaycee's room. While in there, Terry became very emotional and buried her face in one of Jaycee's stuffed animals. Taugher wrote later, *The pain I saw was unspeakable. Whoever stole the daughter also ripped the mother's heart out. Carl, Jaycee's stepfather, was wracked. He told me one of the things that haunted him: If only he had the car keys in his pocket he would not have had to chase the car uphill on a bike.*

Taugher also ruminated on what many others thought: Tahoe was a basin, with few roads leading out of it. Why couldn't law enforcement have sealed off the exit roads in time? In years to come, was some lone hiker going to stumble across Jaycee's remains out in the forest?

Christmas, 1991, was especially painful for Carl and Terry Probyn. Terry told a reporter for the *Sacramento Bee,* "I can't bring myself to have Christmas, not knowing where she is. But I still believe she's alive. It's the people showing up to help that helps me focus."

Carl added, "If she got hit by a car, it would tear your heart out, but there would be an ending. But there is no ending here."

Eight months passed, then ten. Before it seemed possible, Jaycee had been missing for an entire year. On June 10, 1992, there was a candlelight vigil held in South Lake Tahoe to remember Jaycee Lee Dugard. Carl, Terry, and Shayna attended the vigil. Terry told a Sacramento news station, "I'm scared. I'm scared that it's going to go on forever and ever, and we're never going to have an ending. We are living our worst nightmare."

Carl related, "It's like being tortured every day. You know she's gone. I don't know what they're doing to her, but we're being tortured every day, not knowing what's happening to her."

By 1993, the Probyns were willing to try any avenue to keep Jaycee's story alive. They appeared on *The Geraldo Rivera Show,* and Geraldo asked Terry what stresses had been placed on their marriage by Jaycee's disappearance. Terry replied, "It could destroy us if we let it. The whole focus for us is to stay together. When Jaycee comes home, she's going to need that family life. She can't afford for us to be split up."

The marriage, however, was fracturing under the terrible strain. Even though they worked together in 1995 on a video about Jaycee's kidnapping, their ordeal was becoming unbearable. In the spring of 1995, Carl and Terry separated, although they remained on good terms and did not get a divorce. Carl moved out of the house and got his own place. Later, he said to a reporter, "This (abduction) broke up our marriage. We had a great marriage. We never argued." But they could also not come to grips with Jaycee's abduction. There was always the painful thought that she was out there somewhere and needed them.

More years passed, and in 1997, reporter Mike Taugher got a call from Carl Probyn. Carl told him that one of the local alternative newspapers was going to run a story on Carl, pointing to him as having been somehow involved in Jaycee's kidnapping. Taugher, who was about to move to Colorado with his wife, told Carl that he couldn't help him much at present. Carl asked Taugher if he could sue the alternative newspaper, and Taugher thought that he could, if he could prove negligence or gross recklessness.

Carl then asked Taugher if he knew a good lawyer in the area, and Taugher said that he didn't. Before long, the thing that Carl had worried about came true—the El Dorado County Sheriff's Office began digging in the yard of the house that the Probyns had owned on Washoan Boulevard. The investigators also dug under the front porch. The agency wouldn't comment what they were looking for, but the rumor was, of course, that they were looking for Jaycee's body buried on the property. Lieutenant Fred Kollar told a reporter, "Sometimes you want to have someone else come back and look at the case." In other words, new detectives with new perspectives.

Asked about this latest incident, Carl told a *South Lake Tahoe Tribune* journalist, "There is about one percent of Tahoe who think we had something to do with the kidnapping. And this just gives fuel for the fire." The most persistent rumor about Carl was that he had been involved, and "sold" Jaycee into prostitution to pay off a drug debt. Not one bit of evidence ever backed up that rumor.

Then, in late 1997, an incident happened in Lake Tahoe that brought the kidnapping story of Jaycee Lee Dugard back full force. On December 2, 1997, a man and a woman in a van abducted twenty-two-year-old Vanessa Samson off a quiet street in Pleasanton, California. They did it in broad daylight on a workday morning in what was considered to be a safe neighborhood. For the next full day, the abductors—James Daveggio, thirty-seven, and Michelle Michaud, thirty-nine—took turns sexually abusing Vanessa in their van. While one drove, the other continually molested Vanessa on the way to Sacramento and then on to South Lake Tahoe. Daveggio and Michaud got a motel room in South Lake Tahoe, not far from where Jaycee Lee Dugard had once lived. For more hours, they sexually molested Vanessa Samson in the motel room.

When they were done with her, they secreted Vanessa out of the room into the van, and then they drove south on Highway 89. Once they were in the remote Hope Valley, both Daveggio and Michaud strangled the unfortunate young woman to death with a rope. Daveggio and Michaud pulled on the rope around Vanessa's neck at the same time, so that they were equal in the killing. Then they simply deposited her body into a small snow-covered creek known as Crater Wash.

Instead of fleeing the area, the murderous pair stayed for the night across the border in Stateline, Nevada. If not for a passing motorist in Hope Valley, who had exited his vehicle to urinate, Vanessa Samson's remains might not have been found until the following spring, if at all.

Because of a lot of clues pointing their way, both Daveggio and Michaud were arrested by the FBI in Stateline on December 3, 1997. One of the arresting FBI agents was Chris Campion, who joined the Jaycee Dugard case after 1991. Campion, like others, began to wonder if Daveggio and Michaud were responsible for Jaycee's kidnapping.

The *South Lake Tahoe Tribune* soon ran an article with the headline DUGARD LINK INVESTIGATED. There were several reasons for this. One was the daring daylight abduction of Vanessa Samson off a "safe" street. Another reason was the striking resemblance of Michelle Michaud to the dark-haired woman depicted in the sketch of Jaycee Lee Dugard's abductor. Michaud, who was a meth user, had the same type of sunken cheeks as depicted in the sketch. And Michaud's resemblance was so eerily similar, if Michaud's photo was laid side by side with the sketch, the images were uncannily alike in so many details.

Sergeant Jim Watson, of EDSO, told a reporter that the pair was being looked at in conjunction with the Jaycee Dugard case. Terry Probyn was bombarded with questions by reporters from all over the area, who asked what she thought about this latest incident. Terry said, "I agree, and so does Carl, that they (Michelle Michaud and the sketch) are similar in looks, but that doesn't mean it's her." What made this situation so frightening to the Probyns was the fact that details of how Daveggio and Michaud had abused Vanessa sexually and then murdered her were starting to come out. If Jaycee had fallen into the hands of this pair in 1991, it could only be imagined what her fate had been.

One year passed, and then another, without any solid clues as to what had happened to Jaycee. And then in March 2000, another incident that was frightening to both Terry and Carl occurred in the Lake Tahoe area once again. On March 19, nine-year-old Krystal Steadman was coaxed into an apartment by nineteen-year-old T.J. Soria. She was coaxed there so that T.J.s' father, forty-year-old Thomas Soria, could rape the girl. After the rape, Krystal was murdered, and T.J. disposed of her body along a stretch of Highway 50, which led to Carson City.

It wasn't long before the trail led back to the Sorias, and father and son were arrested. During an interview with Fran Soria, Thomas's wife and T.J.'s mother, an FBI agent got around to the Jaycee Lee Dugard case. Fran had no idea what her husband and son had been up to, and the line of questioning scared her. In fact,

Fran was no longer living with Thomas or T.J. in the Lake Tahoe area when she was questioned:

Agent: *I have a really hard question. And it's one that's been eating at me. On June 10, 1991, a little blond-haired girl was abducted in South Lake Tahoe. Her name is Jaycee Lee Dugard. She was on her way to a bus stop on the Pioneer Trail.*

Fran: *I remember the story.*

Agent: *The victim in this case (Krystal Steadman) physically in appearance is very similar to her and I don't know if Tom could have been a part of Jaycee's abduction and I wanted to ask you. And that's why I've been asking a lot of questions about Tahoe.*

Fran: *Yeah.*

Agent: *And I told you I wouldn't hit you with anything. And T.J. with his hair down might look like a composite—well, there were two passengers in a gray vehicle. And you said you had a Mercury Bobcat at the time. When did he (Thomas) get rid of it?*

Fran: *It was totaled in a wreck in 1980.*

Agent: *Then you said you had a Cutlass. How late did you have the Cutlass?*

Fran: *I couldn't tell you.*

Agent: *In '91, did you have the car?*

Fran: *I'm trying to remember.*

Agent: *Since you remember the story, do you remember the artist's conception of the . . .*

Fran: *To tell you the truth, I don't remember. There was something about a man and woman.*

Agent: *Well, they're not entirely sure of the car description. And they're not entirely sure if the woman was a woman. Nothing to scare you.*

> *I'm not thinking about you, but the artist*
> *conception of the woman is very similar to you.*

Fran: *Oh, well, that's nice. Thanks for telling me.*

Agent: *Well, with T.J.'s hair . . .*

Fran: *(Suddenly realizes the implication and gasps)*
So now I'm a suspect!

Agent: *No, not at all. I wasn't telling you this because*
you're a suspect. I'm just trying to explore the
possibility whether Tom could have done
this. I mean, there's things here that raise
my antenna a couple of notches. But nothing
that says this is a done deal. Was Tom taking
trips to Tahoe without you? (In 1991)

Fran: *I'm not sure. I remember them going to Reno*
once by themselves.

Agent: *Did T.J. wear his hair long?*

Fran: *Yeah, he was always wearing his hair long.*

Agent: *When did the trips take place mostly to Tahoe?*
In winter or summer?

Fran: *Winter.*

Agent: *What about summer? Would they not go*
at all?

Fran: *I remember a few.*

Agent: *Around June, July, August?*

Fran: *Yeah, I remember around T.J.'s birthday.*

Agent: *Have you always worn your hair long like*
that?

Fran: *Yes. I don't like short hair.*

In the end, it was a false alarm about the Sorias, especially Fran. She had nothing to do with Jaycee Lee Dugard's case or that of Krystal Steadman. And as time went on, it was proven that Thomas and T.J. Soria had nothing to do with Jaycee as well. Terry and Carl Probyn could be glad of that. When all the facts about Tom and T.J. Soria came out, it was proven just how brutally Krystal Steadman had been raped and murdered.

On June 10, 2001, the ten-year anniversary of Jaycee's abduction arrived. The South Lake Tahoe Soroptimist Club staged a parade for Jaycee named the "Jaycee Lee Dugard Pink Ribbon Parade." Everyone in the area was invited. Hundreds of adults and children showed up, wearing pink ribbons and carrying pink balloons in honor of Jaycee. They marched down a single lane on Highway 50 to a park where Terry Probyn spoke to the gathering.

Terry said that it seemed impossible ten years had passed since her daughter was kidnapped. "It is still as overwhelming as the day it happened," she said. "The person that did this, please give the gift of resolving this. I'm asking that you share, that you find it in your soul to give a gift. It's like a puzzle, but you never know when you're going to get to finish the puzzle. Someone out there has the piece. We need it. You need it."

Terry also took time during the ceremony to remember Krystal Steadman and her family. Like Jaycee, Krystal had gone to Meyers Elementary School. At the gathering, Terry read a letter from Krystal's sister. The letter stated in part: *Please, always keep the lines of communication open with friends and family. Cherish each moment we spend with each other. You never think it's going to happen to you, but it does. Take all the pictures you can as often as you can.*

In the El Dorado County Sheriff's Office, the Jaycee Lee Dugard case over the years was handed down from one team of detectives to another. It was almost like a father handing down a prized possession to a son. All of the detectives treated the case with respect and diligence. They all wanted to give Terry Probyn an answer concerning what had happened to Jaycee. Of course, by this time, none of the detectives held out any hope that Jaycee was still alive. What they imagined was that they would find her remains somewhere. Or, in exchange for some hoped-for leniency on a different case, a criminal behind bars would talk about what he had done to Jaycee.

By now, the detectives had followed leads to every state in the Union and to foreign countries as well. Every year, there would be a new phone call from someone who said he saw a young woman who looked a lot like the way Jaycee might look when she grew older. In many interviews the young woman couldn't remember her childhood and wondered if she had been kidnapped or somehow taken from her own parents. Many of these young women had a strong resemblance of how Jaycee could look as she aged. But one of the EDSO detectives on this quest related, "We would go meet this person, but in fifteen minutes or less, we would know it wasn't Jaycee. There were certain things we knew about Jaycee that this person didn't know. We always came up empty-handed."

The detective also related that there was another scenario that played out over and over again. "Someone would contact us about how in June 1991, they knew someone who claimed they had a boyfriend or a relative who had kidnapped a blond young girl from Lake Tahoe. That person had then taken the girl to an isolated area, raped the girl, and killed her after a period of time." None of these scenarios ever led to finding any traces of Jaycee's remains or anything connected to her.

One of these stories had been very compelling and had to be checked out thoroughly. It concerned a woman who told the detectives she had a friend who lived on the Indian reservation near Carson City. This may have been the Washoe Indian Reservation. At any rate, this person said that an acquaintance of hers had gotten drunk and bragged about abducting Jaycee in Lake Tahoe and taking her to Nevada. There he had raped her repeatedly and then killed her after three days. The informant said that she didn't know if the story was true or not, and had not gone to the police when she first heard about it. She didn't want her friend to get into trouble. Finally the informant's conscience got the better of her, and she told an EDSO detective about it. Like all of the other leads, nothing was found concerning Jaycee. It was just one more dead end.

And so it went, year after year, rumors and tips and leads coming from Oklahoma, Pennsylvania, Texas, and even Great Britain. None of them panned out. All the Probyns had left now of Jaycee were photos, stuffed animals, and memories. Soon the pink ribbons, pink balloons, and marchers were only one more memory. Ten years turned into twelve; fifteen into eighteen. Jaycee Lee Dugard seemed just as lost as ever.

And then out of nowhere, seeming to defy all belief, a young woman, who called herself Alyssa, walked into a parole office in Concord, California, on August 26, 2009. After hours of interviews, she spoke the words that were seemingly impossible: "I'm Jaycee Dugard."

CHAPTER 5

NEWS THAT CIRCLED
THE PLANET

The very first news about the reemergence of Jaycee
Lee Dugard started out as a trickle on San Francisco
Bay Area news stations. Before long, however, the news
became a worldwide torrent. In the very first report-
ings, it was simply stated that Jaycee Dugard was mirac-
ulously alive. On August 26, 2009, the *Contra Costa
Times* ran a very short article about the discovery. It
was, in fact, only three paragraphs long, with an old
photo of Jaycee Dugard when she was eleven years
old. The article stated, *The eyes of the world turned to a rural
street near Antioch on August 26 with the news that Jaycee
Dugard was discovered alive and well, 18 years after her abduction at age 11. Then came that additional stunner:
Authorities said convicted rapist Phillip Garrido and his
wife, Nancy, had held Dugard and later her two daughters—
fathered by Garrido—in a hidden backyard warren of tents
and sheds.* The article went on to report that a press
conference on the UC Berkeley campus would soon

take place. At the press conference, Lisa Campbell and Ally Jacobs would speak about what had led them to suspect something was wrong when Phillip Garrido came to UC with two young girls on August 24.

News radio station KCBS also started broadcasting very brief details about what had occurred in Concord, and the incredible news that Jaycee Lee Dugard had been found alive. Other newspaper articles from the area were just as brief and cryptic, leaving many wondering who Phillip and Nancy Garrido were. Their names didn't mean anything. Over the years, neither Phillip nor Nancy had ever been suspects in Jaycee Dugard's disappearance.

The few journalists who were initially working on the story were soon joined by an avalanche of reporters, news trucks, satellite trucks, and camera crews. The reporters jammed into the UC news conference where UCPD captain Margaret Bennett told them, "We are very proud of the work that Lisa and Ally did on this case. From their bios, you know that both of these individuals are very smart and experienced. We have a lot of interaction between students and the surrounding community at UC. We do get outsiders on our campus, and that's one of the reasons this department is here.

"Because of the beginning of [the] semester, we take extra care to keep students safe. The work Lisa and Ally did set off a chain of events that will undoubtedly change the lives of the three people involved. We're pleased with the role UCPD has played in reuniting this family."

Lisa Campbell started off by giving her take on the events that began on August 24, when a man and two girls walked into her office. And then Ally Jacobs told what had occurred when she became involved. After Lisa and Ally retold the events of August 24 and 25, the floor was thrown open to questions from the reporters. The first question was about the book Phillip Garrido brought with him to UC. The reporter wanted to know, "Was it self-published?"

Ally answered, "It was a book shown on the media a couple of times. It's about schizophrenia. It had a blue cover and was handwritten. Not a very professional job. I tried to read it, but it was kind of difficult to understand. It was very choppy and didn't make a whole lot of sense."

The next question was "What were the actions like between Phillip Garrido and the two girls? Were they afraid of him?"

Ally replied, "No, they didn't seem afraid. Maybe afraid of what they might say. Like their answers needed to be short, clipped, and to the point. They were very rehearsed. That was their dad, and they thought he was God's gift. That was their world. That was their life. It was like all that they knew."

A reporter asked, "Didn't they seem a little young to be his daughters?"

Ally responded, "They seemed a little young. But I have little kids. So I'm not good at gauging the ages of older kids."

"How were they dressed?" was another question.

Ally said, "Drab and nondescript. They were in dresses. The older one had blond hair pulled back in a ponytail. And she had on a little sundress. It was kind of tan or brown."

A journalist wanted to know what had tipped Lisa and Ally off about this situation that something had to be done. Lisa responded, "I was a police officer in Chicago. And I worked with youth then. I interacted with children on a day-to-day basis. Just experience and training helped here. And the energy level of those girls was strange. They weren't vibrant and they were extremely rehearsed. If one moved, the other one immediately gestured toward her. It was if, 'We shouldn't be in a certain position.' The older one— her hands remained on her legs the whole time. She would either look at her dad or at the ceiling. The younger one was a little more engaging, but still there was no activity, no energy level. No response to the environment around her."

To this, Ally added, "It was very similar when I came in contact with them. And some kind of alarm bell went off in my head. There was something up with those kids. You really couldn't pinpoint it. It was like something you'd see in a movie or on TV, where these kids were so robotic and not acting like normal eleven- and fifteen-year-olds would act. Trying to investigate why they were acting the way they were acting without their cooperation was really difficult to do."

There was a question, "So it wasn't really the girls who tipped you off?"

Ally said, "If he hadn't come in with those girls, I would have just let him talk."

A reporter wanted to know, "Did the girls seem brainwashed or emotionally disturbed?"

Ally replied, "The word you used, 'brainwashed,' that was the sense we were getting."

And Lisa added, "They were truly submissive."

A journalist asked, "What was your reaction to the girls' reaction to the admission by their father of rape?"

Ally responded, "He threw that out so quickly. . . ." Then her answer trailed off.

Lisa answered, "He continued to talk. He was going through what was in his book. He said, 'I was arrested, I was convicted, but now I'm doing God's work!' And he mumbled right on past that. The girls didn't have a reaction at all."

Ally added, "We weren't that shocked, because we

already knew he was on parole for those things. So I wasn't shocked about that. But I was shocked by the way he said it. So matter-of-fact. Like if he said, 'I'm wearing a blue shirt.' The girls didn't react at all to his comment."

One reporter asked, "Did he have a GPS device on him because he was on parole?"

Lisa and Ally looked at each other and then shook their heads. Neither one had seen a GPS device attached to Phil Garrido's ankle. But then they had been so busy with other things, they hadn't been looking for one.

Another question was "Did he ever get through to you what he wanted to do on campus?"

Both Ally and Lisa laughed, and they both said no. Lisa added, "He said it was all in the book he brought."

The press conference only fanned the flames of media interest in this case. Soon there were reporters from around the world, scurrying around Walnut Avenue just outside of Antioch, where the Garridos had lived. They were also on the streets of Meyers, near South Lake Tahoe, where Jaycee had been kidnapped eighteen years earlier. And in Southern California, where Terry Probyn and Carl Probyn now lived. By now, Terry and Carl were separated, but still in contact with each other. Their stories were just one more element in this compelling drama that was rapidly unfolding.

When it was determined for certain that "Alyssa" was in reality Jaycee Lee Dugard, a law enforcement officer contacted Jaycee Lee's mom, Terry Probyn, where she lived in Southern California. If Terry had been struck by a lightning bolt, the effect could not have been more dramatic or unexpected. She was literally floored by the news. And just as earth-shattering was when Jaycee was put on the phone, and the first words out of her mouth were "Hi, Mom! I have babies."

Not only was Terry once more speaking with her own daughter, who had been missing for eighteen years, she was suddenly told that she was a grandmother! Incredibly, Jaycee recalled an immense amount of her life before the kidnapping. It was if both mother and daughter were thrust directly back into "pre–June 10, 1991" mode. And another thing was very evident, even though Jaycee had been kept away in a secret compound for years, she was very bright, and knew a lot about the world at large.

Within a short time frame, Terry contacted Carl by phone. Carl soon related to reporters, "Terry told me, 'They found Jaycee! She's alive!' We cried for about two minutes. Then Terry said, 'She remembers everything!'"

Carl soon told a *Sacramento Bee* reporter, "You bet it was a surprise! I had eventually lost hope she would be found alive. Then you pray you get her body back so there is an ending. To have this happen when we get her back alive, and when she remembers things from the past, and to have people in custody is a triple win."

On Thursday, August 27, 2009, mother and daughter were reunited in a secret location in Contra Costa County, not far from Antioch. And for the first time, Terry met her granddaughters, Angel and Starlit. To say the meeting between Terry and Jaycee was emotional was not to do justice to the word. It was as if a ghost had once again returned to the land of the living.

Terry would not speak to the press at that point, but Tina Dugard, Terry's sister (Jaycee's aunt), later held a press conference at the FBI office in Los Angeles. Tina gave insights into just how powerful the reunion had been. Tina said that on Wednesday, August 26, an El Dorado County Sheriff's investigator had called her around supper time, trying to find Terry Probyn. Tina gave the investigator the contact information; and a while later, Tina received a phone call from Jaycee's half sister, Shayna, who was now nineteen. In total disbelief, Tina heard the words coming from Shayna: "They found Jaycee. She's alive!"

Tina related, "I don't know what I felt. I just said, 'What?' I'm sure I repeated the word several times. We both started crying hysterically."

Tina was so wound up that night, she could barely sleep, and almost missed her early-morning flight from Ontario, California, with Terry and Shayna, to the Bay Area. FBI officials met the three women at an undisclosed location. They were all whisked to a secret locale, where there, before their almost unbelieving eyes, stood a twenty-nine-year-old Jaycee and her two daughters. Immediately Jaycee and her mom gave each other a huge, emotional hug. Tina related, "The smile on my sister's face was as wide as the sea." Then Jaycee hugged Shayna and her aunt Tina. Incredibly, Jaycee remembered her aunt, after all these years, and declared, "Auntie Tina!"

Tina Dugard said later, "I went forward and cried and hugged her and held her as tight as I possibly could. It was surreal. It was fabulous. It was one of the happiest moments of my life. I can't even remember what I told her."

Then Tina recounted, "Jaycee looked like a twenty-nine-year-old woman. She's fabulous and she's beautiful. The girls have their mother's blond hair and bright blue eyes and big smile. They both look healthy."

As for Shayna and Jaycee, Tina recounted, "They

were so happy to meet. Jaycee was a girl that Shayna had only known through old photographs, family movies, and media accounts of her abduction." That, and the stories that Terry had told Shayna about her elder daughter. In those stories, Jaycee was never older than eleven years old. It seemed incredible that the girl of eleven was now standing in front of Shayna as a grown woman, with two daughters of her own. In fact, the younger daughter was eleven years old, the same age as Jaycee had been when she disappeared from the lives of Terry, Shayna, and Aunt Tina.

Tina told the *Orange County Register* she had thought back in 1991 that Jaycee would be found within days. When that didn't happen, Tina thought it would occur within a few weeks. Tina added, "Then it was by Thanksgiving. And then, for sure, by Christmas." Tina related that never happened, and Jaycee's present of a Happy Holidays Christmas Barbie remained in its box.

Tina told the reporter, "It's clear the girls have been on the Internet and know a lot of things. It's clear that Jaycee did a great job with the limited resources she had and limited education. The girls are educated and bright."

At one point, Tina said, she was with Jaycee and her girls, and Angel and Starlit pointed up at the sky and told her the names of the constellations. And the next day, one of the girls pointed at a plant in the backyard where they were staying and said, "That's a nasturtium. It's edible. Do you want to eat it?"

Tina related, "It was a beautiful day. We stared up at the clouds and saw fluffy cotton shapes." Then she added, "There was a sense of comfort and optimism. A sense of happiness. Jaycee and her girls are happy. People probably want to think that it's a horrible, scary thing for us all. But the horrible, scary thing happened eighteen years ago, and continued to happen for the last eighteen years. The darkness and despair has now lifted."

Even though the gathered media was enthralled by what Tina Dugard had to say, there was the unanswered question of what had occurred during those "horrible, scary eighteen years." There was also the question of who was Phillip Garrido, and how had he kidnapped and held Jaycee Lee Dugard in captivity for eighteen years, fathered two daughters with her, and kept it all a secret for such a long, long time.

II

IN THE SHADOWS

CHAPTER 6

"HE WAS SPOILED AS A CHILD."

Phillip Craig Garrido was born in Pittsburg, California, on April 5, 1951. Located at the junction of the Sacramento and San Joaquin Rivers, in Northern California, Pittsburg was an industrial city in the 1950s. Not unlike its famous namesake in Pennsylvania, Pittsburg, California's main industry was its steel mills. Most of the city's citizens were working-class families, and the preponderance of them worked in one of the mills around town. Besides steel mills, there were also chemical plants and smaller industries that were adjuncts of the large mills.

The nearby city of Antioch was in the same mold as Pittsburg, with its main industry being paper mills such as Fiberboard and Crown Zee. Along with these were other industries such as DuPont Chemicals, Dow Chemicals, and Kaiser Gypsum. In both cities during that era, the local businesses depended on having the mill workers as their customers. And in that era, there

were no large retail outlets there, such as Kmart or
Walmart and the like. There was a small jcpenney store
in Pittsburg and a small Sears store in Antioch, but
most of the local businesses were mom-and-pop establishments.

Phil's dad, Manuel Garrido, was a forklift operator
for most of his life, and the Garrido family was definitely in the working class of the area. They eventually moved to Brentwood, a town about twenty miles
east of Pittsburg. Brentwood was much more rural,
with surrounding farmland, where tomatoes, corn,
walnut trees, almond trees, and apricots were grown.
In fact, the area had originally been known as "Eden
Plain" in the nineteenth century for its rich soils and
temperate climate. Ironically, in the background,
Mount Diablo (the Devil's Mountain) dominated the
western horizon. When someone wanted to go to the
"big city" from Brentwood, they either drove to Antioch, with its population of around fifteen thousand,
or the even bigger city of Stockton to the east, with
a population exceeding thirty thousand. To get to
Stockton, a person had to drive on levee roads through
the California Delta.

That was another factor of Brentwood. It lay on the
edge of the California Delta, with its thousand miles of
waterways. These waterways turned, twisted, and me-
andered across the landscape, adding to the richness
of the soils. Brentwood was at the juncture of farmland, wetlands, and rivers; and farther to the northwest
lay the industrial zone.

Phil Garrido had a brother, Ron, who was eight
years older than he was, and Phil's mom, Patricia,
became a successful real estate agent in the Brentwood
area. She attended school board meetings, and the
Garrido family lived a stable, if not extravagant, life in
the small town. For most of the people there, it was

quiet, not terribly exciting, but a comfortable way of life. Like many in his generation, Phil was raised on television fare of Captain Kangaroo, Davy Crockett, and Sky King.

Phil's father, Manuel, later said that Phil was a good boy when he was young. "He was never in any trouble. He was well-behaved and polite." Manuel did indicate, however, that Phil's mother spoiled him and doted on him. And for that reason, Phil was never disciplined when he acted out, even by Manuel.

Although Phil had a high IQ, he only achieved average grades in school. More than one person later said that Phil had the ability—but not the drive—to accomplish much in school. Ron agreed with his dad that Phil's mother spoiled him, and Phil never put out much effort in anything he did. Even Phil later on would admit, "I was spoiled as a child." There's no record that Phil joined the Boy Scouts, was in Little League, or played any kind of team sports while growing up in Brentwood.

By the time Phil reached Liberty Union High School, his grades did not improve. He didn't join clubs and he didn't go out for athletics. The one thing he did do, however, was enjoy playing and listening to music. Especially rock-and-roll music. Phil got a bass guitar and joined a rock-and-roll band with some other local boys. Even though he wouldn't apply himself to his studies at school, Phil practiced long hours on his bass guitar. And as time went on, he became a fairly good player. His favorite artists, as the 1960s rolled along, were the Jefferson Airplane and Creedence Clearwater Revival.

The "hippie scene" was just starting to take off in nearby San Francisco in 1967 and 1968, and Phil made his way over to Haight-Ashbury as often as he could. There were free concerts in Golden Gate Park, and in the park's panhandle, put on by the likes of the Jefferson Airplane, Grateful Dead, and other popular psychedelic rock groups. For a rural boy from Brentwood, it was indeed like Alice going down the rabbit hole into another world inhabited by hookah-smoking caterpillars. And it wasn't long before Phil was smoking marijuana himself, just like so many other young people who attended the free concerts were doing.

Mike Kelly, a member of a Brentwood band, the Village Drunks, recalled, "Phil was a nice young guy growing up. He was clean-cut and pretty smart. He was just a normal high-school kid. But the hippie scene came along and he really got into it, with the moccasins, fringe coat, and all."

Kelly added that they were all partying back then in the late 1960s, "smoking weed." Kelly related, "I knew when to stop, but I guess Phil didn't." Apparently, Phil began using more marijuana, and others attest to his use of hashish, illegal pills, such as uppers and downers, and LSD as well. Even Phil would later write of this period in his life: *Marijuana was reaching out to rural California. From that point on my life was slowly changing.* He may have been hedging about the "slowly" part. For others around him, he seemed to be changing very quickly into a "stoner."

Steve Luchessi, another member of the Village Drunks, recounted, "Phil was in the background at Liberty (Union) High School. Not one of the most popular. I thought he was weird, but not that weird. I'm not sure if he was high all the time or just saw things differently. It was almost as if he was trying to keep up with the psychedelic scene, the drug scene. He painted his bedroom black and covered the walls with psychedelic music posters and illuminated them with black lights."

Unlike Mike Kelly and Steve Luchessi, there were some local girls, who as women many years later, had a different take on Phil Garrido. Not wanting to reveal their identities, one woman told a *San Francisco Chronicle* reporter that there were many girls in high school who thought Phil was cute. One of them told the reporter, "You should have seen Phil in early high school. He was the cutest. Girls wanted to dance with him at all the dances."

Another woman, who had been a classmate at Liberty Union High School, said, "He had a cute smile. He wasn't a jock, but a lot of girls liked him. I wouldn't say he was really friendly, but he wasn't standoffish, either."

Perhaps Phil would have had his fling with pot and LSD and moved on. But according to both his father and brother, an incident in 1968 tipped Phil over the edge. Phil was riding his motorcycle when he had a bad accident and was sent to a local hospital. He suffered numerous injuries, including a severe injury to his head. Manuel Garrido said later, "It ruined him. I remember the emergency room calling me and saying, 'We have to operate on his head.' I told them, 'Do whatever you can.'"

Manuel added, "They didn't do enough! My son was ruined after that. The drugs, crazy behavior, all that stuff started then."

Some of Phil's classmates would disagree, saying that the drug use and "weird behavior" had started before the motorcycle accident. But everyone agreed that Phil's "crazy behavior" and drug use increased after the accident. In fact, there were numerous periods when he seemed to be stoned all the time.

Apparently, Phil and his band, the Free Spirit Band, were pretty good and they played at dances in the area.

Even Steve Luchessi, of the Village Drunks, admitted, "He was good, but we kicked his band's ass at the Battle of the Bands."

Even though the band played on, Phil's life was changing in several ways. Phil's mother got a job as a bookkeeper at a construction pipe company in Brentwood. And despite his drug usage, and hard-rocking ways, Phil became a member of a local Jehovah's Witness Church. Just how often he attended was not recorded later. Phil got a job at the pipe company where his mother was employed for a while, and he seemed to have done a good job there. His employer would later say that Phil was a good worker, who always did the tasks assigned to him.

This work ethic of Phil's seemed to change when he was hired by the Fiberboard Company in 1970. Fiberboard was one of the largest pulp mills in the area, and was a few short blocks away from where Phil would later live on Walnut Avenue. At Fiberboard, Phil became more slack in his performance, and he often would not show up for work at all, without giving a reason why.

Then on December 6, 1969, Phil most likely went to a concert that would in some ways exemplify his own later life, with a kind of frenzied madness. It was the Rolling Stones concert at nearby Altamont Speedway, only twenty miles southeast of Brentwood, near Altamont Pass. Although he didn't write about this later, there would be others in Brentwood that said Phil was there. And it would have been strange if a rock-and-roll music lover like Phil had not been there. The concert was the event of the season, and was supposed to be a kind of "West Coast Woodstock." Instead, it would take on a more sinister and deadly mantle.

The Rolling Stones, for some reason, decided to have the Hells Angels "police" the concert. Rather than policing the throng, the Hells Angels ended up terrorizing many of the concertgoers. One man, who was clearly high or intoxicated, was stabbed to death right in front of the stage. The whole incident was caught in the film that the Rolling Stones were making about their tour. Instead of becoming another Woodstock, Altamont became synonymous with the ending of the "Age of Aquarius."

Phil's life changed somewhat again in 1971 when his parents got divorced. According to the divorce settlement, dated June 7, 1971, the divorce documents related that *the court orders that care, custody and control of the minor child, Phillip C. Garrido, be awarded to petitioner (Patricia Garrido) with reasonable rights of visitation to respondent (Manuel Garrido). The court finds that said minor child is self-supporting, and no child support is ordered. No spousal support is ordered.* It was odd that Phil was still considered a minor child. After all, he was twenty years old by that time and holding down a steady job.

The court also found that 180 shares of stock in the Bank of Agriculture and Commerce in Brentwood were Patricia's sole property, as well as $40,000 held in a time certificate. That was a substantial sum of money in 1971. In fact, Patricia was so well-off for that era, she had to pay Manuel $3,800 to make things equitable.

Patricia got sole ownership of a home and property in Oakley, and Manuel got sole ownership of a residence in Brentwood. Patricia was to keep a 1969 Oldsmobile and Manuel a 1966 Ford Ranchero.

After this divorce, Phil moved in with his mother at her residence in Oakley. Phil's job performance at

Fiberboard was becoming more erratic all the time, as his drug usage increased. On September 20, 1971, Phil was terminated as an employee there. The main reason was that he often didn't show up for work, nor did he call in as to the reason why. It may have been because of his increasing drug usage.

Sometime around then, Phil moved with Anthony Garcia into a residence on Bolton Road in Oakley. He was still playing bass guitar for the Free Spirit Band around the area, and he apparently had a girlfriend named Cathy. At least one court document stated that as a fact in its contents. In fact, the document would relate how close Phil and Cathy seemed to be at that time, at least to others residing in the household, and by the actions that Cathy took soon thereafter.

Having lived a few years in virtual obscurity, on March 5, 1972, Phil's life came into focus because of something that happened in the town of Oakley, where he was now living. On March 5 of that year, thirteen-year-old Dave Gregory (pseudonym) was high. His strange behavior was noticed by a school counselor on the playground, and he was brought to the principal's office. There Dave admitted that he had been smoking marijuana, which he'd obtained from a nearby residence.

Contra Costa County Sheriff's Office (CCSO) detective Julian Beach went to the school and spoke with Dave. Dave told Detective Beach that he'd gone to a house on Bolton Road and had money with him. He asked one of the residents there if he had any grass. The man said that he didn't have any on him, but Dave should wait in the front yard. The man went back into the house and returned with a Baggie of marijuana. He charged Dave $10 for it. Dave said that he then rolled a joint, proceeded to smoke it, "got dizzy and felt good." That's when he had been caught by the counselor on the school grounds.

In exchange for not being charged with possession of an illegal drug, Dave agreed to show Detective Beach where he had obtained the marijuana. They drove over to a nearby locale in Beach's unmarked vehicle, and Dave pointed out the residence from which he had obtained the dope. Beach noted that the residence was a single-story dwelling on the corner of Bolton Road. The residence didn't have any identifying house number that Beach could see, but he described it as a single-story green residence, with white trim.

Detective Beach requested a search warrant for that house to look for and seize *marijuana, amphetamines, personal papers, pipes, clips, drug paraphernalia and other illegal drug items.* There may have been previous information about suspicions concerning this residence, because Detective Beach did not go there alone to serve the search warrant. In fact, he was accompanied by seven other uniformed officers and plainclothes detectives.

Around 7:30 P.M., the officers arrived and Detective Beach knocked on the door. A young woman named Cathy answered, and Beach announced, "Sheriff's office, we have a warrant!" Then the officers fanned out throughout the house. Beach went into the southwest bedroom, where he found plastic Baggies filled with marijuana. In a second bedroom, more Baggies of marijuana were discovered, along with rolling papers and a water pipe.

The officers found sixteen Baggies of pot in the kitchen area and other marijuana-related items. It soon became apparent that this was not a small-scale operation, but was a fairly good-sized dope house.

Scales, which were probably used to reduce larger amounts of marijuana down to Baggie size, were found.

Anthony P. Garcia was arrested for being in possession of all the illegal items. When Detective Beach spoke with Garcia, Anthony told him, "Hey, Phil Garrido pays half the rent here, and half of the grass is his!"

Someone else in the house added, "Yeah, Phil and Cathy live in that (southwest) bedroom." If so, then Phil was sharing a room with a young woman named Cathy—something that did not come to light in all the media frenzy later.

Officers searched into the backyard because they could hear loud amplified guitar music coming from a shed. Deputy Hisey wrote in his report, *The music was extremely loud. I knocked on the door to ascertain who was in there. I called out for Phil.*

A young man came to the door and said that he was Phil. The young man had a bass guitar with him, and there were also three other individuals inside the shed. That wasn't all. When the officer looked inside the shed, behind some sleeping bags that had been strung up on a line, there was row upon row of marijuana plants. The officer searched Phil's pockets, and inside his white windbreaker were Zig-Zag papers and a Baggie of marijuana.

Phillip Garrido was read his rights and arrested. Along with Anthony Garcia, they were escorted to the Antioch Police Department. The entire search and seizure operation on Bolton Road lasted from 7:30 until 11:30 P.M. Along with the marijuana, illegal amphetamines and barbiturates were seized.

At their arraignment at Contra Costa County Delta Municipal Court, both Phil Garrido and Anthony Garcia pleaded not guilty. Phil retained James McFarland as his attorney, and Garcia was appointed a public defender, Jeffrey Brand. At the preliminary hearing on May 24, 1972, both Phil and Anthony sat by their lawyers in court. The prosecution called Detective Beach to the stand, and Beach went over details on all the illegal drugs that he and the other officers had found in the house. Beach also stated that he found bills and receipts proving that Anthony Garcia and Phil Garrido lived there. A young woman— Cathy apparently was watching from the court gallery— was asked to leave the courtroom at that time because she might be called as a witness.

On cross-examination, McFarland attempted to trip up Detective Beach on exactly where the officers had found the Baggies of marijuana and certain items. McFarland noted that in one police report, there was mention that a Baggie full of pills had been taken from Phil Garrido's clothing when he was arrested. But in other reports, that was not the case. And now there was an empty Baggie sitting in court as evidence, minus all pills.

By July 6, 1972, there was another hearing, and the charges by then were Count 1: possession of marijuana; Count 2: cultivation of marijuana; Count 3: possession of narcotics. Defense attorney McFarland made a statement that Phil Garrido had not been arrested with probable cause, and said that the officers could not have seen the marijuana growing in the shed, unless they entered the shed. The marijuana was all behind sleeping bags that had been draped up on wires, hiding the view from the front door of the shed. And since the original search warrant mentioned nothing about the shed, McFarland said, the arrest of Phil Garrido was illegal. The judge did not allow this contention, and the proceedings moved on.

One very interesting thing came to light during the prelim. An envelope had been addressed from

someone to "Mr. and Mrs. Phil Garrido." Yet, Phil
had written down on his arrest documents that he
was single. Just who "Mrs. Garrido" was supposed to
be did not come to light. Some people in the area
later wondered if Cathy had been mistaken for being
Phil's wife. Apparently, they were living together at
that point.

The matter slowly moved on, but before trial,
through his lawyer, Phil Garrido decided to make a
plea deal. Phil withdrew his not guilty plea, and admitted to guilt. On September 5, 1972, the matter was
heard before Judge William Channel. In the plea deal,
Phil Garrido was to spend ninety days in jail and have
three years' probation. He was to undergo a search at
any time without the use of a search warrant.

And yet, as would happen again and again later in
court matters, Phil Garrido began trying to reduce his
sentence and probation oversight. Through his lawyer,
Phil began to try and modify what had already been
handed down in sentencing. Even John Davis, his probation officer, seemed to side with Phil on this matter.
Davis told the judge that a prominent recording company in San Francisco had recently signed Phil Garrido's musical group to a contract to cut an album. To
stay in the group, Phil had to practice with them no
later than January 12, 1973. If he didn't, his spot would
be replaced by a member of a local musicians union.
The probation officer wrote that if Phil was sentenced
for a longer period of time or if his "musical aspira-
tions" were more of a hobby than a regular job, he
wouldn't recommend an early release.

The probation officer went on to note that Phil
hadn't caused any problems while in jail and had followed all the rules there. The probation officer recommended an early termination of Phil's jail sentence.

Backing up this contention were two people, not

named in court documents, who knew Phil Garrido. In a letter to the judge from one individual, there was the statement: *Phil is an outgoing person who makes friends easily and keeps friends. He worked all through high school, saving money for a car. He loved music since he was a young boy. His main interest in life is to be successful in the musical world.*

The letter went on to state that Phil was very accomplished on bass guitar and appreciated by his band members. According to the writer, Phil had close relations with his family and got along with them. In ending, the writer stated, *I feel that he has realized his problem, and got into trouble because of the place he stayed to practice his music.*

A second letter writer who knew Phil wrote, *Phil is a real likeable, well-mannered boy. He has always been ambitious and progressive. He mixes well with older and younger people. He works hard and cooperates with everyone.*

The letter went on to state that Phil grew up in a time when young people were confused about the world and their role in society. As time went on, the letter writer contended, Phil realized his mistake about using illegal drugs, and he wouldn't do so in the future.

There was even a letter written by Phil Garrido to the judge. In it, Phil stated, *While living in Mr. Garcia's house in Oakley, I had a place to practice with a group band. I became involved in cultivating cannabis for personal use, at the above house. A house where I was arrested. My main reason for living there was to have a place to practice and I very foolishly became involved in the cultivation of the drug.*

Phil had specifically mentioned, *"I became involved in cultivating cannabis for* personal *use."* By this means, he seemed to imply that he had not been part of cultivating it for sale, which would have carried a stiffer penalty. Also, near the end of the letter, Phil wrote that he had learned his lessons and would not use illegal drugs again. Later events would prove this to be an empty promise.

At the time, however, Phil Garrido looked like a good candidate for early release from jail so that he could go cut a record in San Francisco. The judge so ordered, but whether Phil and his band ever cut a record in San Francisco was not later reported upon in court documents.

That same year, 1972, there was another incident that would have much more devastating consequences for Phil, as far as the law was concerned. It occurred on April 16, 1972, when Phil was out on bail for the charges against him on the drug raid case. In the parking lot of the Antioch Public Library on Eighteenth Street, not far from Antioch High School, Phil offered a fourteen-year-old girl some barbiturates. She accepted, and the details become murky at this point. From one later report, it seemed that there might have been one more underage girl who accepted a ride, and there might have been one of Phil's friends in the vehicle. Whatever occurred, Phil and the fourteen-year-old girl ended up at a motel farther east on the highway that led to Oakley.

Of the few details that surfaced later, Phil gave the fourteen-year-old girl more barbiturates at the motel room. While she was stoned, he raped her. In fact, this sexual activity seemed to go on for many hours, possibly into the next day. Apparently, Phil even raped her while she was passed out. The girl woke up the next morning in the motel room and phoned her parents. She told them what had happened to her. A police officer went to the motel and discovered the situation.

Much later, the Antioch Police Department (APD) noted, *The appropriate action was taken.*

The appropriate action was an arrest of Phil Garrido on April 17, 1972, even while the matter of the drug charges against him were still going through the legal system. Phil was charged with rape, contributing to the delinquency of a minor, and providing illegal drugs to a minor. Despite the serious charges, there were a lot of problems with the case for the prosecution. In one story, the fourteen-year-old girl did not want to go to trial, and there was a lot of noncooperation on her part. In another story, the girl was such a bad witness, it was the prosecution that did not want to go to trial. And in a third story, Phil Garrido's defense attorney said that he would paint the fourteen-year-old girl "as a little dope-smoking whore." This last story was apparently more than just a rumor. A prominent district attorney (DA) in another county would later attest to this statement. Things were very callous in 1972 regarding rape cases. Often the victim was portrayed as a slut who somehow had the rape coming to her. Whatever the reason, the charges were dropped in "the furtherance of justice," as the court termed it.

Once again, Phil Garrido had dodged a bullet as far as spending time in jail or prison. But he was not through kidnapping, raping, and holding women and girls, with whom he desired sexual intercourse, against their will. He would later state that he did these things, "Because I couldn't help myself." The law would look at the situations in a very different light.

CHAPTER 7

CHRIS AND KATIE

Despite Phil Garrido's brushes with the law, one girl in the Brentwood area was in love with him. Her name was Christine "Chris" Perreira, and she was a very pretty girl who also had gone to Liberty Union High School. Two years younger than Phil, she had been active in many school clubs, including the pep squad and Future Homemakers of America.

In one photo of Chris in high school, she is depicted joining other girls for a trip to the Sunvalley mall in Concord. The caption below the photo stated, *Boarding the bus to await its departure to Concord, Future Homemaker members discuss activities to participate in while in Concord. The February 4 field trip destination was Sun Valley Shopping Center where members learned how to use their purchasing power correctly.* In that era, Sunvalley was the largest mall for miles around, and a trip there was a real treat for the girls in rural Brentwood.

In another high-school yearbook photo, Chris, adorned in moddish clothes, has a large smile on her face as she gazes upon floats that appear to be a circus parade. This occurred in one of the buildings on campus, and the caption stated, *Christine Perreira casts a smile as she watches the "circus" pass by. As you may have guessed, the animals aren't real, but it's always fun to imagine.*

At the time, Chris couldn't imagine what her life would become when she started dating Phil Garrido. In fact, all of Christine's photos, including one of her amongst the pep squad, seem sweet and innocent in light of what was to happen later. The caption below that photo stated, *Pep Club Buttons Help Raise Spirit. On Homecoming Week Pep Club provided frivolity to the Homecoming rally.*

Phil somehow managed to convince Christine that the fourteen-year-old girl had been lying about being raped in a motel room near Antioch. After all, hadn't the charges against him been dropped? And as for the drug charges in the Oakley case? Phil said that he'd changed his ways about dope. By this point, Phil was apparently no longer with Cathy. By March 1973, Christine was so infatuated with the young rock musician, she and Phil eloped to Carson City, Nevada, and got married. Soon she was working as a blackjack dealer at Harrah's in Reno, right on the main drag of Virginia Street. Harrah's in that era was one of the top-line casinos in the area.

It was Chris's job that mainly supported them. Phil made extra money playing with his band at parties, high-school dances, and taverns around the area. But the group wasn't exactly making a fortune doing it.

Apparently, the other members of his band liked Phil. He was a fairly accomplished bass guitar player and he had a good stage presence. But as time went on, the other members of the band became more and more concerned about Phil's increasing drug use. He constantly smoked marijuana and took LSD and cocaine whenever he could. And he couldn't seem to keep his hands off girls, even if they were underage. His fellow band members attested to Phil's wandering ways and penchant for teenage girls.

On top of that, Phil was absolutely addicted to porn. Pornographic magazines and books were strewn around his house, and he liked pornographic movies, especially *Deep Throat*. He also liked *Behind the Green Door*. This was ironic in light of the fact that Phil would one day move to Antioch, California. Antioch's most infamous former citizens, the Mitchell brothers, Jim and Artie Mitchell, were by the 1970s making a string of pornographic movies including *Behind the Green Door*. In that movie, the Mitchell brothers used the Ivory Soap model Marilyn Chambers and turned her into a sex goddess. It was just the kind of fantasy Phil liked. Young, blond and good-looking.

Just how far Phil's drug usage had gone was later attested to by a friend of his in Reno named Gregory Sheppard. Sheppard said of Phil, "I first met Phil when he came into Shep's Discount Liquor, the store owned by me and my mom. I became a friend of Phil Garrido. We were both musicians and we played a lot together. He played bass guitar. During that time, I saw him taking LSD, pot, cocaine, downers and uppers. Sometimes we'd be playing our guitars and he would take three tabs of acid."

Another person who knew Phil during this period was Reno taxi driver William James Emery. Emery smoked marijuana with Phil and noted later, "He was usually stoned or in the process of being that way. When he was stoned, he was more extreme in everything he did." And about one porno movie that Phil showed Emery, concerning lesbians having sex, Emery said, "Phil became very excited. It was of extreme

nature. Manual, oral, and anal action." Emery spoke
of the lesbians using synthetic dildos and vibrators.

By 1976, matters became very rocky in Phil and
Christine's marriage. She later stated, "He began beating me when he got angry. One time, he took a safety
pin and went after my eyes. He left a scar on my face.
He would smack me around, and he threatened me
when I tried to leave him. I was always looking for a
way to find out how to get away. He always told me
he'd find me wherever.

"I did get away once, but he came after me. He
pulled up, turned around, and forced me back into
the car. He was a good manipulator and a monster. He
was pretty much capable of anything."

Phil may have done whatever he could to keep Christine in his life, but he was restless with married life. He
wanted a lot more; and when he was high, he took whatever he wanted. On the night of November 22, 1976,
what he wanted was sex with a woman other than his
wife. Phil was an opportunist, and when he spotted a
pretty young woman at a market in South Lake Tahoe,
California, near Stateline, Nevada, he decided to act on
his impulses. The pretty young woman turned out to
be twenty-five-year-old Katherine "Katie" Callaway.

In 1976, Katie Callaway lived on Venice Avenue in
South Lake Tahoe. She was a blackjack dealer at one of
the nearby casinos in Stateline, Nevada, a job not
unlike that of Phil's wife, who was working at Harrah's
in Reno. Katie later related that on November 22, 1976,
"I was on my way to my boyfriend's house with a hot
dinner I prepared for him. I stopped at a market to
pick up some coffee and some rice and some oil. It
was Ink's Market at Al Tahoe (a section of the city of
South Lake Tahoe). I picked up the items that I

needed, and got back into my car and started to back out, and someone tapped on my window on my side of the car.

"I turned around, and it was a young man out there. I rolled down my window, and he said, 'Excuse me. I didn't mean to scare you, but do you think you could give me a ride down the street? My car won't start. It's cold.'

"I had some friends who lived just down the street, and I had the whole passenger side filled with food. So I told him, 'Well, if you don't mind holding some of this food, I guess I could.'

"So I let him in the car. He was about six feet tall, and very slender. He had on a blue denim jacket and pants that matched and a brown sweater, and he appeared to have very short hair, but [that was because] it was pulled back in a ponytail. We started toward Stateline, because that's the way I was going, and I asked him where he wanted to be let off. He said, 'Do you know where Ski Run [Boulevard] is?'

"I said yes, and he said, 'Well, it's in that area.' Then he added, 'I'm not familiar with this area, but I know where it's at. I don't know the name of the street I'm staying at.'

"I said okay, and turned up Ski Run, because I was going that way, anyway. We approached the street I was going to turn off on, and I asked, 'Is it much farther?'

"He said, 'No, it's just the next block.'

"I said, 'Okay. I'll just drive around the block.' And he indicated a place on the right. I pulled in and looked over, and there was no house. Just an empty lot. I looked at him and asked, 'Are you sure this is the place?'

"He grabbed my key and started to take it out, but it locked in. He turned off the car and grabbed my hands and grabbed my neck with his other hand. He pushed my head down and said, 'All I want is a piece of ass! If you do what I tell you, you won't get hurt. I'm dead serious! I mean it! I'll hurt you if you make me.'

"I said, 'Okay, all right! What do you want? I'll do what you want.' And he pulled out some handcuffs from his pocket, and he cuffed my hands behind my back. And then he said, 'Okay, we're going to go for a ride. I want to make sure nobody sees you.'

"He strapped my head down to my knees with what I thought was a belt. But it turned out to be a strap. Then he put a coat over me. We started somewhere, and I said, 'Where are you taking me?'

"He answered, 'Somewhere far away.'

"I said, 'Why can't we stay here?'

"He answered, 'Look, there's no use arguing. I've got this all planned out. You might as well understand that you're going with me.'

"We headed down the road, and I said again, 'Is this place very far?'

"And he said, 'Yeah, it's pretty far.'

"Then I asked, 'Can you tell me when I'm going back? A couple of hours?'

"He said, 'No, no. You'll be back sometime tomorrow.'

"I told him, 'Did you notice I don't have any gas to go anywhere?'

"He said, 'Don't worry. I know where there's a gas station where I can stop and no one is going to see you.'

"Before we stopped at the gas station, he pulled over and said, 'I'm going to have to tape your mouth and blindfold you, because I don't want you trying to call the attendant.' But I talked him out of the blindfold, because I wore contacts. He had wanted to put some Kleenex and some tape over my eyes. But I told him with the contacts I couldn't stand that. He just put some light-colored tape over my mouth. It was about two and a half inches wide and about four inches long.

"We pulled into a gas station, and I was thinking it must be one that was self-service. I was trying to figure out the amount of time it took to drive there and where there was a self-service station where the attendant couldn't see inside the car. He tried putting regular gasoline into my car, but it needed unleaded. He jumped back to my car, very nervous and upset. And he said, 'Why didn't you tell me your car won't take gas? What's wrong with it?'

"I couldn't tell him because my mouth was taped shut. All I could say was 'Mmm, mmm.'

"He said, 'You want to tell me something, right!'

"I shook my head yes.

"He said, 'I'm going to undo you, and you'd better not scream. Because if you scream, I'm going to jump in the car and cram it.'

"He untied my mouth, a tiny, tiny bit, and he was very nervous. He was about ready to tape it back shut. And I said, 'Unleaded gas.'

"So then he went back and put unleaded gas in the car, and I was trying to think where we were. Because some gas stations in the Tahoe area then didn't have unleaded gas. He put the gas in, and we took off. After a while he said, 'I know you're uncomfortable, so I'm going to pull over as soon as I can and release the strap around your neck and take the tape off your mouth.'

"He stopped approximately five minutes past the gas station and pulled over. I recognized it as an area around Cave Rock (about ten miles from the California/ Nevada state line, within the state of Nevada on Lake Tahoe's eastern shore). He took the strap off around my neck and he took the tape off my mouth. But he left my handcuffs on. Then he picked me up, put me in the backseat on my side, and put the coat back over me. But it didn't quite cover all of my face. He didn't realize that I could see a tiny bit.

"As we drove off, I was kind of watching the terrain to see where we were going. I tried engaging him in conversation, because I was terrified, and I just wanted to kind of get an idea of how to cope with this person. Trying to figure out what his motives were. Trying to keep myself alive. As I did, I noticed the terrain starting to gradually change.

"I wasn't sure where we were going, but then I saw a neon sign and I guessed we were in Carson City (about thirty miles from South Lake Tahoe). I realized we were heading in the direction of Reno.

"We drove to a place where he said there was a shed." (Actually, the shed Phil mentioned was part of a storage/warehouse complex.) "He was gone for a while, but he came back to the car and was very upset. He said that he had lost the key to the shed. He said he was going to have to go off again and find something to pry open the door. He seemed to mention something about going to his house or his car to find something. I still had the handcuffs on, and a coat over my head. We drove off for about five minutes, and it seemed like we drove on a dirt road. He went to some place to look for a tire iron, but he couldn't find one. Then he asked me if I had one in my car.

"I said, 'I think I have one in the trunk.' I said it because I didn't want to cross him at all. I just kept thinking that if I let him go on with his fantasy, I'd have a better chance of staying alive.

"He found a tire iron in my trunk and we drove back to the shed and there was a loud rock band playing. I thought maybe we were out by some discotheque. But he said it was a band practicing in one of the nearby warehouses. The band was loud enough to cover up the banging and the prying of the lock off the warehouse door. He finally got it open, came back, and took the coat off my head. He said, 'Now, am

I going to have to blindfold you, or are you going to keep your eyes closed? I'll be watching you, and I'll have to hurt you if you open your eyes.'

"I said, 'I'll keep my eyes closed.'

"He got me into an area inside the warehouse, and we walked until he said, 'Here we are. You can open your eyes now. I'm going to be right back. I'm going to pull the car around the side of the building. But I'm going to be in sight. So you'd better not try to get away!'

"He went away, and I didn't know where he was. I thought that I was in the middle of the desert somewhere. If I tried to run, I wouldn't even know where to start. He came back and released my hands. He locked the warehouse door. I didn't even know the size of the room I was in because of the way it was set up. Once he released my handcuffs, he told me to undress."

CHAPTER 8

PHIL'S PORNO PALACE

Katie Callaway continued with her story: "I told him I had to go to the bathroom, and he found a little jar for me to urinate in. I got undressed, and I was freezing in there. I got under a filthy, furry, fake fur–type blanket that he had on an old mattress. It was filthy, but I was freezing. He sat down on the mattress, and I was shaking so badly because I was terrified. I think that he felt sorry for me. He told me that I was the only person that ever made him feel bad for what he was doing."

Phil had rigged up the room with a large mattress, which was covered with a satin sheet and dirty fake-fur blanket. He'd decked out the room with hand-cuffs, dildos, pornographic magazines, drugs, and bottles of cheap wine. He also had a movie projector to show pornographic movies and multicolored lights.

Katie related, "Then he just sat on the mattress and talked to me for about an hour. Just conversation. I think he was trying to relax me. He brought out some marijuana and hashish. And some cheap wine, too. He told me to drink some wine. It would relax me, and besides, he wasn't going to let me go anywhere. After that, he undressed and started having sexual intercourse with me. I just lay very still. I was tolerating it.

"The intercourse was continuous. Ten times, maybe twelve. I couldn't believe it. He entered me from behind, too. Anally. He was very rough and very forceful. He got a vibrator, made me get up and sit on an audio speaker. Then he put the vibrator in my vagina. It really hurt. This just went on and on. I was in there for five and a half, or six, hours.

"He got some scissors and cut off all my vaginal area hair. And around that time, somebody came to the door and banged on it. My attacker put some pants on and went out there. I heard, like, a sliding aluminum door. He was speaking with someone. I thought he was going to bring in some friends. And then he came back and was kind of giggling. He said, 'It's just the guy next door. And the guy kind of wanted to know what was going on in here.' And he said the guy told him that he wanted to hear a tune on the radio. But he (the abductor) knew the guy really kind of knew what was going on in here. Something like that.

"Later, a police officer came and banged rather loudly on the aluminum door. The abductor put on his pants and boots to see who was banging. And he came back, and I was still completely naked. He said to me, 'I think it's the police. Are you going to maintain? Are you going to be quiet?'

"I thought it was a setup or something, and I said okay. He went back out, and it was the first time I ventured beyond a wall of plastic that was immediately in front of me in the warehouse. I fought my way through a couple of walls of carpet to peek outside. And I saw, from the waist down, an officer. So I started yelling, 'Help me! Help me!'

"And the officer just stood there, with no reaction

at all. And so did my abductor. So I ran out of there completely naked. And I thought, 'My God! He's not going to help me!'

"And when the abductor didn't try to run, or the officer didn't do anything, I thought, for sure, it was a setup. I thought this guy (the police officer) was a friend of his and they were just having a good time or something. I ran out farther, and I saw the police officer's car, and then I thought, 'He really is a policeman. What the hell is going on here?'

"The abductor said, 'This is my girlfriend. We're just having a good time.'

"And I said, 'No we're not!'

"The officer asked, 'Whose car is that?'

"And I said, 'It's mine.'

"The officer asked, 'Who drove it here?'

"And I said, 'He did,' and pointed at the abductor.

"The officer then said to the man, 'May I see your driver's license, please?' And the abductor said, 'I don't have a driver's license. I didn't drive the car. She did.'

"'No, I didn't,' I replied.

"Then the officer said, 'Go back in the warehouse and put on some clothes.' I went back inside and put my clothes on, and the officer let the abductor back inside, too. I was scared the abductor was going to make me a hostage or something. I was trying to put my clothes on as fast as I could. And the abductor was begging me not to tell on him. That it would be terribly embarrassing. He was pitifully begging me. I just wanted to get out of there and back to the police officer before he did anything rash.

"I got half of my clothes on, one sock, my jeans and coat, and just left the rest. Then I ran back outside, and I think the officer finally realized that I was terrified. Every time he took a step sideways, I was right beside him, taking one step with him. Eventually he believed me. He told me to go sit in the car, and he called in other officers. When they came, they asked me if I wanted to press charges, and I said yes. I didn't see them arrest the man. I wasn't looking. And then he was gone."

Just why the strange reaction by the officer—when Katie Callaway came running naked out of the warehouse, crying for help—was later addressed in a court hearing. The officer was Reno Police Department (RPD) officer Clifford Conrad, and he testified that in the early-morning hours of November 23, 1976, he was patrolling the south side of Reno. Conrad said, "I stopped in the warehouse area to check a suspicious vehicle and suspicious circumstances. The vehicle was from California and the warehouses are normally rented by people from the Reno area. The vehicle shouldn't have been there that time of morning. So I checked further and found the lock on the warehouse door broken off. I tried the door to see if I could open it, and it would come up about four inches. And I kept trying the door until someone came there. It was a garage-type door that rolled from the bottom to the top. The man who answered the door had on a blue pair of pants and nothing else. It was not a warm evening. It was cold.

"I questioned him about if the warehouse was rented to him, and he said no, it was to a friend of his. I'm not sure if he gave me the friend's name or not. But he said his friend lived on Market Street. He said he had lost the key. I asked him for his name, date of birth. Things like that. He said his name was Phillip Garrido. I wanted to check with our dispatcher to see if they would obtain an address and just everything to check his story.

"While I was talking to Mr. Garrido, a young woman stuck her head out behind some type of plastic material on the left-hand side of the garage, as you were looking in, and said, 'Help me.' So I asked her what she wanted. She just said, 'Help me' again and she ran out. She had on no clothing at all. She ran around the back of me and said, 'Help me. He is trying to rape me,' is the way she put it. She also said that she was afraid of him, and she repeated that he was trying to rape her."

It's hard to know at this point if Officer Conrad misunderstood Katie Callaway. He heard it as, "He's trying to rape me." More likely she had said, "He raped me."

Conrad continued, "I talked to him for another minute. And he went inside to get his jacket, after he asked me if he could."

As to this strange occurrence, the prosecutor asked Officer Conrad, "You saw a broken lock on the door. You had a man who came to the door with only his pants on, and nothing else. You had a young lady who ran out, who was naked, crying something about rape. Why did you allow Mr. Garrido to go back into that warehouse when Miss Callaway was in there?"

Conrad answered, "The circumstances that I was led to believe by Mr. Garrido were that he was married and lived down the street, and this was his girlfriend."

"Is that what Mr. Garrido said to you?"

"He implied that. He didn't exactly come out and say it."

"How did he imply it?"

"He said he lived down the street, he was married, and this was a friend of his. He even called her by name. He called her Kathy."

"But Miss Callaway had said something about rape when she came out?" the prosecutor asked.

"She said, 'He is trying to rape me,' are the words she used."

"You didn't feel at that point that there was any danger or anything like that?"

"No, sir."

"And how long were they inside that warehouse together?"

"I would say about thirty seconds to a minute at the most."

"Before this incident, had you ever investigated rape charges before?"

"No, sir."

After both Katie Callaway and Phil Garrido came back outside of the warehouse, after they put on some articles of clothing, Officer Conrad placed Katie in the backseat of his patrol car and continued his conversation with Phil. Conrad related later, "I was still trying to check why he was there and why the broken lock. He said that he and a friend used the place for storing musical instruments and playing there, and that he lost the key to the lock, so he broke the lock off. I asked him how long he had known Kathy and where he had met her. He was being evasive. He said, 'I don't have an answer to that.'"

Another police officer, named Erick Soderblom, soon came on the scene. Soderblom later said, "On my arrival at the Mill Street Warehouse, I observed Officer Conrad and Officer Bradshaw engaged in conversation with a male subject and female subject. I went over to the female subject, who was later identified as Miss Callaway, and began speaking with her to ascertain what the problem was at the warehouse. Miss

Callaway told me that she was the victim of a rape and kidnapping.

"She appeared to have some sort of a red mark or abrasion about her wrists. The marks or abrasions had the appearance of having been made by a handcuff. I was familiar with the marks made by handcuffs. I'd seen those types of marks and abrasions roughly six times per day for over four years. The marks and abrasions on Miss Callaway—they were like a red line that joins on each side of a wrist in a circular pattern, two lines parallel and adjoining a second or a third singular line.

"She appeared to be upset. The male seemed to be quite calm. It was quite illuminated there, both with the vehicles' lights and with the area lighting." Soderblom believed Katie Callaway as soon as she began telling her story to him. What she was saying seemed to fit the situation.

Katie filled out a criminal complaint against her attacker with Officer Soderblom. Meanwhile, Officer Conrad was waiting for his sergeant to arrive. While he did so, Conrad went with Phil into the warehouse so that Phil could retrieve his shirt and jacket. Once Conrad was in there, he spotted a vial of what appeared to be hashish. When the sergeant arrived, he agreed with Officer Conrad that illegal drugs were present. Phil Garrido was read his Miranda rights and then arrested. He was taken to the Washoe Medical Center for testing of alcohol and drugs. After that, he was driven to the Reno City Jail, had his mug shot taken, and was placed into a jail cell.

Reno PD officer Carolyn Jean Carlon became part of the situation concerning Katie Callaway. Carlon went to the Washoe Medical Emergency Center with Katie Callaway and was there as a physical examination was done. A doctor named Dr. Boss took pubic hair samples from Katie and handed them to Officer Carlon. Carlon put them in an envelope, wrote the case number on the envelope, and took the envelope to a Reno PD evidence locker. Also stored into evidence was the comb that Dr. Boss had used, in case there was trace material on the comb.

Officer Soderblom was also present at the examination and related, "After the initial investigation had occurred, when Miss Callaway was at the Reno police station being interviewed by Officer Carlon, I took samplings of Miss Callaway's hair. Each sample was taken separately and bagged and tagged, and then placed into evidence."

Soderblom prepared a card with a case number and wrote on the separate cards, *Four hair samples, one piece of white paper with tape and hair-like particles*. That last item came from a jacket pocket of Phil Garrido's coat. The hair sample on that seemed to match the hair samples taken from Katie Callaway's head. Soderblom also bagged and tagged a piece of Kleenex with some hair strands and silver-colored tape as well.

RPD detective Dan DeMaranville also became involved in this matter. He met with a very upset and shaken Katie Callaway and interviewed her about her ordeal. Katie told DeMaranville about how she had been kidnapped, her terrifying ride from Lake Tahoe, and being taken into the warehouse. Katie related about her rape, "He just kept doing the same thing over and over!"

She was stunned by how long her ordeal had lasted. She initially thought he would rape her and it would be over in a short period of time. Instead, it went on for hour after hour. DeMaranville agreed with Katie that if Officer Conrad had not come along, her attacker probably would have taken her somewhere and killed her after he was done with her.

After her interview with DeMarnaville, Katie was taken to the Washoe County District Attorney's Office. At the DA's office, she gave statements to Deputy District Attorney (DDA) Michael "Mike" Malloy. And before long, she was making more statements to FBI agents because it was obvious she had been taken across state lines.

One of the RPD officers in the case had a very unusual name. He was Nevada J. Wise, and he worked as a criminalist for the Reno PD. He was a lieutenant in charge of technical services in 1976, which was comprised of the crime lab, evidence and property rooms, and photographic laboratory.

Lieutenant Wise went to the warehouse, where the alleged crime had taken place, and he searched and seized items from Katie's Ford Pinto. One item was a belt that Katie said had been used to restrain her. Lieutenant Wise and other technicians gathered items from the vehicle, from the ground, and from inside the warehouse. These items were taken to the Washoe County Criminalistic Laboratory for examination. Among the items was a pair of scissors, a padlock, and a broken metal hasp. A key to the padlock was also found on the floorboard at the rear of the driver's-side seat. This was undoubtedly the key Phil had dropped and had been searching for on the night of November 22.

Also seized were a pair of handcuffs, a key to the handcuffs, and a roll of tape on the passenger-side dashboard. An imitation "furry" blanket was taken from the warehouse; marijuana was seized, along with a small bottle containing a hard brownish material believed to be hashish, a roach, a roach clip, and a hash pipe. Anything that could possibly be narcotic in nature was bagged and taken to the narcotics laboratory for analysis. One of these items was a small container with some kind of residue. The residue would later be analyzed as being trace amounts of LSD.

Detective DeMarnville was also out at the warehouse and he investigated the crime scene. DeMarnville noted that Phil had rigged up different colored studio lights in the interior of his "shed." DeMaranville also noted: *I found a bed. Marital sex toys, handcuffs. A piece of tape, silver in color. There were some baggies, containing a substance believed to be marijuana.* DeMaranville wrote of finding cigarette rolling papers and what appeared to be semen stains on the mattress as well.

Vincent Vitale worked as a criminalist at the Washoe County Sheriff's Office (WCSO). He had a bachelor's degree in chemistry and a master's degree in biochemistry. One of the items Vitale looked at was samples of hair taken from the crime scene. Vitale put samples of hair taken from the head of Katie Callaway onto slides, next to samples of hair taken from Phil's shirt and also from the belt that was seized. The hairs matched. The same thing held true for head hairs found on a piece of tape. As far as pubic hair went, a sample taken from Katie Callaway and one found on the pair of scissors *could have come from the same individual.*

At first, Phil Garrido had "lawyered up" and would not talk to detectives at the jail. However, within a few hours, he had a change of mind and agreed to speak with Detective DeMaranville. At first, Phil barely spoke at all. To put Phil at ease, DeMaranville began talking about unrelated things, such as what Phil did for a living. Phil was happy to tell DeMaranville about his career as a rock musician.

Then slowly the subject turned to the kidnapping of Katie Callaway. Phil was at first hesitant to talk about it, but further questioned as to why he had done it, Phil suddenly blurted out, "Because it's the only way I can get my sexual satisfaction!"

As the interview progressed, Phil began to have tears in his eyes and eventually started crying. De-Maranville didn't know if this was genuine or an act. DeMaranville later stated: "He seemed remorseful. But I think a lot of it was a put-on. Of course, he appeared remorseful, but I think a lot of that was because he got caught."

In another outrageous statement by Phil Garrido to Detective DeMaranville, he started shifting the blame of why it had all occurred in the first place. Phil said, "She was attractive, and she shouldn't have given me a ride."

DeMaranville later added, "He (Phil) wouldn't have had any other choice but to get rid of her (after he was done sexually abusing her). The guy's not stupid. He wasn't going to turn his victim loose and have her go right to the police, which is what she would have done."

Around the same time that Phil was being interviewed, Reno police officers contacted Phil's wife, Chris Garrido, at her work area in Harrah's. They told Chris the basic outlines of what Katie Callaway was alleging. Chris agreed that officers could search the residence where she and Phil lived on Market Street. Asked if Phil owned a pair of handcuffs, Chris admitted that she had bought him a pair from a local pawnshop in the recent past.

Chris accompanied the officers to her residence, and they discovered numerous pornographic magazines and books there. One officer was going to look at some Polaroid photos, and Chris asked him not to. She said that those photos had been taken by Phil of her naked, and the photos depicted her "pubic area." The officer complied and did not look at or seize the photos. Just what else the photos might have depicted was never known.

Because Katie Callaway had been kidnapped in California and transported to Nevada, the FBI was now involved. Special Agent Gerald Adams was an agent in South Lake Tahoe, and he met Katie Callaway and had her retrace her path on the night of November 22 through 23, 1976. Agent Adams went with Katie to Ink's Market on Highway 50, and then up Ski Run Boulevard to Willow Avenue. They turned left on Willow and then to a vacant lot, where Katie said she had been attacked initially. This was clearly on the California side of the border, and she obviously had been transported to a warehouse in Reno, Nevada, where she was raped.

Two different cases began to go forward against Phil Garrido for the abduction and rape of Katie Callaway in December 1976. One was a federal case, because he had kidnapped her in California and taken her across state lines into Nevada, and the charges mainly concerned the kidnapping. The second case was a state of Nevada case, to be held at a superior court. The charges there were for the rape and other related charges in the commission of the rape. The first to take a crack at Phil in a trial would be the Feds.

CHAPTER 9

INSIDE PHIL'S MIND

Phil Garrido might have thought he was being very clever by having a storage room in a warehouse turned into a "sex parlor," where he could restrain a victim and have sex with her. But the fact that he had kidnapped Katie Callaway in California and taken her to Nevada made his plight infinitely worse. A federal grand jury in Reno, Nevada, indicted Phil on kidnapping charges. In legal language, they stated: *On or about the 22nd day of November, 1976, Phillip Craig Garrido knowingly transported in interstate commerce, from South Lake Tahoe, California, to Reno, Nevada, one Katherine Callaway who had theretofore been unlawfully seized, kidnapped, carried away and held by Phillip Craig Garrido; all in violation of Title 18, United States Code, Section 1201.*

In a document that Phil had to fill out about his financial situation, he listed one dependent—his wife, and that he was self-employed. As to property he owned, all he listed were musical instruments.

Compared to the worldwide attention Phil Garrido would receive in 2009 for the kidnapping of Jaycee

Lee Dugard, his 1976 case barely made the newspapers at all. A short article in the *Reno Gazette-Journal* stated MUSICIAN HELD IN KIDNAP CASE. The entire article was three paragraphs long and related in very sketchy details about the kidnapper, the victim, and the fact that the FBI was involved because the victim had been taken across state lines. By comparison, an article just above it, entitled TEEN-AGE GIRL LEADS WILD CHASE, was much more lengthy, and related about a teenage girl who had led cops on a one hundred mile per hour chase in the area.

Oddly, it wasn't Phil Garrido as much as Officer Conrad who received much more print the next day. And even more oddly, Conrad received praise for his actions in the arrest of Phil Garrido. Granted, Conrad had spotted the car with a California license plate and a broken lock at the warehouse on Mill Street. But he also had let Phil Garrido reenter the warehouse with Katie Callaway, which terrified her and could have led to a very dangerous situation.

The title of the article was POLICEMAN GIVEN PRAISE FOR RESCUE OF WOMAN. In the article, a Reno police detective stated, *"Officer Clifford Conrad did a heck of a job."* The detective said that Conrad had stopped to see why a car was parked at that late hour in front of a warehouse. The detective added that a warehouse storage unit had rugs on the floor and walls, pornographic magazines, a movie projector, marital aids, a spotlight, wine, and hot water.

In the federal case, a judge assigned a defense attorney, Willard Van Hazel, for Phil Garrido from the Office of the Federal Public Defender. And it soon became apparent in what direction Van Hazel's defense was going to go. Van Hazel asked that Phil be examined by a psychiatrist because it was possible that he was mentally ill. This motion was granted, and Reno psychiatrist Lynn Gerow went to the jail, where Phil was incarcerated, to examine him. In a report to federal judge Bruce Thompson, Gerow related that Phillip Garrido was a tall, thin white male, appeared "unkempt and unshaven," but he presented his story in a "clear and logical fashion."

Phil told Dr. Gerow that he had extensively used LSD, marijuana, alcohol, and cocaine for the previous six years. Phil said that he had particularly abused LSD. Then he stated that from 1970 to 1974, he took LSD on an almost daily basis, and had done so more sparingly up until his arrest. Phil also related that he took "four hits of acid" after he had kidnapped Katie Callaway on the drive to Reno.

Phil complained of residual effects from the LSD, such as "flashbacks." Phil said that he had never been hospitalized for psychiatric treatment, and didn't have "head problems" other than an occasional migraine. Phil told of one incarceration in the Contra Costa County Clayton Farm for possession of an illegal substance. He did not mention his guilty plea on the 1972 Oakley charges, or speak of it at all. Nor did he mention anything about his alleged rape of a fourteen-year-old girl in April 1972 near Antioch.

About Phil's family history, the report noted: *He reports considerable emotional conflict with his parents during his formative years. He graduated from Lincoln Union High School in 1969.* (It was actually Liberty Union High School.) *Thereafter he worked on and off as a musician and began using drugs immediately. He was married in 1973, and his wife currently works as a dealer in a local casino.*

Phil brought up his religious beliefs in what Dr. Gerow called "recent increasing religiosity." Gerow noted that there were several references to God and

Jesus. Phil stated that he had become more religious in recent weeks, and Gerow wrote that Phil's verbal productions were not delusional in quality: *He based his new religious interests more appropriately on the considerable guilt and fear he was experiencing since being incarcerated. He believes strongly that LSD increases his sexual powers. He was preoccupied with the idea of sex and admitted to a history of several sexual disorders. He looked and acted depressed. He would occasionally cry during the interview.*

Phil denied any suicidal tendencies, and the report stated that he was "oriented" in all three spheres. His memory for immediate, recent, and remote events was at times spotty, but there was nothing specific to *make one suspect the presence of a chronic organic brain syndrome.* Phil did complain of hallucinations at times, but Gerow noted that was common for someone who had used a lot of LSD. Then Gerow noted, *His judgment was very poor. His insight minimal. His intelligence appeared to be average.*

Dr. Gerow's diagnosis fell into two categories. In one, Gerow stated that Phil showed the symptoms of *a mixed sexual deviation and chronic drug abuse.* The latter might have made the former worse. Gerow related that a man with satyriasis, such as Phil experienced, often thought about sex constantly and masturbated frequently. Phil seemed to fall into this category. Someone with satyriasis could have organic dysfunctions in the temporal lobe or cerebral syphilis, and Gerow recommended that neurological testing be performed on Phillip Garrido.

As far as Phil's ability to help his attorney in his defense and understand what was going on in court, Dr. Gerow stated that Phil was competent to do those things. Gerow added one more thing: *It is also my opinion that at the time of the crime, the defendant as a result of mental illness or defect did not have substantial capacity either to appreciate the wrongfulness of his conduct or to conform his conduct to the requirements of the law.* If indeed, Phil Garrido did not understand what he was doing was wrong at the time of the crime, then he had not formed *intent* to commit a crime.

With that report in mind, a federal district judge ordered on December 28, 1976: *The United States Marshall is directed to take the defendant, Phillip Craig Garrido, from the Washoe County Jail to Dr. Peterman's office at the above address for purposes of said examination (an EEG and a neurological consultation). Dr. Peterman is directed to make a written report of his findings and to furnish copies of the same on or before January 13, 1976.*

In a self-report about himself just before the exam, Phil stated that he had attended high school and got mostly B's and C's, with an occasional D, on his report cards. Phil also noted that in the early 1970s he had taken up to five "hits" of LSD in one day. Despite taking LSD prior to the rape of Katie Callaway, Phil related that he could remember the events quite well.

After Dr. Albert Peterman ran his tests, he stated that there was no history of head injuries, skull fracture, or concussion. Just why Phil did not bring up his motorcycle accident or head trauma that he incurred, along with surgery at an Antioch hospital, is unknown. (And it would lead some detectives in the future to wonder if this accident ever took place at all. The only people to mention it would be Phil and his father, Manuel.)

Dr. Peterman also noted that there was no history of convulsive disorders or history of epilepsy in the family. Phil did suffer from migraine headaches, but he was able to counteract that by not eating certain foods to which he was allergic. A month previously,

Phil had a cyst removed from his scalp, which had now healed.

Dr. Albert Peterman wrote that an EEG performed in his office that day on Phil Garrido was entirely normal: *The examination reveals a quite apprehensive, somewhat withdrawn, thin, young man who is alert, well-oriented and cooperative. He did burst into tears on one occasion when I asked him to do some calculations to test organic brain function, but otherwise was reasonably well composed.*

Dr. Peterman related that Phil could do serial sevens and retain five digits in forward and reverse order. The cranial nerve function was intact; pupils and eye-grounds were normal; visual fields were full to confrontation. There was no carotid bruit; muscle strength and stretch reflexes were fine; there also was no particular tremor or movement disorder.

Dr. Peterman added, *He states that he is looking forward to going to court, has found religion and feels that his life will change for the better. I see no evidence either by history, examination or EEG of brain damage per se, although there is considerable evidence of anxiety and depression and personality disorder as noted by Dr. Gerow.*

Just before trial, Phil Garrido's attorney, Willard Van Hazel, wanted the judge to issue special instructions to the jurors. These included: *If the evidence in the case leaves you with a* reasonable doubt *as to whether the defendant was sane at the time of the alleged offense, you will find him not guilty even though it may appear that he was sane at earlier and later times.* This was in essence a "temporary insanity" ruling. Van Hazel noted, *The law does not hold a person criminally accountable for his conduct while insane since an insane person is not capable of forming the intent essential to the commission of a crime.*

Van Hazel added one more important issue on the motion. That jurors were not to take into account that Katie Callaway had been raped. Van Hazel stated that issue was a Nevada case and not part of the federal case. A judge looked at this motion, and then wrote upon it, *Offered and rejected.*

CHAPTER 10

A FEDERAL CASE

At Phil Garrido's federal trial, both the prosecution and defense examined witnesses in a fairly straightforward path that had been laid down in previous police reports and interviews. It was on cross-examination and redirect that new and different avenues were explored. This began right away when Phil's attorney, Willard Van Hazel, asked questions of Katie Callaway after her direct testimony was finished.

Van Hazel wanted to know, "Did the defendant ever threaten you with a weapon or display a weapon?"

Katie replied, "No. But he said that he would not hurt me unless I attempted to get him caught, or whatever. He said he would just bash my head so as to knock me out. The only weapon, and it probably couldn't even be considered a weapon, but I was considering it at the time, was a pair of scissors."

Van Hazel asked if the scissors had been used in California or in the car ride. She said, "I didn't see them until I was inside of where he had me. Then he cut off my pubic hair with them."

"Did he ever simulate a weapon? Like someone in a bank robbery saying, 'I've got a gun here, give me your money.'"

"No, but he was six foot four. He didn't really have to do a whole lot. I'm five foot five and weigh one hundred five pounds."

Van Hazel also asked about the circumstances when Phil had first contacted her. Katie recalled, "He was dressed very nicely. He had on a denim jacket and denim matching pants. It looked like he had his hair pulled back, very neat. He had on a brown sweater. I may have seen him in the store. I was walking in the back of the store to gather items real fast, because I was late for my boyfriend's, and it seemed like I glanced down an aisle and saw him, full face, standing there for just a second."

In an era when rape victims could still be castigated for their attire, Van Hazel asked, "Was your jacket zipped while you were in the store?"

"I don't remember."

"Were you wearing a brassiere that night?"

"No."

"When he got in the car, did he make any suggestive moves or suggestive conversation? By that, I mean of a sexual overtone."

"No, none whatsoever."

Van Hazel wanted to know what conversation had taken place as they drove along toward an area where Phil said that he had friends. Katie replied, "I talked maybe sideways, and probably seemed very cold to him, because I just don't talk to strangers. I am a twenty-one dealer, and I see millions of people a day. I just don't engage in conversation with strangers."

Asked about the conversation of when he had first handcuffed her, Katie responded, "He asked me, 'Are you expected anywhere?' And I said, 'Well, I'm expected at my boyfriend's for dinner. I have to get to work at nine A.M.' And he said, 'Well, if you are real good, I will try and have you back by dawn.'"

Van Hazel asked about when she was first attacked in the car, "Did you sound your horn?"

"No."

"Or scream?"

"No."

"Did he have his hand over your mouth at the time he first grabbed you?"

"No. At first I thought he was going to try and grab me and kiss me. But then one hand went for the keys and one hand went for my neck. He turned the car off. I kept trying to push my head up, because I didn't understand what was going on. I thought he was kidding. It happened so fast. I had never been assaulted before, or attacked, or anything. I was waiting at any second for a weapon to be brought out. I didn't make any fast defensive moves because of that. I was just taken by surprise by the whole situation."

Van Hazel asked, "Now, I take it that you were in fear at this time and you were acting in such a way not to antagonize him. Is that correct?"

Katie said, "I was completely passive. I was trying to deal with the whole situation as logically as I could without allowing terror to take over. The fact of being bound, my hands handcuffed, my head strapped down to my knees and being at the complete mercy of someone. I had no idea what he was going to do with me or what was going on in his mind at the time."

"Now, I believe you stated at one point he said if you tried to do something—if you tried to do anything, that he would use a certain amount of force to overcome you. Did he say he would kill you?"

"He said he would knock me in the head and knock me out."

"Did he ever say to you, 'I will not kill you. I will just use whatever force I need to'?"

"That is true. He said, 'I am not going to hurt you unless you try—for my own protection, I will hurt you.'"

"Did you ever suggest to him that if he had sex on his mind, that perhaps you could get the whole thing over right then and there?"

"Yes, I did."

"And what did he say?"

"He said, 'You might as well get that out of your mind. You are going with me. You have got no choice, I have got it all planned. I am just not going to let you go now, so might as well not ask again.'"

"Did he say he would bring you back to the Tahoe area when he was done?"

"I asked him if he was going to give me gas money so I could get back. He said, 'Don't worry, don't worry.' That's all he would say."

"Now, when the defendant talked about a sexual fantasy or that he couldn't help himself, and although he had a nice wife, this was just something he had to do. Where did that conversation occur? In California, or Nevada, or aren't you sure?"

"It must have been in Nevada. He told me I had a long ride ahead of me and I tried to engage him in conversation. You know, try and figure out what kind of person abducted me and what state of mind he was in. Like I said, how to best deal with it. And I tried to talk to him more of on a peer-type basis. The same age group, type of person, you know, talk to him as a friend. And I asked him what aspect got him off doing this to young ladies. And he said that it was just fantasies that he had to live out. He said he couldn't help himself almost, but he had to do it. He said that he had a completely happy life with his wife. They had a very happy sexual life and he was completely satisfied there. But

he had to do this, and his wife knew and understood."
(That was Phil's take on it. Christine most likely did not
know, and would have been appalled if she found out.)

"Did he mention what his wife did for a living?"

"He said she was a (blackjack) dealer. I asked him
why he told me that if he didn't want to do anything
about, you know, knowing him. He also told me his
name was Bill, and then he slipped up later on and
he said, 'My wife said 'Phil' the other day,' but I continued to call him Bill, so he wouldn't have any idea
and think I knew his real name. And when I mentioned that I was a twenty-one dealer, he kind of chuck-
led and said that his wife was a twenty-one dealer also.
And I said, 'Oh, then you are from Reno?' And he responded, 'Well, just because I told you that, she could
be from Las Vegas or anywhere, you know. It doesn't
mean we are from this area.' He said he wasn't from
the area. He was just up here doing a few things. No
one even knew his real identity, where he was right
now. He could be gone in a week, anyway, so it really
didn't matter. He indicated to me that he was a complete transient in the area."

Van Hazel asked, "Did you say anything in response,
of when he talked about his sex fantasy? Did you say
anything about fantasies or anything like that?"

"I completely went along with everything. I said,
'Oh, yes. Oh, I like that, too.' You know, I tried to completely stay on good terms with him. Like, 'I'm all for
what you're doing.'"

"In that conversation, did you say you often wondered what it would be like to be raped, or something
like that?"

"Oh, yes. I said, 'If everything you are telling me is
true, that you are not going to hurt me, that all you
want to do is give me pleasure and just make me feel

good, even though you've abducted me, under force, then I guess it is not going to be so bad.'"

"Coming down that hill (into Carson City), did he talk about anything other than his sex fantasy? Did he refer to religion, for instance?"

"Yes. He talked about Jesus. He said he was going to turn himself over to Jesus next year."

"Now, going through the evening, did he say any other things that were revealing as to who he might be or what he did?"

"I don't know if he indicated then if he was a musician or not, but he kept saying, 'Someday I'm going to let you know who I am. Someday I just might come back and tell you who I am.' As if I thought he was somebody famous or something."

Asked about the band she heard at the warehouse complex, Katie replied, "There was a loud, loud band. He said it was a band practicing. At one time when we left to go get the tire iron, we came back and I asked something about the band. And he said, 'Oh, did you think that is the same band? Didn't you recognize the other band we heard the first time we were here?' It was like he was trying to confuse me."

Asked if she thought Phil had put in a tape to simulate a live band playing, Katie answered, "It was playing when we drove up. Which means he didn't have time to go turn on anything. And I thought maybe they were his friends. His band members. And I thought if I tried to run, all of those people were his friends."

Van Hazel wanted to know if Phil had drugs there, and Katie replied, "I had sarcastically said on the way there, 'Gee, I wish I had a joint right now,' meaning to relax my nerves. And he said, 'Oh, well. I've got some stuff back at the shed that will blow your head away.' When we got there, he had some hash in a glass vial

and he had some marijuana in a small Baggie. Paraphernalia, a roach clip, a pipe, things like that."

Asked if she used any dope that Phil had, Katie
replied that she had. "I tried some hashish. It was very
strong. It intensified all my paranoid feelings extremely, and I didn't smoke any more. I just wanted
to be fully competent and fully alert, because of the situation I was in. It intensified everything. He had also
asked me to drink some cheap wine. And he kept in-
sisting I take a few drinks because I was shaking so terribly. I drank not even half a glass of the wine."

Van Hazel wanted to know if Phil had anything to
drink. Katie responded, "Yes, he got almost to the point
of intoxication. He got giggly and kept saying, 'Oh, I
hardly ever drink. I'm really loaded from the wine.'"

Wanting to know how Katie reacted when Officer
Conrad let Phil back in the shed with her to put on
some clothes, Katie said, "I don't know why he sent
him back in. The abductor scared me so bad, I didn't
even get my clothes on. He could have done anything
to me at that time. His life was in jeopardy and he
knew he was caught. And at one point, the abductor
said he was going to fight me in court, and I would
never win."

Van Hazel asked why at first she had not told Officer Conrad that she had been raped and wanted to
press charges. In fact, initially Katie had mentioned
that she just wanted to go home. To this, Katie said, "I
was very confused. I was very frightened. I was almost
in a state of unbelief of the whole situation because of
the officer's reaction and because of Mr. Garrido's
reaction when I first cried for help. You know, there
was no immediate response, and no immediate reaction. Mr. Garrido was looking at me very sorrowfully
and pitifully. And I was just answering the officer
questioning me with yes and no answers. As far as, 'Is

this your car? Did he drive it?' And it was all going back and forth and getting nowhere. I just wanted to get out of there. My nerves were shot. It had been a long ordeal. A horrible ordeal. I wanted to get away from there, from that person. At that point, I was almost at the snapping point. I was almost at the point of thinking of picking up the scissors and trying to kill him. It was a very traumatic thing. At that point, I couldn't take it any longer."

These words rushed out of Katie's mouth so quickly, Judge Thompson told her, "Just wait until you get a question."

Asked how Phil's demeanor had changed over time, Katie replied, "In the car, he seemed very nervous, very uptight. Later in the warehouse, he was a lot calmer. He would get very distant looks, like he was just spaced out. And I had no faith that he was going to take me back home, like he said he would."

Van Hazel may have wished that he had never asked one final question. "Did you gain the impression that the defendant believed you when you resorted to this ruse?" (He was referring to her acting as if she might enjoy being tied up and raped.) "Did he act nice toward you?"

Katie replied, "Oh, yes. I am sure that is what made him act so nicely toward me throughout the whole thing, [it] was because of my attitude for my own protection. He said I was the only one who had ever made him feel bad about what he was doing."

The words "the only one who had ever made him feel bad" implied there had been more than one. In other words, more than just the girl Phil had taken from the Antioch Library in 1972 to a motel room and raped. How many more—or who they were—got shut off very quickly in questioning.

CHAPTER 11

INCRIMINATING EVIDENCE

After Katie Callaway's lengthy testimony, there was a string of other witnesses. One of these was her boyfriend at the time, David Wade. Wade said that on the afternoon of November 22, 1976, he had asked Katie to stop by a store and pick up some coffee. She was supposed to have shown up at around seven o'clock, but did not show up at all that night.

The next witness was Forrest Susan Dougherty. She and two friends were at a tavern called Rojo's in South Lake Tahoe on November 22. Dougherty testified, "As we were leaving, we were walking toward the car to get in. I saw Katie pulling out of a parking space in front of Ink's Market. I observed her pulling out and backing up, and I saw her and another person, a man, in the car. I observed the fact that he appeared to have very short hair and I was trying to figure out who he was. I didn't know any of her friends that had hair that short." (Phil had tied his long hair back in a ponytail that evening.) "Katie headed toward Stateline after that."

Van Hazel asked, "Mrs. Dougherty, were you interviewed by an FBI agent by the name of Gerald Adams on or about November 23, 1976?"

She replied, "I guess that was his name. I was interviewed by an FBI agent."

"Do you have a recollection of making this statement to him, and I quote: 'Then I saw a white male with very dark short hair, may have had some curl to it, and his ears were visible.'" (Phil had very straight hair.)

Dougherty replied, "I don't recall saying that his hair had a curl to it."

After Dougherty, William James Emery testified that he had been living in a storage shed in the warehouse where Phil had taken Katie Callaway. Emery said that he had met Phil before that and knew that he was a musician. Emery related, "He asked if I would watch his shed and make sure that nobody broke in or anything, because he played music. And he gave me specific signs of the vehicles that were allowed in front of his storage shed. He gave me a phone number and I was to call him if some car was there that wasn't supposed to be there."

Asked about the night and early-morning hours of the time in question, Emery said, "I was getting off from driving a taxi for Whittlesea. And about twelve-fifteen A.M., I got out of the taxi and looked down the two rows of storage sheds, and there was a vehicle parked in front of the gentleman's (Phil's) shed. I didn't recognize it. I walked up and looked at it, and it had a California license plate. It was a blue Ford Pinto. I went back to my storage unit and lifted up the door about three feet and went in and changed clothes."

Emery was asked if he knocked on the shed door,

and he said that he had done so twice. He added that no one responded, which makes him unlikely as the one Phil had spoken to at some point before the police officers arrived. Emery continued with his testimony, "I sat outside for a while by my shed and I let my dogs play, to see if somebody would come out (of Phil's shed). And I sat there for quite a while, maybe an hour, and nobody came out and there wasn't any noise. But the hasp was down, so I knew somebody was in there. I went into my shed, got a piece of paper and pencil, and wrote down the license number and took the phone number that he gave me. I rode my bicycle up to the service station and called his house. I didn't get any response. So I rode about three more blocks to his house and knocked on the door. But nobody responded." (Christine might have been working a late shift and dealing cards at a casino at that time.) "So I went back to my shed and then went to bed."

Both federal prosecutor Leland Lutfy and Willard Van Hazel wanted to get at why Officer Clifford Conrad had acted the way he did at the storage shed area on November 23. Lutfy had Conrad testify basically to the same things he had written in his report. Lutfy also asked, "During the times that you had the conversation with the defendant at the scene, were there any questions that you asked him he did not understand?"

Conrad said there were none. So then Lutfy wanted to know if Phil was able to answer each and every question. Conrad replied, "He was evasive on some. I asked him how long he knew Miss Callaway, and where he had met her. Things like that. And he said, 'I don't have an answer to that.'"

* * *

On cross, Willard Van Hazel got to a key point in Officer Conrad's initial report. Van Hazel said, "She (Katie) stated something to the effect, 'He is trying to rape me'?"

Conrad replied, "Yes, sir. Those were her exact words."

"Exact words?"

"Yes, sir."

"And it couldn't have been, 'He raped me.' Past tense?"

"No, sir. When she said it, she said, 'Trying.'"

As to another key point, Van Hazel asked, "Why did you have her go back in and detain what would have been a suspect at that point?" (In other words, let Katie go back in alone and detain Phil outside.) "You had a suspect in your presence, didn't you?"

"Not at that time," Conrad responded.

"Could you observe them when they went back inside?"

"No, sir."

"Did either the victim or the defendant appear intoxicated or under the influence of anything?"

"No, sir."

"There was no slurred speech on the part of the defendant, Mr. Garrido, as though he had been drinking?"

"No, sir."

"Did you smell anything on his breath?"

"I believe I had a cold at the time."

"At the time you were questioning either one of them, [did you] smell any odors that were suggestive of marijuana or hashish?"

"No, sir. I didn't."

"When did you first become aware that there might have been narcotics involved in the crime scene?"

"After Officer Bradshaw got there. I asked Mr. Garrido if there was anyone else inside of the shed, since we couldn't see the rear area. And he said no. And I asked him if I could go in and look, and he said yes. As soon as I walked in, a small cigarette on the floor and a small vial and roach clip and a few other things became visible. I picked it up (the marijuana cigarette) and I couldn't smell anything then. So I asked—I can't remember if it was Officer Bradshaw or Officer Soderblom—to smell it. And they said it smelled like marijuana."

"What was the demeanor of the defendant when you first met him? Did he appear frightened or appear apprehensive to you?"

"No, sir."

"When Miss Callaway ran out screaming, 'Help me!' what did the defendant do? Did he appear to run?"

"No, sir. He just stood there."

"When they both came back out again, after getting dressed, did the defendant's demeanor change at any point?"

"I would say about a couple of minutes before we placed him under arrest and I was asking more specific details about the victim, Miss Callaway, and that is when he said, 'I don't have an answer.' That's about the only time he got excited. He became more short. Not actually hostile. More defensive."

A couple of criminalists testified about items found at the crime scene, and these were introduced into evidence. Among the items were a belt, a pair of scissors, a lock, a broken hasp, and a key. There were also hair samples, a pair of handcuffs, a piece of tape with hair on it, a shirt, and a jacket.

During a break, when the jury was out of the courtroom, Van Hazel brought up an important issue with the judge. Van Hazel said, "Before proceeding with the defense, Mr. Garrido and I have conferred about trial strategy. . . ."

Judge Thomspon stopped Van Hazel right there, and he said, "You listen to this, Mr. Garrido, very carefully."

Phil replied, "All right."

Van Hazel continued, "The substance of that advice I gave him has been in the course of presenting the line of defense. And I understand the defendant is raising an issue of insanity or lack of specific intent. I am afraid, or have cautioned my client, that if he takes the stand, which would almost seem necessary to sustain that defense of not knowing that what he did at the time was morally wrong. He exposes himself to incrimination on outstanding charges in the state of Nevada. And also charges, which I believe are pending, in the state of California, carrying major penalties."

Judge Thompson responded, "Let's discuss first the possibility of the introduction by the government of other similar acts."

Leland Lutfy replied, "Well, if he takes the stand, I am sure going to want to go into that, Your Honor."

Judge Thompson replied, "On what basis, do you think you are entitled to go into it?"

Lutfy answered, "We believe we can show the defense is coming up with an insanity or some kind of defense based on LSD abuse. That this man was in some kind of fantasy and could not differentiate between fantasy and reality. We think by pointing to and questioning the defendant about prior specific acts prior to this incident, we can show he is following a pattern of attempting to kidnap, and raping, other women."

By bringing this up, it certainly seemed that Lutfy

was going to try and get information into trial about Phil's rape of the young woman in Antioch in 1972. The judge asked, "How does that relate to the proposed defense?"

Lutfy replied, "Because I think that the jury has a right to be able to see that the defendant is claiming that here is one instance he couldn't differentiate between reality and—"

Judge Thompson jumped in, "How do you know he is claiming it in this one instance?"

Lutfy responded, "I don't know. I don't know what he is claiming. I don't really know at this point anything other than the fact that I have been served with a notice of some kind of a basis like that. And we do have evidence, we do have information of other acts by this defendant."

This statement was interesting in its own right: "Information of other acts." It brought up the possibility that there were more acts than just the rape of the young woman in Antioch in 1972, perpetrated by Phil Garrido. Otherwise, if that was the only one, Lutfy most likely would have said, "Information of *another act*."

Judge Thompson asked, "On what basis is that type of evidence ever admissible? On the face of it, it is prejudicial. So you have to have some reason to offer it."

Lutfy responded, "He (Garrido) had the intent prior, and this is a consistent act with prior intent to—"

Judge Thompson interrupted again. "I don't know how often he used LSD. I don't know whether or not he used it then. We have no evidence at this point that he used it during the course of this event. Apparently, one of the elements to be considered is whether he should be fearful that you can offer evidence of other similar acts. And it is not admissible just because it is a similar act close in time. There has got to be some basis for it. I don't know what he is going to testify to. It seems to me that if his only defense is that he didn't know what he was doing (was wrong), it is equably arguable that he didn't know what he was doing a month before."

Lutfy tried again. "We can show a similar pattern of behavior in a prior offense relative to the handcuffs. It goes to intent. I think it can show the jury—the jury has a right to see that and determine whether or not this man was fantasizing one time, or whether or not it was a thought-out plan of kidnapping and raping a woman. I am not stating at this time the government intends to go into that. I just want the opportunity to be able to, if we so desire, on cross-examination."

Judge Thompson responded, "You can offer it, but you are going to offer it in the absence of the jury and not mention anything like that in the presence of the jury until you obtain a ruling."

Then Judge Thompson asked Phil if he was going to testify in his own defense. Judge Thompson said, "Mr. Garrido, I want to advise you that it is a decision you have to make. In the final analysis, you can listen to Mr. Van Hazel and consider his advice, but it has to be your decision as to whether you are going to testify. At the moment, the government has rested, and the only thing the jury has to consider is the testimony of Miss Callaway and the corroborating circumstances. You have indicated that you intend to present a defense of drug abuse and that you are not in control of yourself, and that you should not be held legally responsible for your conduct because of it. I don't know if there is any way that you can prove the extent of your drug abuse without testifying yourself. You might consider that. I don't know whether these horrible side effects that Mr. Van Hazel envisions would happen or not. I have indicated somewhat that

I think that the other evidence (prior bad acts) might be irrelevant, but I haven't decided. I have to tell you this also, Mr. Garrido, that if you decide to take the stand and testify, any testimony that you give can be used in any criminal prosecution. You are not testifying under any form of immunity whatsoever. Do you understand?"

Phil replied, "Yes, Your Honor."

In a city known for gambling, Phil Garrido decided to roll the dice and hope that the jury would believe him when he said that drugs had made his mental processes so erratic and flawed that he couldn't control his own actions when he kidnapped and raped Katie Callaway.

CHAPTER 12

OBSESSION

After short testimony by Gregory Sheppard as to Phil Garrido's drug use, Phil took the stand on his own behalf. Willard Van Hazel asked Phil, "Are you married?" Phil replied, "Yes, I am." Van Hazel then asked, "Happily?" Phil answered, "Very happily."

So Van Hazel wanted to know, "Do you find your wife attractive?" Phil said, "She is beautiful."

"Mr. Garrido, how long have you been using drugs? And by that, I mean either hallucinogens, like acid, or cocaine or marijuana?"

Phil replied, "When I graduated high school, within that first month after graduation, is when I was first introduced to marijuana. And within a month after that, I was introduced to LSD."

"You were arrested for that, possession of marijuana, weren't you?"

"In 1969, and also with LSD." Phil made no mention of the 1972 drug bust in Oakley, California.

Van Hazel asked if Phil had been using drugs, including LSD, up to his arrest, and Phil said that he had. Asked what other kinds of drugs he used, Phil replied that he sometimes used uppers and downers, but his drugs of choice were marijuana and LSD. Phil said that he would also use hashish whenever he could afford it.

As to the most LSD Phil had taken on one occasion, he said he had taken ten hits of LSD. And by that, he added, "I took it all at once. All ten at once. The only time that I ever had any bad trips was in the younger part of my experience with LSD, as far as a frightening experience."

Van Hazel asked, "Does LSD act as a sexual stimulant on you?"

Phil replied, "Beyond a doubt, it does."

"What kind of physical reactions do you have with LSD?"

"Within the first half hour, you start to get off. And then I start to get body temperatures. You get warm and then chills. And I would get dry mouth. I usually always become nervous."

Asked if he took LSD on the day he kidnapped Katie Callaway, Phil said that he had. "Four hits. I got it in South Lake Tahoe."

Van Hazel wondered if Phil had sexual fantasies in conjunction with his drug use, clear back to 1969. Phil related, "The effect was—I was able to masturbate myself while I was either watching a movie or looking at magazines. The movies were at a drive-in. I would take my automobile and I would put up on the side windows two towels, some type of something to keep anybody from seeing me, and I would sit in the backseat." As far as magazines went, Phil said he masturbated at home with those.

Asked if he'd purchased pornographic films or videos, Phil said he had done so within the previous two years. And as far as masturbating in public, Phil answered, "I did it in restaurants, bathrooms, different type of amusement places, such as a bar. I did it while looking in windows."

"Windows of homes?"

"Yes, sir."

"What were you looking at?"

"Women."

"What were the women doing?"

"They were either unclothed or partly clothed. I have done it by the side of schools, grammar schools and high schools. In my own car while watching young females."

"How old were they?"

"From seven to ten."

"Did you expose yourself on those occasions?"

"A few times."

"What would you do?"

"Open the car door. The pants were to my knees."

Van Hazel wanted to know if there were certain types of pornographic photos at home that turned him on. Phil answered, "Well, I always looked at women that were naked. But there have been a type of bondage pictures. Women in handcuffs. Chained."

"Did this sexual fantasy become increasingly real to you, so that you could visualize it without pictures by just closing your eyes?"

"Yes."

"Were you increasingly obsessed with it?"

"Yes. From the first time I went to a drive-in and started masturbating myself."

Van Hazel took Phil back through the events of November 22, and then asked, "Didn't you know you could be caught and criminally punished for it?"

"Criminally, yes. I did know that."

"Didn't you think it was wrong?"

"No."

"Well, who told you it was right? Did your parents bring you up to believe that was a morally right thing to do?"

"No. My parents never instructed me sexually at all."

"You didn't learn in school that it was right, did you?"

"No."

"But you didn't think it was wrong?"

"Not at that point in time, no."

"Did you tell Miss Callaway that you had a sexual fantasy?"

"Yes."

"Did you tell her you couldn't help yourself?"

"Yes, I did."

"Was it true?"

"Yes."

"Did you tell her you were sorry you were doing this?"

"Yes."

"Why were you?"

"Because she was so nice to me."

"But you weren't sorry enough to stop, were you?"

"No."

Van Hazel asked that if all Phil wanted was sex, why didn't he just take her into the bushes somewhere in South Lake Tahoe. Phil replied, "I had this fantasy that was driving me to do this. Something that was making me want to do it with no way to stop." In other words, he wanted to take her to the room he had already set up in the warehouse. That room that Detective De-Maranville had called a "porno palace" was part of Phil's sexual fantasy.

Van Hazel said that Katie Callaway mentioned that it almost seemed at one point like Phil wanted to be caught. Van Hazel asked why Phil hadn't sought psychiatric help if he knew he had a problem. Phil replied,

"I don't know. It must be like a person that has any other kind of trouble, and he doesn't seek help."

Following up on the reasons that it seemed like he almost wanted to get caught, Van Hazel brought up the fact that Phil had mentioned to Katie Callaway his name, his wife's occupation, that he owned a shed, and that he was in a band. Phil, in response, said that Katie was very nice to him and that he was just having a conversation with her. "She was convincing me that she was enjoying it."

Van Hazel asked, "You really thought she wanted to do that?"

Phil replied, "In my own mixed-up mind, yes."

Van Hazel stated, "In the state of Nevada, in some counties, we have places where people can go to seek sexual gratification. A bawdy house. A whorehouse. Why didn't you go to those?"

Phil responded, "I went once when I was younger, and it never did nothing for me. I have had the advantage of being with many women. With their will."

"But that isn't your sex thing?"

"No."

"That isn't what drives you?"

"No."

"And yet you've stated that you live a clean life."

"I don't go breaking into people's houses. I don't go to hurt anybody."

Van Hazel finished his questioning after that.

On cross-examination, the federal prosecutor Leland Lutfy asked, "Do you know what the terms 'right' and 'wrong' mean?"

"Yes," Phil replied.

"Is it right to beat your wife?"

"No."

"You and your wife have an understanding about the sexual activity?"

"Yes." (At least in Phil's mind, they did.)

"Did she know where you were the night that you kidnapped Miss Callaway?"

"No. The only thing my wife knew was that I went to South Lake Tahoe to get LSD."

Lutfy wanted to know how many of Phil's friends used LSD, and he said a few of them did. Then Lutfy asked if any of them took LSD and went out and kidnapped and raped girls. Phil replied, "I know nothing of their private lives."

Asked if Phil had good sexual relations with his wife, he said that he did. Lutfy then wanted to know why Phil didn't harm his wife during sex. Phil answered, "Because I love her."

"Is it only people that you don't love that you harm?"

Phil replied, "I didn't feel that I was harming Katherine Callaway, so I don't feel I was harming anybody."

"You didn't think you were harming her! You put handcuffs on her."

Phil still replied that he didn't think he was harming her.

"You didn't think you were harming her when you grabbed her by the back of the neck and [put] her head down to her knees?"

"No."

For the questions of whether he thought he was harming her for tying her up with a belt, placing tape over her mouth, and telling her to keep her eyes closed, Phil answered no to each question.

Lutfy said that when Phil masturbated at the drive-in, he had put towels up on the windows, so he must have known that what he was doing was wrong. Phil replied that he had done so because when he first started masturbating in public, he'd been embarrassed about it then.

When Phil had gone to places near schools and masturbated in his car, Lutfy said that he could have just as well gone into the middle of the street and done it. Phil agreed that was so, but he didn't do so because he didn't want to get caught by the law.

"You didn't want to get punished, did you?"

"No."

"You *did* want to punish Miss Callaway, didn't you?"

"No."

Lutfy asked if Phil thought that lots of people went to public places and masturbated. Phil replied that he didn't know. So Lutfy asked if Phil knew anyone else who did those types of things. Phil answered, "Privately, no. But you read about it in magazines."

"Did your parents ever teach you right from wrong?"

"Yes."

"Did you get slapped when you were a boy when you did something your parents said was wrong?"

"Very unfortunately, no."

"Did they ever verbally tell you, you were wrong. You shouldn't do this?"

"Up to the point when I was ten years old. After that, I was spoiled. My father never did take any restrictions of beating me or disciplining me, and my mother spoiled me."

"Do you feel your father should have done that?"

"Yes."

"Why do you think he should have done that?"

"Because of what I have learned."

"Do you think you shouldn't do things that are wrong?"

"Yes."

Lutfy asked if Phil Garrido had been seen by psychiatrists before the present trial. Phil agreed that he had done so. Asked if he had lied to those psychiatrists, Phil answered, "I don't really want to bring that up, because it might be prejudicial against me, but I will if I must answer it."

Judge Thompson spoke up and said to Phil, "All he asked you was 'Why didn't you lie to the doctors?'"

Phil answered, "Because I have been working very steadily the last two months with a minister getting close to God."

So Lutfy asked, "Do you feel you have discovered God?"

"Yes."

Asked how long ago he had discovered God, Phil replied that it had been within the last three months. Lutfy then asked if Phil had mentioned about God and Jesus to Katie Callaway on the ride to the storage shed in Reno. Phil said, "I told her I believed in Him and that someday I would like to turn to Him."

"Someday? It wasn't going to be that day, was it?"

"No."

"Do you think God would like the things you have done?"

"Absolutely not. I am ashamed of them."

The defense attorney Van Hazel took one more crack at trying to convey Phil's state of mind at the time of the crime to the jurors. Van Hazel asked, "Mr. Garrido, were you ashamed when you did what you did to Miss Callaway?"

Phil answered, "No."

"You were not ashamed?"

"No, I couldn't feel shame. I didn't even realize the reality of shame for what I was doing."

"The only reason you are ashamed now is because

you fear going to prison or being convicted of a crime. Is that where your shame comes from?"

"No."

"Well, what is the difference between then and now?"

Phil replied, "Because I have come close to God. Because I feel God. Because God has shown me what is real."

"But you were talking about God that night?"

"Yes. But I did not say I had contact with God."

"Since November twenty-second, you have had contact with God?"

"Yes. I have studied very hard and I have learned what it takes to find God."

Whether this line of reasoning would resonate with the jurors would be crucial on the way they reached their verdict.

CHAPTER 13

FANTASY WORLD

From direct testimony by Phil Garrido, the trial now went to the opinion of psychiatrists who had examined him. And the psychiatrist for the defense and the psychiatrist for the prosecution would have almost diametric conclusions.

First on the stand was Dr. Charles Kuhn for the defense. Kuhn had been a bomber pilot during World War II. After that, he studied at Ohio State University and got his medical degree. Later he obtained a degree in psychiatry and had done his residency in Miami and then Detroit. Since 1975, Dr. Kuhn had been in private practice in Reno, Nevada.

Dr. Kuhn said of his examination of Phil Garrido, "I went to see Mr. Garrido at the Washoe County Jail and spent an hour with him there. Then I wrote up a report and submitted it. The diagnosis I gave on the report was one of drug dependence, both on LSD and cannabis. The most salient part of his behavior and medical background that impressed me was his judgment, or lack of it, during the commission of the crime. There is no question in my mind that Mr. Garrido has an intelligence somewhat better than average.

"There are many things in his behavior that do not reflect his use of his intelligence. And from my point of view, there is always a need to look at why that is so. One example I can give right off the top would be his strangely erratic judgment in seeking a girl to abduct in South Lake Tahoe, for example, instead of Stateline, Nevada."

Willard Van Hazel wanted to know why that was important, and Dr. Kuhn said, "I would think that if one were only interested in fulfilling this sexual fantasy—and, in fact, if they were driven to do so—there is nothing in the sexual fantasy that has any geographical significance. And unless a person were pretty fogged up one way or another, they wouldn't incur the involvement of the federal law, which almost every person would know they were doing by crossing state lines.

"I think that many of the aberrations in Mr. Garrido's sexual fantasies and sexual behavior might be viewed in the same light if they were to occur in a more circumscribed way or to occur in a less intense way. I think there are a great many people amongst us who engage in various perversions, some of which Mr. Garrido described. Certainly there are a great many people that engage in a number of deviant type of autoeroticism, and that sort of thing. Very few people engage in it to the extent that he did—daily or thereabouts—over a period of years without it becoming disruptive to the other kinds of functioning. And I think that is relevant. I think it does reflect some force or some explanation for his ability to conduct himself in such a preoccupied, obsessed way without having mental illness or without having seriously impaired intelligence."

Dr. Kuhn agreed with Dr. Gerow's report that Phil Garrido had "mixed sexual deviation," exemplified by his voyeurism and exhibitionism. Dr. Kuhn also said that he had done some "reality testing" on Phil. By this, he meant, "The function that allows us to discern what is real in terms of actions from what isn't."

Van Hazel asked, "In your opinion, did Mr. Garrido have some difficulty in separating this sexual fantasy from reality?"

Kuhn responded, "I believe there are two different issues involved in terms of degree of control or the degree of awareness of Mr. Garrido and this type of behavior. One of the issues involves the sexual aberration itself and the implications of that in terms of how that determines or shapes his behavior. The other issue is, of course, the drug involvement and the prolonged or lasting effect of that. In some respects, I feel that the question that is being raised is how do I view the effect of his drug use in terms of his ability to conform his behavior with what the law demands.

"My point of view on that is that I feel that he, and many other people in similar positions, don't, or can't, get involved with certain real issues, such as legal issues or a moral issue. It isn't a question of whether he is thinking or feeling something is right or wrong. It seems to me that in most cases these people don't even raise that question. That is not a part of their behavior— whether they are in the private confines of their own bedroom or not. One of the issues of reality testing would be the normal change in one's thinking or one's attitude when they leave the bedroom. Without the influence of any of this drug involvement, I think Mr. Garrido would pause carrying out sexual fantasies. I am describing his inability to use a reasonable degree of self-control or self-discipline when it comes to doing things that are clearly wrong, clearly illegal, and clearly self-destructive."

Van Hazel asked, "Surely, Doctor, everybody that takes drugs does not go out and commit these types of offenses, do they?"

Dr. Kuhn replied, "I don't believe that the drug, in this case LSD, is responsible for creating either the obsession or the content or quality of the fantasy. I really don't believe the drug did that. I think the drug permitted it to flourish, so to speak, and survive, and ultimately the drug permitted it to get acted out."

Van Hazel then said, "When we talk about fantasy, Doctor, it sounds like Disneyland, Fantasy World. It is something stronger, more vivid than that, correct?"

Kuhn answered, "Yes. I think that is a poor choice of words on my part. It would be much better to refer to it as a sexual preoccupation or obsession. It is a very complex ideation. It is something that pushes its way into a person's conscious thoughts and, in this case, into his actions. One of the issues that I am trying to deal with is what did he have available to keep it in check. It seems to me that was very limited."

"Why?"

"Because of the drug."

Van Hazel then asked, "Now, Doctor, do you have an opinion on the issue of whether the defendant lacked, as a result of mental disease or defect, substantial capacity either to appreciate the wrongfulness of his conduct or to conform his conduct to the requirements of the law?"

Dr. Kuhn said, "Yes, I do. I am fairly strong about the latter part of that alternative. I think that the defendant did not have adequate control to conform his behavior."

"You have not stated you believe that the defendant was psychotic at any point. Is that correct?"

"That is correct. What is important (in this case) is what I would call impulse neurosis. It is not an official name of anything, but it is fairly typical of most perversions wherein the person's attention and anxieties mount over a period of time in a way that is not particularly unpleasant, but rather exciting, stimulating, though sometimes sort of scary.

"As the tension does mount, they are driven to do some particular act such as engage in a type of voyeurism or exhibitionism or much more complex kind of sexual ritual, which is what in this case we are considering. The effect of this is that throughout the whole act, their physiology does change. They become stimulated, their heart rate changes, their breathing changes, and at times it seems almost uncontrollable. An irreversible, driven sort of behavior. The outcome or the end result of it is, of course, that the sexual, not necessarily coinciding with the sexual gratification—they experience a very pleasurable release of tension."

Van Hazel asked, "Doctor, do you believe that Mr. Garrido would be a menace to the health, safety, and morals of himself and others without psychiatric treatment?"

Dr. Kuhn replied, "I certainly do."

During a break, Judge Thompson had some unfinished business to attend to. And it was explosive business. Judge Thompson said to the prosecutor, "Mr. Lutfy, there have been certain matters that we have discussed that so far have been excluded from the testimony in this case. I want to tell these two doctors what you desire to prove, either through cross-examination of Mr. Garrido or with respect to his conduct."

Lutfy replied, "We offer to prove, Your Honor, that

approximately an hour prior to the kidnapping of Katherine Callaway, that Mr. Garrido at that time attempted the kidnapping of another woman, in which he entered her car, by asking for a ride. He got in the vehicle, went a certain distance with her, directed her to a different street, the same as he did with Miss Callaway. Upon stopping the vehicle, again Mr. Garrido grabbed this woman, put one handcuff on this woman, and was unable to put the other one on. She jumped out of the vehicle, struggling with him. And after that, she promised that she would not tell the police or tell anybody about what he had done. He agreed to unloosen that handcuff. The vehicle was moving, then she jumped out of the car and ran up the street and took off. I believe under rule 404—"

Judge Thompson interrupted him and said, "I didn't ask you for a legal argument. What else do you want to prove?"

Lutfy said, "We want to show that conduct, Your Honor."

"That is all?"

"That is all."

Judge Thompson said, "All right. This is forever, you are not going to change your mind, this is all you want to prove?"

Lutfy replied, "As far as the testimony is concerned."

"With respect to other so-called bad acts?"

"That is correct."

Judge Thompson turned to Dr. Kuhn and said, "Would that information be important to you in reaching a psychiatric opinion in this case, or would it have any influence on your opinion whatsoever?"

Dr. Kuhn replied, "Not at all, sir."

Judge Thompson then turned to Dr. Gerow and said, "If I asked the same question of you?"

Dr. Gerow responded, "It just tells me, Your Honor,

part of the state of mind prior to the alleged offense, in that he formed the intent."

"Would it change the opinion you have reached with respect to Mr. Garrido in any respect?"

Dr. Gerow said, "No, sir."

Judge Thompson stated, "Well, then, I rule out that evidence."

Because of the judge's ruling, no juror would hear about Phil Garrido and an attempted kidnapping in the Lake Tahoe area one hour before that of Katie Callaway. And later, no parole board member would ever hear of this as well, unless they scoured the federal court transcripts.

Leland Lutfy wasn't taking Dr. Kuhn's testimony at face value, and asked him on cross-examination, "During your examination, you didn't think Mr. Garrido had any kind of thinking disorder?"

"No, I didn't."

"You didn't think he had any kind of organic impairment?"

"No, I didn't."

"Would consistent LSD abuse somehow or other change someone physically?"

Kuhn replied, "That is somewhat controversial. I think it does, myself, but it is not something that is demonstrable in terms of any lab study."

"You said at the time of the report that he did have the ability to assist his counsel in the preparation of his defense?"

"Yes, I did."

"You also said at that time that he had a rational and factual understanding of the nature of the charges and proceedings against him?"

"Yes."

Lutfy asked, "How do you know what length of time Mr. Garrido used LSD, if ever?"

Kuhn said, "I don't. But much of our work is based on calculated guesses regarding the validity of what people tell us."

"Is your opinion of Mr. Garrido's mental state another calculated guess?"

"Not so!"

At that point, Van Hazel angrily jumped in and said, "Your Honor, I will object to the framing of a question of that type to a professional person!"

Judge Thompson asked, "What is your objection?"

Van Hazel replied, "I think it is one thing to cross-examine him. It is another to badger a professional witness."

Judge Thompson said, "Overruled."

Lutfy continued, "Did you ever have occasion when you are examining somebody that they lie to you?"

"Many times."

"Is the defendant psychotic?"

"No."

"Is he neurotic?"

"Not technically, according to our nomenclature. I think he is."

"You can be neurotic and still know right from wrong, can't you?"

"Oh, yes."

"Can you be a sexual deviant and still know right from wrong?"

"Yes."

"Do you think he knew right from wrong?"

"Yes."

After Dr. Charles Kuhn's testimony, Leland Lutfy brought on the prosecution's psychiatrist to present his findings on Phil Garrido. Dr. Lynn Gerow had gone to medical school at McGill University and interned at Walter Reed General Hospital in Washington, D.C. Later he specialized in psychiatry and practiced at Letterman General Hospital and Langley Porter Neuropsychiatric Institute in San Francisco. Within the past few years, he had a private practice in Reno.

Asked about how he formed his report on Phil Garrido, Dr. Gerow said, "On the material that was supplied to me by the defendant's attorney, and the history that Mr. Garrido supplied to me and my examination. I felt that he was competent to stand trial, and I felt that he was responsible for the act in question. The defendant did not have a psychiatric disorder or a mental disorder. He gave me a clear, concise statement of the events in question in sequence, told me what happened from early on November twenty-second, until the next morning. There was nothing in what he told me, nothing in the mental-status examination, that one could say that he wasn't responsible and competent."

Dr. Gerow agreed that during tests he administered on Phil Garrido, Phil had good remote memory, recent memory, and could do calculations. Dr. Gerow even asked Phil the meaning of a proverb. The proverb Gerow used was "There is no use crying over spilled milk." Phil said that he knew the meaning of it, but he had never heard it before.

Dr. Gerow asked about another maxim, "People who live in glass houses shouldn't throw stones." Phil did interpret that one correctly, and said, "People who are vulnerable about something should be careful. Should cover their flank in that regard."

As to why Dr. Gerow was asking about these proverbs or maxims, he replied that he wanted to see if Phil could think and interpret abstract meanings. And Dr.

Gerow added, "You are looking either for a thought disorder or some kind of organic impairment."

Lutfy asked, "Did he evidence any of these?"

"No," Dr. Gerow replied.

One adage in particular was interesting to Lutfy. It concerned "Those who dance must pay the fiddler." Phil's response to that was that he had committed a crime, and should pay for that crime.

Lutfy asked, "Did you find anything strange about that response?"

Dr. Gerow answered, "It seemed like a fairly appropriate abstract response from somebody in jail."

"Did you conclude whether or not Mr. Garrido had a sexual preoccupation?"

"He does."

"What do you conclude as a result of that?"

"Nothing. He had a lot of things, one of which was a sexual preoccupation. But that in itself didn't lead me to any diagnosis. He had a history of being a Peeping Tom, or voyeur. He gave a history of being an exhibitionist and taking off his clothes in front of little girls. He gave a history of impulsive masturbation. These things led me to believe he was sexually deviant and had that mental disorder."

"What does it mean to be a sexual deviant?"

"It means that your sex life is primarily directed toward inanimate objects, or in some way not normally channeled."

"Can you be a sexual deviant and still differentiate between right and wrong?"

"Yes."

"Can you be a sexual deviant and still conform your conduct to the requirements of the law?"

"Yes."

Lutfy asked if Phil had told Dr. Gerow about the events of November 22 and 23, in connection to Katie

Callaway. Gerow said, "He went into a great amount of detail."

Lutfy then asked, "Is it still your opinion, after hearing all of this from Mr. Garrido about what he did, that he could conform his conduct to the requirements of the law?"

Dr. Gerow replied, "I think he could."

"And it was still your conclusion, as a result of hearing all of this, that Mr. Garrido knew right from wrong at the time of the incident that occurred?"

"Yes, he knew right from wrong."

On cross-examination, Willard Van Hazel had Dr. Gerow testify about what Phil Garrido had mentioned in reference to hallucinations that he suffered from, in relation to taking LSD. Dr. Gerow related, "He said he had hallucinations, and he was seeing things that weren't there. Like he would look at a grain in the wood, and it would move a little bit. Those are very common in people that abuse LSD and other hallucinogens."

Van Hazel then asked, "How would you characterize his judgment?"

"Poor judgment."

"Very poor?"

"Very poor."

"You used the term 'religiosity' in your report. What is that?"

"One of the things he was preoccupied about was religious events. He talked at length about the Bible. He had a Bible with him when I saw him and talked about the Lord and God, and he talked about it to enough of an extent that I felt he was preoccupied by those things, and therefore I used the term 'religiosity.'"

Asked about Phil's use of LSD as a sexual stimulant,

Dr. Gerow replied, "Without LSD, he was not sexually stimulated to any great degree."

After both Leland Lutfy and Willard Van Hazel were through with Dr. Gerow, Judge Bruce Thompson asked him a few questions, with the jurors listening in. Judge Thompson asked, "In your opinion, can LSD have a long-lasting effect on the brain function?"

Dr. Gerow said that it could. So Judge Thompson then asked, "Of what sort?"

Dr. Gerow replied, "Taken in sufficient quantity, in some individuals, it will produce dementia. What I mean by that is memory disturbance, orientation problems, and they break down socially. They don't have the normal social give-and-take that they once had."

Judge Thompson asked, if in Dr. Gerow's estimation, "Was there any indication on Mr. Garrido that brain damage had occurred?"

Dr. Gerow replied, "No indication of brain damage."

After Dr. Lynn Gerow stepped down, there was a moment of drama in the courtroom. The next witness was supposed to be Dr. Albert Peterman, the neurologist. Judge Thompson asked why that witness was not ready to take the stand, and Lutfy replied, "He was told to report to our office and then come here. He has not been to our office. Our secretary has been trying to reach him. She has not been able to do so."

Judge Thompson heatedly responded, "You tell him to be here at ten-thirty tomorrow morning. And if he isn't here, I'll get out a warrant for his arrest!"

Dr. Peterman *did* show up the next day, without incident, for a short period of testimony. Dr. Peterman told the jurors about the neurological examination he performed on Phil Garrido. Asked what his conclusions were, Dr. Peterman said, "I found that he had a normal examination. I was asked specifically if there was any evidence of brain damage. I did not feel that there was. I didn't find any impairment of his brain functions or nervous system."

Defense attorney Van Hazel had a few questions as well. He asked, "Doctor, would all instances of drug addiction show some type of organic change or disorder that the tests would pick up?"

Dr. Peterman replied, "No, they would not."

"And would the answer be precisely that if I asked you in the instance of addiction to LSD?"

Dr. Peterman said, "In the instance of addiction to LSD, I would likely find nothing on examination."

After Dr. Albert Peterman, both sides rested their cases. It basically now came down to whether the jurors thought that Phil Garrido had been so addicted to drug use that he could not control his actions when he kidnapped and raped Katie Callaway. In other words, whether his capacity to reason had been so impaired, he really didn't understand what he was doing when he took her to the warehouse in Reno.

CHAPTER 14

"RIGHT NOW HE'S A DANGEROUS MAN."

It didn't take long for the jury to reach a decision on Phil Garrido's federal case. On February 11, 1977, they came back with the following decision: *We, the jury, duly empaneled in the above entitled case, upon our oaths do say that we find the defendant, Phillip Craig Garrido, guilty of the offense charged in the Indictment.*

Compared to all the media attention that Phil Garrido would garner in future years, there was very little attention paid to him in 1977. A short article in the *Reno Gazette-Journal* stated, KIDNAP VERDICT RETURNED. *A federal court jury has convicted a Reno musician of kidnapping a South Lake Tahoe woman on November 23rd. He faces Washoe County charges of possession of a controlled substance, rape and sex perversion.*

If Phil Garrido hoped for a light sentence in the federal case, he was greatly disappointed. On March 11, 1977, Judge Bruce Thompson handed down a sentence of fifty years in a federal penitentiary. Phil wasted no time firing his lawyer and appealing the sentencing. Willard Van Hazel related to Judge Thompson,

*On or before March 16, 1977, Mr. Garrido wrote a letter to
the Office of the Federal Public Defender counsel, and the appointment of a new counsel, which indicated Mr. Garrido's
desire to file an appeal for reduction of sentence under rule 35.*

Van Hazel could not have been too happy about the
reasoning in Phil's actions. Phil was now claiming: *in-
effective assistance of trial counsel.* In other words, he was
blaming the trial performance of Willard Van Hazel.
Under the circumstances of the case, however, Van
Hazel had put up an extensive defense considering all
the factors detrimental to Phil. The most obvious
having been Katie Callaway's eyewitness account of
what had occurred. But Phil did not see things that
way. Instead, he retained a new counsel, Kenneth
Cory, from the federal defender's office.

Phil's letter, with misspellings intact, went as follows:
*My appointed councel from beginning to end has not been in
my behalf. Van Haizel has tried his best to keep me from trial.
By telling me there was no defence. I stayed with him because
I have no insight on the law.*

Phil wrote that he and Van Hazel had at one point
planned to change his plea to guilty, hoping for some
kind of plea deal. Phil even claimed that the judge in
the case did not want to accept his plea. At that point,
he and Van Hazel had returned to a plea of not guilty
in the case.

Then Phil claimed in the letter that "Van Haizel"
did not come to see him until four days before trial.
Phil also said that his counsel kept trying to change his
mind about defense tactics. He also claimed that Van
Hazel actually wanted him to go to prison.

Phil even claimed that the defense attorney had
told the judge that he thought Phil should have state
time added on to federal time. At least that was Phil's
take on the matter. Phil then stated that Van Hazel

never tried to help him and only turned in a lukewarm performance to keep from looking completely incompetent in court.

Before Phil Garrido could go very far in his federal case appeal, he had to contend with charges against him in the Washoe County court system. The grand jury in Washoe County had brought a bill of indictment against Phil on three charges: forcible rape, an infamous crime against nature, and possession of a controlled substance. The "infamous crime against nature" charge, still being used in Nevada in 1977, concerned anal intercourse. DDA Michael Malloy became the prosecutor in the case.

Ron Bath, a Washoe County public defender, was Phil's attorney in this case. Right off the bat, Bath put forward a motion to have Phil examined by psychiatrists, as had been done in the federal case. This was so ordered by Judge Ernest Bowen, and as in his federal case, the psychiatrists were Dr. Charles Kuhn and Dr. Lynn Gerow. In a pretrial hearing, Bath stated to a judge just what the purpose of the psychiatrists for both the defense and prosecution would be: *According to Mr. Malloy, he was also requesting with respect to the psychiatric examination, the issue of whether this individual knew the difference between right and wrong at the time of the offense.*

In the end, as far as a trial went, it wouldn't matter whether Phil knew the difference between right and wrong, because there was no trial. Phil made a plea deal through his attorney and changed his plea to guilty. By doing so, Phil signed a statement that he waived his rights to the privilege of self-incrimination, trial by jury, and the right to confront his accuser.

What he admitted to was *That on the 22nd and 23rd of November, 1976, in the county of Washoe, State of Nevada, I did willfully and unlawfully have carnal knowledge of and with Katherine Gayle Callaway, a female human being against her will.*

Where Phil gained in the bargain was that the "infamous acts against nature" charge was dropped, and so was the possession of an illegal substance. For signing the agreement, Phil was to receive a period of imprisonment in Nevada from five years to life.

In March 1977, Judge Roy Torvinen held a hearing about all of these matters. Judge Torvinen asked Phil, "Are you satisfied with the legal representation you received from the public defender's office?"

Unlike in his federal case, Phil said, "Definitely, I am."

Judge Torvinen then asked Phil, "Has there ever been any threats or coercion of any kind except for the fact of the prosecution in this case to induce you to plead guilty?"

Phil replied, "No, sir."

There was an interesting exchange between attorneys and Judge Torvinen on April 11, 1977, concerning the case, with Phil also present. Phil's attorney, Ron Bath, addressed the judge and said, "We're not making light of the offense that Mr. Garrido has pled guilty to. However, I would like to point out to the court that this is one of the things that took place across state lines, and everybody is trying to get a pound of his flesh. But he's presently under a fifty-year sentence in the federal jurisdiction. I can relate Mr. Garrido's feelings that he's extremely remorseful over this thing. It's something that happened with extreme use of drugs. He's hoping to benefit from the time spent in prison to better his life, and I think he's a candidate for the court's consideration in this matter."

Malloy spoke up and said, "I don't know which of us, Mr. Bath says, is getting the pound of flesh—the federal government or the state of Nevada, or both. Anyway, I don't know that I'm getting a pound of flesh. He says he's referring to California. I don't mean to make light of it, either, but this is an extremely serious offense.

"We could take first custody of him because he's in state custody now and has been all along. In this case, we could send him directly to the Nevada State Prison and leave it up to the federal government to take him from there. As crowded as the state prison is, it doesn't matter where he does his time, and the federal prisons aren't as crowded. I don't object to sending him to federal prison first and have the state of Nevada place the hold. I think the sentence should be for the crime committed, and maybe by the time he's released, he won't be so dangerous, because right now he's a dangerous man.

"Mr. Bath informed me that Mr. Garrido has to do a minimum of two-thirds of the federal sentence before paroled. And he got fifty years in the federal prison on the federal sentence."

Judge Torvinen asked Phil if he had anything to say. Phil replied, "Well, the only thing I do say is that I'm very fortunate that this happened to me because my life was in a crash course. Before I ever came into using marijuana, my life was clean. I had no arrest record, but association with marijuana led me to harder drugs, and I've used LSD for the last seven years. And if it wasn't for the drug LSD, I wouldn't be here right now. But this has given me a chance to find something more important than anything, and that is God. And I can straighten out my life."

Judge Torvinen then pronounced sentence upon Phillip Garrido. "Upon the entry of the plea of guilty to the indictment, Count one, forcible rape, a felony, it is the judgment of the court that the defendant is guilty, and it is the sentence of the court that he be sentenced to the Nevada State Prison for a term of life. As I understand the statute, it is with the possibility of parole. The sentence is to run concurrent with the sentence of the interstate kidnapping by the federal government, that I understand is fifty years. He is sentenced first from the federal court, and it will be the order of the court that he fulfill the federal sentence before required to maintain the balance of the term under the Nevada state sentence. Counts two and three will be dismissed."

Phil spoke up and added his two cents to the proceedings. "Your Honor, I would like to say one more thing that I didn't want to say before. I feel I will be able to be helped more in the federal prison because of the facilities and psychiatric treatment."

Phil Garrido was transferred to Leavenworth Federal Penitentiary in Kansas on June 30, 1977, to begin serving his term for the kidnapping case. And almost immediately, he put in motion an appeal on his sentencing. This went through the Ninth Circuit Court of Appeals, and was dealt with by two circuit judges and one district judge. A part of the appeal dealt with his mental state at the time of the offense. Phil argued that if he was too influenced by drugs to know what he was doing, he shouldn't be sentenced as if he had full capacity of his reasoning.

While in the federal prison, Phil also wrote a letter to Judge Bruce Thompson. In it, he wrote, *When living at home and going to school, my life was free from the influences*

*of drugs. I had been raised in the country and lived in a very
clean home. I was the baby of the family and spoiled in the
long run.*

Phil then noted that drugs were starting to make
their way into Brentwood by 1969, and he began smoking marijuana. From there, it was just a short step for
him to the use of LSD. Of LSD use, he wrote, *It took
me to another style of living and thinking, in the long run I
lost much of my reasoning powers. Seven years of using made
me fall from reality.*

Phil then related that on his own initiative he was
seeing psychiatrist Dr. Kiehlbauch in Leavenworth
Prison and said that he was making great progress on
mental health issues. He had also finished high school
and was preparing to take college courses. He was in
carpentry shop in prison and planned to enroll in an
apprentice carpentry program, which would last for
four years. He also enrolled in drafting school. Phil
said that after four years of that, he planned on taking
two years of computer courses. (At that time, comput-
ers were just in their infancy and mysterious except for
a handful of professionals.)

Phil wrote, *I have set my goals and find myself well on my
way. It shall take seven years of schooling to complete the
courses. In all respects my life has changed. Of course, that is
because I wanted to, knowing this is my chance to get my life
in line. Drugs have been my down fall. I am so ashamed of
my past. But my future is now in control.*

Phil ended the letter by stating that all he wanted
was a chance. What exactly he wanted from Judge
Thompson, he didn't state. Perhaps he wanted a fa-
vorable report from Judge Thompson to the court of
appeals.

On his behalf, Phil also got letters from the warden
at Leavenworth, a psychiatrist, and his caseworker
there. Warden IRL Day wrote on April 12, 1978, to

Leland Lutfy, who had requested information about Phil's time in Leavenworth since being incarcerated. Lutfy had requested to know about Phil's medical, psychiatric, and educational progress so far. Day said that follow-up letters would be coming from the psychology staff. And then Day added: *Mr. Garrido has been involved in individual counseling with our psychology staff. We trust this information will be helpful to you.*

A report put together by Phil's case manager, R. Rose, noted, *Mr. Garrido was initially designated close-custody and regular duty status. The classification team assigned Mr. Garrido to work in the carpentry shop and recommended that he seek educational instruction to prepare for future college enrollment and that he also seek counseling to improve his self-control in avoiding future chemical abuse.*

The report noted that in carpentry shop, Phil was responsible for using woodworking equipment in making cabinets. He got on-the-job training and weekly classroom training. His work supervisor rated Phil as average in his skill, work habits, and care of equipment. *His supervisor states that he shows regular attendance on the job, gets along well with the others, reacts well to authority, and accepts responsibility.* In fact, Phil was receiving meritorious good time for his responsibilities in the carpenter shop.

Rose related that Phil had been an active participant in the educational program on a half-day basis since August 1, 1977. Phil's initial goal was to get a GED, which he accomplished. His supervisor stated that Phil had elevated his academic level significantly, and Phil had enrolled for eight hours of college course work for the summer of 1978. *Mr. Garrido's supervisor within the Education Department states that he is an exemplary student and cooperative in all respects.* Phil's long-range goal was to complete the computer college course and perhaps one day be involved in that field.

The report noted that in Phil's spare time, he practiced playing guitar, participated in church activities, exercised in the athletic yard, and occasionally went to institution movies. Phil phoned his mother on a weekly basis and also wrote to his father and brother. No one had come to visit Phil while he was incarcerated in Leavenworth.

Mr. Garrido appears to be in good physical and mental health and complains of no health problems at this time. It would not be anticipated that health problems would seriously restrict future employability.

Clinical psychologist John B. Kiehlbauch and psychologist trainee Ian Fluger put together a psychological evaluation of Phil in regard to Phil's asking for reduction of sentence. The report began that Phil appeared as an adequately nourished, "pleasant-appearing" twenty-seven-year-old male. Phil was verbal from the initial contact, cooperative, candid, and volunteered information readily, even information that was critical of him.

A short history of Phil's arrests was followed by the comment: *Mr. Garrido is the product of a prosocial middle class family, now broken, from which he inculcated generally appropriate values, though he describes himself as over-condoned and pampered by his parents. He describes himself as a semi-professional musician. There is a current marriage of unknown prospect, and no children have resulted from it.*

The report noted that Phil had done very well in raising his academic standards and in carpentry shop. He also had been faithful to his mental-health regime, which focused on developing basic personality strengths and *resolving immediate conflict areas and self-awareness in lifestyle patterns.* Phil still said that he had flashbacks from LSD usage, but these were diminishing in frequency and in severity.

Several tests had been administered upon Phil, including the Wechsler Adult Intelligence Scale (WAIS), Minnesota Multiphasic Personality Inventory (MMPI), Bender Visual Motor Gestalt Test, Rotter Incomplete Sentence Blank (RISB), Thematic Apperception Test (TAT), Rorschach Psychodiagnostic Instrument (RORS), and Mental Status Examination (MSE).

Testing revealed that Phil's IQ was at the upper end of the average range, being 110. His functional intelligence seemed to be improving as time passed away from LSD usage. The MMPI revealed that he fell within average boundaries. The Bender Visual Motor Gestalt Test showed that Phil was average, except for a strong sense of "approval-seeking behaviors."

The RISB reflected Mr. Garrido as a "sensitive young man" who was religious and sought to address his problems. It was noted that when he approached a new project, he did so with extreme zeal and diligence. He reflected careful attention to detail in things that he pursued. There was also one more significant sentence: *He might appear compulsive in many of his pursuits.*

The TAT showed that Phil had an active imagination and also understood symbolism. He had religious feelings that helped him in his daily life.

The RORS showed that he was mainly "form determined," but also responded to color cards. Phil had a tendency toward using fantasy to resolve his needs.

The MSE revealed a prosocial attitude in that he was cooperative and sincere. Phil was a likeable young man and engendered positive feelings in others. Recent memory was good, but distant memory was still clouded by his past drug use. Phil's concepts of time, space, and person were adequate.

In summary, the report stressed that Phil Garrido

was a young man of average intelligence who used his intelligence to achieve his goals. He had progressed very well in both his educational training and therapy while in prison.

And now came the most important part of the report. The psychologist recommended that Phil's current sentence be moderated to parole eligibility and that he be paroled when his therapy goals had been fulfilled. The psychologist also recommended that Phil be part of a mental-health treatment program once he was released from prison. The psychologist thought that Phil's transition into the community at large was positive, and the likelihood that he would reoffend was minimal.

In essence, the psychologists at Leavenworth were asking that Phil be let out of prison sometime in 1981, after he had completed his courses in the penitentiary. They also contended that once he was let out of prison, his chances of doing anything like another kidnapping and rape were "minimal."

Leland Lutfy wasn't buying any of this. His motion declared in part, *Mr. Garrido treated this girl (Katie Callaway) no better than he would a side of beef.* Lutfy believed that Garrido, despite his protestations that he was a changed man, was still a very dangerous individual.

In the end, the United States Court of Appeals took all of this information into account and denied Phil Garrido a reduction of sentence. For the time being, he wasn't going anywhere beyond the walls of Leavenworth Federal Penitentiary. And yet, changes were coming to him from an unexpected quarter. A young woman named Nancy Bocanegra was about to enter the walls of the prison as a visitor, and neither her life nor Phil's would ever be the same.

CHAPTER 15

NANCY

In the years to come, there would be a great deal of mystery about just who Nancy Bocanegra Garrido was. In fact, the misinformation blended with the actual information until it was difficult to separate fact from fiction. There would be stories that Nancy was born in the Philippines and that she and her family emigrated to the United States. The truth of the matter was, Nancy was born Nancy Bocanegra on July 18, 1955, in Bexar County, Texas.

In school, Nancy was bright, but also quiet and shy. That was an aspect about her that would carry through into her later years—she blended into the background, and virtually no one could remember anything about her. Unlike Phil Garrido in his high-school days, where people remembered him either as being "dreamy" or a "weirdo," Nancy was barely remembered at all.

One of the very few people to shed any light at all on this period of Nancy's life was her brother David. He said that she was a "normal kid." She had friends and went out with them, doing what average teenage girls did.

Nancy and her family moved from Texas to Denver, Colorado. It was there that Nancy studied nursing and eventually got a job as a nursing aide. And Nancy, like Phil Garrido, was a Jehovah's Witness. Basically, Jehovah's Witnesses believed in the literal truth of the Bible, and that the Bible stories were not mere myths or vague examples of how to live one's life. Jehovah's Witnesses had tight-knit communities at their Kingdom Halls. And they often sent out pairs of individuals to proselytize about their beliefs.

One story is that Nancy Bocanegra first met Phil Garrido at Leavenworth Federal Penitentiary when she went to visit her uncle who was in that prison. The year was 1980, and almost immediately Phil, who was now divorced, began courting Nancy. When Phil was on his best behavior, he could be very charming. Even the prison psychologist attested to that. And to diminutive and pretty Nancy Bocanegra, Phil was charming indeed.

Another story is that Phil and Nancy met in prison because of their common thread of being Jehovah's Witnesses. Phil did attend Jehovah's Witness religious services while in prison. This ambiguity about Nancy would become a common theme about most of the rest of her life from 1980 onward. Except for very few occasions, there was no actual documentation to nail down facts about her life. One thing is certain, however; she and Phil began a long-distance relationship by mail. And as time moved on, Nancy made numerous trips from Denver to Leavenworth Federal Penitentiary.

Then on October 14, 1981, Phil and Nancy were married in Leavenworth. Two inmates acted as witnesses, while a pastor performed the ceremony. A prison official took a photograph of the pair, and this, too, would become one of the few legacies of Nancy's life during that period of time. In the photo, Phil and Nancy were wrapped up in each other's arms. Phil had a dark moustache and deep blue eyes. He also exposed his hairy chest above the unbuttoned portion of his shirt. Phil looked as if he was ready to go out to a disco, rather than facing an indeterminate amount of time being locked behind prison bars.

Nancy, on the other hand, looked absolutely enraptured by Phil. In the photograph, she holds on tightly to him. And while Phil stared directly at the camera, Nancy gazed adoringly at Phil.

Eventually Nancy moved to the city of Leavenworth, just to be closer to Phil. Even here, her time in Leavenworth was nearly a complete cipher. One of the few people to note her time there was her landlord, John Saunders. Saunders basically recalled her, not because of the impression she made on him, but because of the lack of one. He said that she "must have been a good tenant," because she got her deposit back when she moved.

All information about Nancy was hard to come by, even when she lived for a while in Leavenworth. As it turned out, she lived on South Broadway on a tree-lined street. While not the most luxurious part of town, it was a pleasant street with nice homes and rental units. The Carroll Mansion, a large Victorian home built in 1867, was not far away from where Nancy resided at the time.

As usual, Nancy found a job as a nurse, and here, too, it was the lack of anything negative that defined her. She went to Leavenworth Penitentiary at every opportunity to see Phil, and for five years they lived this married but separate life.

* * *

In May 1984, Phil had his first parole board hearing. The five-member review board decided that Phil was still too much a danger to society and denied his request for an early release. They also wrote in the report, *The board finds that further evaluation of your progress is necessary. Release at this time would depreciate the seriousness of the crime.*

Phil tried again in March 1986, with the same results. Nonetheless, Phil was about to get a change of scene. He was transferred to the medium-security prison at Lompoc, California. This facility was considered one of the "cushiest" in the federal system. This move prompted Nancy to follow him, and she did so by moving in with her mother-in-law, Patricia Franzen, on Walnut Avenue, near Antioch. Even being there, it was still a 250-mile drive for Nancy down to Lompoc, which was on the central California coast.

It was while living with Patricia Franzen that Nancy had one of her very few interactions with the law. In fact, her brother had said of Nancy that she never even had a speeding ticket.

On October 18, 1987, while riding with Patricia in her vehicle, near Brentwood, Nancy was a passenger during an automobile accident. This happened at the intersection of Walnut Avenue and Dainty Avenue. The accident involved an uninsured motorist, and it was serious enough that both Patricia and Nancy were named as plaintiffs in court papers against the uninsured motorist.

The court papers recorded as reasons for the action: *wage loss, hospital and medical expenses, property damage, loss of use of property, loss of earning capacity.* Even though whose hospitalization and medical treatment were not mentioned, it's quite possible that Nancy was part of that situation. Why else name Nancy in the court action if Patricia Franzen was the only one involved?

Eventually the court action wasn't necessary, because Patricia's Allstate policy covered uninsured motorists. And then, like a ghost, Nancy Garrido disappeared into the background as usual. She was so invisible, many people on Walnut Avenue didn't know that she was living in Pat Franzen's house. Even next-door neighbor Helen Boyer said later that she hardly ever saw Nancy out in the yard. And when Helen did, Nancy only spoke a few words to her.

On November 5, 1987, two examiners from the U.S. Parole Commission met with Phil Garrido at Lompoc. And once again, Phil told them about how he had changed since kidnapping and raping Katie Callaway in 1976. On the surface, it appeared as if he really had changed. Phil had a good conduct record in prison, a good work record, and excellent reports from staff members and psychiatrists. Not only that, he had a wife and mother waiting for him in Antioch. Phil said that because of being in prison, he no longer had any taste for illegal drugs, which, he said, had been his ruination. And Phil spoke at great length about his religious beliefs and how those beliefs had made him a changed man.

The examiners bought it. In January 1988, Phil was discharged from serving federal prison time, and he was transferred to Nevada state custody. This was because he still had to serve time for his sentencing in the Washoe County court system when he made his plea deal. In what would become a very complex entanglement of different judicial entities, Phil was granted a U.S. Parole Commission's Certificate of Parole, even though he still had to spend time behind prison bars in

Nevada. The certificate, in part, read: *Said prisoner has substantially observed the rules of the institution, and in the opinion of the Commission said prisoner's release would not depreciate the seriousness of this offense or promise disrespect for the law, and would not jeopardize the public welfare.*

Katie Callaway would have had a very different opinion if she had known that Phil Garrido had just been granted this certificate by the U.S. Parole Commission. She absolutely would have thought it depreciated the seriousness of the crime *and* that Phil was still a threat to the public welfare. Instead of a fifty-year sentence, Phil had served less than eleven years of federal prison time.

Phil was transported from Lompoc to the medium-security Nevada prison near Carson City. He wasn't there long, before he was up for his third Nevada Parole Board review. And this time, the results were going to be very different than what had come before.

CHAPTER 16

"THIS IS MY FIRST DRINK IN ELEVEN YEARS."

Much of the confusion and mismanagement in regard to Phil Garrido began in 1988, when he was transferred from federal custody and supervision and placed under the care of the state of Nevada. By August 1988, Phil was up for his third parole board hearing on his Nevada case; and because his federal parole report had been so glowing, it influenced his Nevada parole board hearing.

This time, the Nevada Parole Board weighed Phil's good prison record against his "future dangerousness" to society. On a sliding scale of one to ten—ten being the best—Phil scored a six. This was just barely adequate for the possibility of parole. Even with that score, two of the five on the board voted for no parole. But it was the other three that mattered.

In a decision that would have far-reaching consequences, especially for Jaycee Lee Dugard and her family, the board voted for an early release for Phil Garrido. He was to move to his mother's residence near Antioch, California, and obtain a steady job. He was to submit to drug testing and attend substance-abuse meetings. The parole board seemed to have taken a look at his 1969 drug arrest when he was sent to the Clayton Juvenile Facility. But there is no indication at all that they took into account his 1972 plea deal on the more serious drug charges when he was discovered playing his guitar in a shed filled with growing marijuana plants in Oakley. This would have added points to his score, making him ineligible for parole.

On August 29, 1988, Phil was released from Carson City State Prison and had to stay in a halfway house in Oakland, about forty miles west of his mother's residence on Walnut Avenue. This halfway house was particularly meant for paroled sex offenders. Once in a while, Phil was able to travel with Nancy or his mother to other places in the Bay Area. And by now, his legal standing with Nevada and California was becoming a tangled mess.

A state of Nevada document, entitled "Investigation Request, of August 12, 1988," shows how complicated things had become. The Nevada report noted that *the subject (Phil Garrido) is being supervised by Federal Probation Officers for the offense of kidnapping and is serving a fifty year sentence. He has been instructed to report to US Probation Officer Gordon Brown at the Federal Building, 13th and Jackson Streets in Oakland, California.*

Phil, however, could not stay out of trouble. Even though he was never to have contact with his rape victim Katie Callaway again, apparently he did just that. After her terrible ordeal at the hands of Phil Garrido in 1976, Katie had gone overseas for a lengthy period of time. But she missed her friends in the Lake Tahoe area, and eventually she moved back there and once again began work in a casino at Stateline. This time, it was at the posh Caesars Palace casino as a croupier at a roulette wheel.

Katie recalled later that she was working the roulette wheel at Caesars when a man came up to her table and sat down. He obtained some chips, and then, in an all-too-familiar voice, he said, "Hi, Katie."

Katie said later, "I knew it was Phil Garrido right away. He ordered a drink and said, 'You know, Katie, this is my first drink in eleven years.'"

Katie was terrified. She had been assured by the federal parole board that Phil Garrido would not even be eligible for parole until 2006. And here he was at her roulette table in 1988.

Katie was absolutely stunned by what was happening. The man tried engaging her in small talk, but she was nearly frozen with fear. After a short time, the man cashed in his chips and left. As soon as he did, Katie went to her pit boss and told him she had just been contacted by the man who had kidnapped and raped her. Casino security was able to catch the man before he left the casino. However, because he wasn't carrying any identification, they let him go.

Katie later contacted Phil's parole agent and learned that Phil was at a halfway house in Oakland. Even though the parole agent agreed with Katie that Phil would go into his best behavior when he wanted to impress authorities, he could be dangerous when he was set on breaking the law. Unfortunately for Katie, Phil had served his time, according to the parole board, and there was nothing to be done about him unless he reoffended.

Katie was so rattled by what had just occurred, she soon pulled up stakes from Lake Tahoe and virtually went into hiding in another California town many miles away. She never wanted to have another encounter with Phil Garrido.

After the halfway house, Phil went to live with his mother and Nancy on Walnut Avenue. Nancy was working as a nurse, as usual, taking care of handicapped people in the area. She was quiet, efficient, and generally liked by the people she took care of. Almost no one on Walnut Avenue had any contact with Nancy. The one exception was Helen Boyer, who lived next door and who was on friendly terms with Pat Franzen.

Helen said of Nancy, "She hardly said a word to me. She was friendly, but did not make much conversation." At the time, Boyer thought that Phil was okay as a neighbor. He was more outgoing and talkative than Nancy.

Helen also noted that Phil started doing a lot of work on the yard. He planted screening shrubbery, put up a fence, and worked on a shed in the far backyard. Before long, he had effectively created two backyards— one near the house and another toward the rear of the property. As far as the shed went, it was starting to become like the one he had used as a musical workshop when he had been in Oakley in 1972. He soundproofed the walls and ran wires and cables from the main house out to the shed. For all intents and purposes, it looked just like a place to play his electric guitar. But Phil soon had other ideas what the shed would be used for. He had never forgotten the "porno palace" he had created in the warehouse in Reno. That image was so powerful that he began thinking of kidnapping another victim to fulfill his fantasies. And this time, he wanted a blond young girl.

CHAPTER 17

ENTREPRENEUR PHIL

Nancy went on quietly with her work, and Phil busied himself around the yard as the 1980s came to an end. Phil conformed to his parole schedule and seemed to be adapting to a new life on Walnut Avenue. But there was always something murky going on around him, much of which would not come to light until much later. On August 16, 1990, a white male about Phil's age was reported as chasing two adult females in Oakley. It wasn't until September 2009 that one of these women came forward and said that the person who had chased her looked the way that Phil Garrido did in that year.

Of course, the most mysterious event in Phil Garrido's life occurred in the days just before, during, and after June 10, 1991, when Jaycee Lee Dugard was kidnapped off the street near South Lake Tahoe and disappeared. And exactly what happened only came to light after August 2009. In the intervening years, Phil and Nancy, by all outside scrutiny, went on with their quiet life on Walnut Avenue. It was true that more boards appeared on the fences that Phil worked on, and Nancy was even more reclusive than ever.

All of this might have gone on as usual, but on March 18, 1993, Phil was arrested on a federal warrant for breaking the rules of his parole. He had not reported to his probation officer; he tested positive for marijuana and was not going to mandated counseling sessions. Phil was incarcerated at a federal detention center in Dublin, about forty miles southwest of Antioch. Soon he was transferred to the nearby Pleasanton Federal Correctional Institution.

All while Phil was there, Nancy remained at home on Walnut Avenue. What was not apparent at the time was that Nancy was not alone with Pat Franzen. Unknown to anyone else at the time, there was one more person locked in a shed on the back of the property. She was a twelve-year-old girl who had disappeared from the world at large.

While in his cell, Phil practiced his guitar and composed several songs. One of these he later entitled "Baby Blue." It was a love song to a young girl with a repeated line that she was a "dream come true." Another song he composed stated that every girl in the world wanted to be in love. And yet a third concerned a girl kept in the darkness. Phil also related in the song that everyone "in the human race" was "abused."

Phil was not incarcerated for long, and by April 29, 1993, he was released to "home confinement," and he had to check in at a halfway house in Oakland once again. And for Pat Franzen, who always wanted a daughter, the advent of Phil back in the household also brought a new surprise. A young girl named "Alyssa" emerged within the family. Pat later said, "I was pleased she was around."

If the emergence of "Alyssa" in the household was pleasing to Pat Franzen, it was soon doubly so when another young girl, a baby this time, appeared on the scene. Her name was Angel. Angel was a beautiful baby and Pat was "pleased" indeed to have the two girls around. Pat Franzen had no idea that Alyssa was actually the mother of the infant. Phil told his mom that Angel was his daughter by another girlfriend whom he'd had. Just who that girlfriend was, Pat didn't know.

Nancy not only took care of Pat, but she got a job at the Contra Costa County ARC agency, which attended to needs of disabled people in the county. Nancy's job was as a nurse and physical therapy specialist. Before being hired, the agency had run a routine background check on Nancy, and she had an absolutely clean record. In fact, she had a very impressive résumé as far as nursing skills went. Nancy's patients grew to like her, and she was always kind to them and attentive.

By 1995, Phil seemed more productive than ever and bought an inexpensive printing press, which he placed in a tent in the backyard. He decided to start a printing business, printing out business cards and brochures for local enterprises. He named the business Printing For Less. And Phil had Alyssa start creating graphic designs, even though she was so young and only fifteen years old at the time. Interestingly enough, Phil had Alyssa create a business card for his business, depicting a young beautiful blond woman on the card. The young woman looked like a more mature version of what Alyssa might look like someday.

Phil's business flyers pronounced: *Printing For Less— Affordable Advertising. No One Beats our Quality, Services or Prices! Just Schedule An Appointment And Start Your Layout.*

Phil's printing business may not have been the most professional in the region, but it was certainly one of the most inexpensive. For small businesses in eastern and central Contra Costa County, that was a real plus. Phil started making money from his new venture. And word spread from one small business owner to another about Phil's very reasonable prices and good, if not exceptional, workmanship.

The businesses in the area that Phil serviced with his printing business began to become very diverse. Establishments such as East County Glass and Window Company and Wayne's Barbershop in Pittsburg became Phil's regular customers. Phil's printing business turned out flyers, business cards, pamphlets, envelopes, and coupons.

Marc Lister, who owned a glass company, later said of Phil's production, "He did a good job for me and I was more than happy to introduce him to my friends in the automotive (glass) industry. He was cheap, reliable, and there was never any graphical errors or misspelled words."

And the owner of East County Glass and Window Company, Tim Allen, said of Phil and his workmanship, "I admired his professionalism and efficiency. He did good work."

Phil was being on his best behavior during this period. Janice Gomes, who owned a business in the area, later said about Phil and his approach, "He seemed very friendly. Very open and wasn't pushy. 'Oh, don't make a decision now,' he said. 'If you find that you are interested, give me a call.' So then I got business cards from him and was impressed. I told everyone about him, and they told their friends. He was very competitive, so over the years quite a few people were using Phillip's services."

The printing business was doing so well, in fact, that Nancy quit her job with Contra Costa ARC in 1998 and began to look after Phil's mother, Pat. By now, Pat was in the early stages of dementia and needed full-time care. Once in a while, Nancy would help Phil in his printing business, but her main job was looking after Phil's aging mother. Apparently, Nancy did a good job, and Pat would later call her daughter-in-law "an angel."

Supervision of Phil became even more lax in the spring of 1999. Phil received a letter from the United States District Court about his federal parole. The letter stated in part: *You will be happy to know that you are no longer obligated to report to the U.S. Probation Office. I want to thank you for your cooperation over this period of supervision and I hope that you will continue to do well. Best Regards, Mark Messner, U.S. Probation Officer.*

Matters were very chaotic now between California supervision of Phil and that of Nevada. In a faxed transmission from the Nevada Division of Parole to a California parole agency, Julie Johnson wrote: *Yesterday the Division requested emergency reporting instructions on the above subject (Phil Garrido) but was denied by your agency. Since your agency does not provide dual supervision our agency had to monitor the subject through his U.S. Probation and Parole Officer Mark Messner.*

The fax went on to note that Phil had seemingly acquired a stable life, was married, and ran his own printing business. And then the fax added, *Ordering the subject to return to Nevada to await acceptance from your state would be disruptive and unproductive for the subject who has managed to change his behavior.*

Finally, in June 1999, Phil was ordered to report to a California parole office and see Parole Agent A. Fulbright. One of Fulbright's early reports on Phil stated that Phil had made *good proper adjustment.*

And later in a report, it was noted that Phil took an antinarcotic test. The results came back with a positive result (and the exact name of the drug was blacked out), but a further notation related: *The issue was a case conference with the unit supervisor and decision was made to disregard further positives due to the subject's (blacked out) which he has to take, which makes him test positive for (blacked out).* Apparently, Phil was taking some kind of prescription medicine that made his drug tests seem as if he was testing positive for an illegal drug. In fact, he may have been taking illegal drugs, but his prescription medicine was masking his findings.

Phil did not want to be on parole at all, however, and Agent Fulbright noted in one report: *Garrido is seeking counsel of an attorney.* Phil went even further than that. He wrote the parole commission, stating that he had been released early from federal prison because of his good behavior: *The reason for my release 26 years early, was due to the complete recovery and successful reorientation back into the community. Years of hard work went into this recovery. At this point, every professional involved in my case recognized any further supervision would no longer be of any benefit to me, and so I was released back into the community under no supervision.*

Phil went on to write that it was clear to him that Nevada had dumped him off, to be monitored by California, because Nevada didn't have the resources to do so themselves. Phil added that if he had been in Nevada prison for twelve years, instead of federal prison, he might not have been rehabilitated at all. Phil wrote that the federal government had the resources to isolate a chemical problem in his brain and alleviate it by the use of medication. And he was outraged that the state of Nevada was now saying that parole supervision would help him readjust to life outside of prison. Phil claimed that he had already readjusted very well to leading a normal life in the community. He stated that Nevada's probation laws were outdated and needed to be reviewed by a federal agency.

Despite this letter, Phil was staying on Nevada/ California parole supervision—whether he liked it or not. He did, however, get a good report from Parole Agent Fulbright a few days later. The report stated: *Prognosis is good.*

In November 1999, Phil reluctantly agreed that California had the right to oversee his probation, and he signed an agreement to that effect. Phil started sending in his monthly reports, which were mainly self-reports of what he was doing. And in return, Agent Fulbright generally gave Phil good marks. In one, Fulbright wrote, *Garrido has completed over ten years of Federal Parole supervision. He is available for supervision and in compliance with his conditions of parole.*

And then there was one more sentence that Phil Garrido dreamed about. Fulbright wrote, *Recommendation: Discharge from parole supervision.* Nevada, however, ignored Fulbright's recommendation. And so the often erratic dual supervision of Nevada demanding that Phil Garrido still be on parole, and California doing the actual supervision, continued. Most of the time, one state barely knew what the other was doing in regard to Phil Garrido.

Fulbright did speak in person with Nancy in May 2000, and she said that Phil was very busy with his printing business. A few months later, Fulbright noted that there were no changes to Phil's reports. By now, however, Fulbright was becoming increasingly frustrated with dealing with the Garridos. Fulbright wrote in one report, *Why did I take this case?*

Things were pretty much the same throughout the year 2000. In fact, Phil's printing business was doing so well, he started doing business on the Internet, and Alyssa dealt with most of the customers online. Phil's operations expanded to J&M Enterprises, an auto-salvage yard outside of Pittsburg, and a recycling center in that city owned by Maria Christenson. Both businesses thought that Phil did good work for a lot less money than his competition.

Janice Gomes, who had been using Phil's service for some time, also ran a child safety program entitled National Community Empowerment Program. In the summer of 2000, Janice ordered business cards from Phil concerning this enterprise. But when he arrived with them, Janice noticed that "Child Safety" was mis-spelled as "Child Saftey."

Janice pointed this out to Phil, who responded, "My daughter's doing them."

Janice wondered why Phil's daughter would be doing the business cards and told Phil that his daugh-ter was not a good speller. In response, Phil said, "She's a good speller for six."

Janice thought this was cute, and she kept a batch of misspelled cards.

By 2001, Phil's parole agent was giving him even more leeway, if that was possible. A report noted: *Con-trolling offense is non-sexual. Offending sexually is more opportunistic or situational than a primary deviant sexual orientation. These cases can be reasonably handled on a control service caseload.* This assessment was astounding in light of the premeditation concerning Katie Calla-way's abduction and rape. In that case, Phil already had a room rigged up to meet his sexual fantasies. Just how this was "opportunistic" was not explained in this report.

In 2002, Phil got a new parole agent, R. Rodriguez.

And in Rodriguez's reports were the notations, *Subject has (blacked out) and is on (blacked out), and will always test positive for (blacked out)*. The visits by Rodriguez progressed throughout 2002, with notations such as, *Attempted home visit. No one answered the door. Left business card with instructions for subject to call me*. Phil did phone Rodriguez and came to the Concord office a few days later. A month later, Rodriguez wrote, *Mom showed me their room.* (Phil and Nancy's room) *First room off the livingroom. Big house.*

Two months later, in October 2002, Rodriguez visited the Garrido home once again on Walnut Avenue. In this report he related, *Me—wife. Doing ok. (Phil) will come into office to (drug) test*. That very same day, Phil provided a urine sample at the Concord office for drug testing.

In December, Rodriguez went to the Garrido home, no one answered the door, and he left his business card once again. In a later report, Rodriguez drew a sketch of the home. The sketch depicted a living room, kitchen/dining area, two bedrooms next to a bathroom, and Phil and Nancy's bedroom. There was a small sketch of the back porch and backyard door. But there was no sketch of the backyard or tall wooden fence that seemed to be the end of the backyard.

And so it went through 2004, 2005, and 2006, with home visits, visits to the Concord parole office by Phil, and the usual drug testing. Even when there was a new parole agent for Phil—Juan Castillo—the notations about him were generally very brief and even cryptic at times. Things such as, *Subject states all is well*. Or, *Wife says no contact with police or any problems*. More than once, however, there would be reports about Phil, apparently coming from Nancy: *He just stepped out*. In fact, there seemed to be a lot of occasions when Phil had "just stepped out," and it was not recorded as to where he had gone. If he had gone beyond a twenty-five-mile limit, without first telling his parole agent, that would have been in violation of his parole. But no agent apparently ever checked on this issue.

Throughout 2006 and 2007 and into 2008, the reports varied little in their notations: *April 6, 2006—Garrido registers with local law enforcement as a sex offender. August 23, 2007—Local law enforcement queries Garrido in law enforcement database. March 28, 2008—Local law enforcement queries Garrido in law enforcement database.*

Only one notation stood out for its dissimilarity to the rest: *November 30, 2006—Garrido's neighbor reports to local law enforcement several tents in Garrido's yard with people living in them and that there are children present. The neighbor is concerned because Garrido has sexual addiction. No action taken by responding officers.*

That one terse sentence—"No action taken by responding officers"—was going to come back and haunt the parole agents and Contra Costa County Sheriff's Office. But as far as most people were concerned in early 2008, Phil Garrido was just a fairly successful, if eccentric, entrepreneur.

CHAPTER 18

THE BLACK BOX

By the middle of 2008, Phil's grip on reality was dangerously eroding. He had managed to keep the backyard compound secret for seventeen years, but his own erratic actions were making that more difficult to do as each day passed. He could be seen walking down Walnut Avenue at times, singing loudly or acting strangely. And chief amongst his strange actions was a box that he had invented where he claimed that he could project his thoughts into other people's minds without saying a word. Over time, Phil would also claim that through this box he could channel the words of angels and even of God.

Phil began writing notes about his "magic box" and developed them into a rough handwritten book entitled *Origins of Schizophrenia Revealed*. It was the same book he would one day take with him to UC Berkeley, and it dealt with his supposed transformation from being a "sexual predator." And in a candid statement, he wrote, *Not all people who suffer from these types of problems are happy with their behavior and do experience major depression after ejaculation.*

Phil said he started looking at things differently when he accepted God into his life: *Because of my background I began to examine issues of how certain behaviors cause a great deal of pain in myself and those who are victimized by those behaviors especially our family and my wife. Building from those personal experiences I prepared a way to deal with these issues in my own mind.*

Phil wrote that in the past, he would look at an attractive woman and desire to assault her sexually. But in his new way of thinking, he could look at an attractive woman and merely think, *See how beautiful she is to look at.* By this new means, he could admire her attractiveness without having to assault her sexually. And Phil added that this new outlook helped alleviate the pain he had caused his wife. By "wife," it wasn't clear if he meant Nancy or Alyssa.

Phil said by this new thought process, he was able to control his overzealous masturbation. He had masturbated, in part, trying to reach a "high" that could not be attained. And he wrote: *I discovered one of the most imaginable freedoms imaginable, it was like the feelings one has when he is with someone new for the first time, except this time it was with my wife.* Phil related that his intercourse with her now was like the feelings a person felt when they met someone for the first time, and wanted to be with them every moment of the day.

Phil stated that one day after intercourse, he realized that he no longer had to do the things that had so stimulated him in the past. Those, of course, had meant kidnapping and bondage. And then he wrote, *I began to weep, telling her, "I'm sorry for the things I did in the past."* Phil wrote that he was overwhelmed with a feeling he had never experienced before.

Ever since then, Phil related, he had experienced the same feeling. He no longer desired other women whom he saw. He had a new love and desire for his own wife. And in a very revealing statement, he added that in the past, after ejaculation, he no longer wanted to be with that woman or even touch her.

Phil Garrido also decided to start a corporation under the Articles of Incorporation with the state of California. The name of Phil's corporation was originally called the Phillip C. Knight Institute. In time, however, it would be called God's Desire. As Phil noted on his incorporation form: *The specific purpose of this corporation is to create a religious organization. This corporation is a nonprofit Religious Corporation and is not organized for the private gain of any person.*

Phil added that his organization would not be affiliated with any "political party or framework" and was under the Internal Revenue Code, wherein it would not be taxed.

Once again, Phil could not help bragging about what he perceived his mission would accomplish. In a separate paper, he wrote his parole agent at the time, Juan Castillo: *This presentation will gain national attention, bringing scientists, physicists, psychologists, educators and religious leaders from around the world, turning their attention towards California on that day. So it is imperative that you be aware that I am moving towards a powerful disclosure concerning my past and how these issues can be managed. It will also help me with full access to any correctional institution anywhere in the United States of America.*

* * *

As time progressed, Phil Garrido became even more enthusiastic about the "black box" that he had created. It was about the size of a small suitcase and had two headsets and a microphone attached to it. Originally his conception for the box was to create "whispering voices" that would be like those heard by people with schizophrenia. Eager to try this box out on others, Phil took the black box to Jim and Cheyvonne Molino's business in Pittsburg. The Molinos were customers of Phil's in his printing business.

Later, Cheyvonne Molino related about the box, "He said he had a project he was working on and it was the development of a cure for schizophrenia. If a normal person put a headset on—that was attached to the box—they can hear what a schizophrenic walks around hearing in everyday life. That's how he explained it to me."

In a demonstration, Phil had Cheyvonne put on a headset, and he put one on as well. Then Phil turned away from her and began whispering into the microphone. By use of the black box, he altered the whispering sounds that she heard.

Phil tried this black box out on other customers of his; and over the next few months, he tinkered with it as well. As time progressed, his claims about the box became much more grandiose. Phil began asserting that he could hear the voices of angels and even God being channeled through the black box.

One of Phil's customers, Marc Lister, knew about these expanding claims by Phil and also about Phil's demonstration of the box at various parks around Antioch where homeless people gathered. Lister said that Phil started taking the box to those parks and demonstrating to homeless people about the box's mystical functions. And Lister added that over time, Phil also had Nancy, Angel, and Starlit accompany him to the parks. Once in a while, even Alyssa was allowed to go along to the parks.

Phil Garrido also started a blog on the Internet and styled himself as the "manwhospokewithhismind." The fact that all of this ran as one word gave an indication of the frantic pace that he set for himself in this matter. In one posting, Phil referred to a "cultural trance," wherein large bodies of people accepted something as being true, when, in fact, it was not. As an example, Phil gave the perception that before Columbus proved otherwise, many people in Europe believed that the world was flat. In today's world, Phil said, everyone accepted the "fact" that no one could produce voices that others could hear, simply by thinking and transmitting their thoughts to others without ever opening their mouths. Phil related that he was going to prove that the opposite was true. By means of the box he had devised, Phil claimed, he could send a person his thoughts without uttering a word.

In humanity's present condition, Phil wrote, people see what they expect to see. Hear what they expect to hear. Think what they expect to think. By doing this, he claimed, they actually kept themselves from a higher truth.

Phil related that he was going to use an "age-old book, the Bible," but he would interpret it in new ways. Then he quoted Isaiah 6:9— *"Go and tell this people: 'Be ever hearing, but never understanding, be ever seeing, but never perceiving.'"*

In the summer of 2008, Phil made a disclaimer

before posting on his Web site, This freedom has not come due to something great about myself, instead this ability is to open doors that will honor the Creator and his eternal purpose for mankind. With that disclaimer in place, Phil wrote that it had all begun for him when God removed a problem from his shoulders. Because of things that had been removed, he said, he was now a free man. Phil did not go into further detail at that time as to what the problem had been.

According to Phil, the posting was to gain the attention of unbelievers, including "scientists, psychiatrists, and educators." Phil related that the Creator's work was all over the world and his message was a wake-up call. Then Phil said he was doing this, not to be controversial or challenge anyone's religious beliefs. Rather, he was going to present his case in a rational and orderly manner.

Phil quoted Jeremiah 9:24 from the Bible— *"Let him who boasts, boast about this: that he understands and knows me, that I am the Lord, who exercises kindness, patience and righteousness on earth, for these I delight."*

Phil noted that in August 2008, he went to UC Berkeley's Free Speech Stage and publicly spoke about his convictions and provided a live demonstration with his magical box. He said the demonstration was a platform to begin making the public aware about the voice of God and its power to save lives.

This mania on the subject showed how far Phil was now willing to go, even if it endangered the elaborate web of deceit he had constructed in his own household. Had one parole agent ever looked at that posting, the agent would have noted that by Phil going to People's Park, he was traveling beyond the twenty-five-mile limit to which he was confined. If he wanted to go beyond twenty-five miles, Phil was supposed to let the parole office know about his planned trip.

Without parole agent approval, Phil, Alyssa, Angel, and Starlit began taking numerous trips to People's Park in Berkeley so that Phil could demonstrate his black box. There were always numerous homeless people there, and one of Phil's main draws was handing out sandwiches and bottles of water to them. Then when he had a captive audience, Phil would demonstrate his black box to the throng by use of an amplification system. It may not have been the "Miracle of the Loaves and Fishes," but there would always be several people there who shouted back to Phil that they could hear his voice, even though he hadn't uttered any words to them.

Phil was even breaking down his carefully built web of deceit more than that. He posted that he had sent law enforcement agencies and university departments an invitation about a demonstration and lecture on the device he had created. Phil added an interesting caveat: If you feel the following documents are in any way fraudulent, the California State Courts are open to you. Anyone under the influence of illegal drugs, or if you think you are being led by voices, seek professional help immediately.

Then in another posting, Phil presented his document that had been sent to law enforcement agencies, and he was going to take it to the UC Berkeley campus. The document began that he had a new insight that could help people who were hearing voices to make them stop before they committed a violent act against themselves or someone else. And he cited a recent incident where a deranged woman had thrown her children into San Francisco Bay to drown them. She had apparently been hearing voices that "told her" to do so. Phil wrote that his new insights could have helped her before she had become overwhelmed by her own inner voices and what she perceived to be external voices speaking to her.

Phil related that the document was to open minds of religious leaders, scientists, psychiatrists, physicists, and educators worldwide. And he was sending law enforcement copies of the document so that they could, in his words, "separate church and state." With that information, Phil said that even law enforcement agents could benefit by reaching a "higher state of qualified control" when dealing with the public.

Included in the package were six Declarations and Affirmations confirming demonstrations of his box, wherein he was allowed to *speak in a tongue unknown to mankind.* The Declaration of Affirmation stated that the individuals signing it actually watched Phil demonstrate what he could do with the device he had constructed.

The Declaration of Affirmation also stated that the person signing it agreed that they had witnessed Phillip Garrido's ability to control sound with his mind, and that he had developed a device for others to witness the phenomena. These affirmations came from a variety of Phil's business customers. Some of them were impressed by the black box; others just signed the affirmations to get rid of Phil and have him quit pestering them on the subject.

Tim Allen, who owned East County Glass and Window Company, said later, "The way he described it is that he could hear people think. He could hear voices. God would talk to him and he could hear the voices through this box, and that I could understand what he was thinking telepathically. I shut my eyes. I really wanted to hear something, but all I could hear were kind of hollow sounds like a shell."

A few of Phil's customers told him that they were not going to sign any affirmation and not to bring up the subject again. Maria Christenson said, "I never let him in when he wanted to bring it in. I didn't want to sign it. He was mad at me because he wanted to bring that box, so I could hear the voices. And I just said no."

Not content merely to have affirmations, Phil hired a private detective, who had once been a cop, to attest to the validity of all of his statements about the black box. The detective was very skeptical about Phil's assertions, but he dutifully went along with Phil to a number of Phil's customers' establishments. The detective was basically there to witness the people signing their names to the affirmation form.

David Bocanegra, who rarely spoke to his sister, Nancy, since she had married Phil, did so around this time. Nancy was very excited and told David about Phil's black box from which he could hear the voices of angels and of God. David said later, "It was just really off-the-wall. I couldn't believe my sister was with this guy!"

And by now, Nancy was part of one more of Phil's schemes. For months, she had been taking care of an elderly neighbor named Dilbert Medeiros. Just before Medeiros moved to a nursing home, he gave the Garridos $18,000 for a church that they said they were starting. Medeiros later said that this $18,000 was only a loan. The Garridos said it was an outright gift.

Nancy also displayed some bizarre behavior while living on Walnut Avenue. This came in the form of various aliases that she used. Amongst these were Nancy M. Garrido, Nancy P. Garrido, Nancy Garrida and Nancy Garrizo. She also created several false addresses where she claimed she was residing.

Phil didn't create as many aliases and false addresses, but he did create one address that was strange in its own way. It was in August 1993, around the time he was sent back to prison for six weeks for a parole violation. Phil created an address in Antioch, California, but there was no such address and nothing even close to that in Antioch. Just what Phil was doing making this false address did not come to light later on, nor did the fact that he, like Nancy, seemed to have used the same address in Antioch at some point. Of course, no residence existed at that location.

On April 14, 2008, Phil Garrido's life became a lot more restricted. He was finally categorized by the probation department as a high-risk sexual offender. Under "Jessica's Law," he could not reside within two thousand feet of a public park, a public school, or a private school. Since he lived on semirural Walnut Avenue, he met those requirements.

In addition, he had to sign a form that he would not consume excessive amounts of alcohol or use illegal drugs, and that he would actively participate in a psychiatric program. He was not to have contact with females between the ages of fourteen and eighteen. (Under the circumstances, his signature here was fraudulent in the extreme.) He was not to have any contact with the victim of his crime—in other words, Katie Callaway.

Curfew was to be from ten o'clock until six o'clock the following morning. Many of the other things he agreed to would be harder to prove. He was not to view television shows or movies geared toward the types of crime he had committed. Nor was he to view television programs or movies that would "stimulate sexual fantasies." He was not to possess handcuffs or any kind of restraints. And he was not to possess costumes, masks, or items that would conceal his identity. That last part was interesting. On the previous Halloween, according to some neighbors, Phil had been seen going around the neighborhood wearing a gorilla suit. He had been accompanied by two young blond girls.

One thing that was not restricted was use of a computer for the Internet. Perhaps Phil had told his parole agent he needed this for his printing business. At least on the surface, it seemed as if Phil had a steady job and a stable lifestyle. After all, he and Nancy had been married for twenty-seven years, and she had not cited any domestic abuse by Phil.

Phil had to wear a Global Positioning System (GPS) device now, and the device was placed on Phil's leg by a parole agent. Phil was required to charge his GPS device twice a day, for one hour each time. One charging was to be at 5:30 A.M. and the other at 5:30 P.M. He was not to tamper with the device, force a boot over the device, expose it to extreme heat, or submerge it in water.

As 2008 progressed, the local fire department was called to the Garrido residence on May 21 to assist Phil's elderly mother. None of the fire department personnel noted anything out of the ordinary at the residence, other than it seemed to have a lot of clutter.

These problems with Phil's mother apparently became even more severe in June 2009. On June 3, 8, and 22, the fire department was called out to the residence on Walnut Avenue. All that was listed in Phil's later parole report for each occasion was: *Health of elderly female.*

It's hard to know what effect his mother's medical emergencies had on Phil. After all, he even had admitted that she was the one who always had "spoiled" him. Perhaps it further eroded the wall of secrecy that he had built around Alyssa, Angel, and Starlit. It was in the summer of 2009 that Phil began to take Angel and Starlit with him more frequently on printing business trips, and especially on his mission concerning God's Desire. Phil's grip on the elaborate web of deceit was steadily decreasing and he was on a collision course with the unexpected events at UC Berkeley that would turn his world upside down.

III

THE RECKONING

Jaycee Lee Dugard spent the first nine years of her life with her mother, Terry, a single mom. When Terry married Carl Probyn, the family moved to South Lake Tahoe, California. *(Yearbook photo)*

Jaycee eventually liked the move and enjoyed her classmates at Meyers Elementary School. *(Yearbook photo)*

Jaycee Dugard had been missing for eighteen years when, on August 25, 2009, University of California, Berkeley policewomen Ally Jacobs (left) and Lisa Campbell (right) became suspicious about a man with two girls on campus. *(Cathy Cockrell/ UC Berkeley NewsCenter)*

Jaycee Dugard announced her true identity at the Concord, California Parole Office. Reporters showed up at the nearby Concord Police Department soon after the news broke. *(Author photo)*

For her work in breaking open the case, Officer Ally Jacobs received a thank-you from the entire city council in her hometown of Brentwood, California, where she lived with her two young sons. *(Author photo)*

After the revelation that "Alyssa" was actually Jaycee Lee Dugard, law enforcement investigators descended upon the home of Phillip and Nancy Garrido near Antioch, California, where Jaycee and her two daughters, fathered by Phil, had been kept in seclusion. *(Author photo)*

Just two of the many officers and investigators, after a long, hot day of work at the Garrido home. Temperatures in the area that August reached over 100 degrees. *(Author photo)*

The Garridos' green van was hauled away as evidence to a police yard for further investigation of its interior. *(Author photo)*

Reporters from around the world descended upon Walnut Avenue once the incredible story broke about Jaycee Dugard, her daughters, and the kidnappers. (Author photo)

While reporters were interested in all the police activity, the police were just as interested in the reporters. Most officers had never seen a media frenzy like this before and captured it on camera. (Author photo)

Young Phil Garrido attended classes in the small town of Brentwood, California, about fifty miles east of San Francisco. *(Yearbook photo)*

Phil was bright and popular with girls in school, but he made only average grades and didn't join any clubs. He was much more interested in playing bass guitar in his rock and roll band. *(Yearbook photo)*

Many people who knew him said that Phil Garrido was different after he had a motorcycle accident and started taking illegal drugs. He turned from being a "nice, clean-cut kid" into a "dope-smoking stoner." Soon he was using LSD almost on a daily basis. *(Mug shot)*

Despite Phil's yen for illegal drugs and sometimes bizarre behavior, his high school sweetheart, Christine Perreira, eloped with him to Reno in 1973. *(Yearbook photo)*

Phil got into very serious trouble in 1976 when he kidnapped Katie Callaway in South Lake Tahoe, California. He took her across state lines into Nevada to a warehouse in Reno and raped her for hours. Only the lucky arrival of a police officer at the warehouse saved Katie. *(Mug shot)*

Phil got an early release from federal prison and served his probation near Antioch in a house his mother owned. In 1993, while living there with Nancy, Phil broke the rules of his probation and was sent back to prison for a short time. (Mug shot)

Phil's mug shot was taken again when he was arrested for Jaycee Dugard's kidnapping in 2009. At the time, he had a distinctive growth near his nose. (Mug shot)

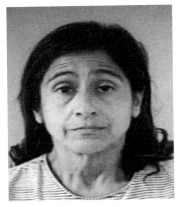

At the time of her arrest, Nancy Garrido looked care-worn and dazed. (Mug shot)

There were concerns that other missing Bay Area children might have been kidnapped by Phil and Nancy Garrido. Blond-haired Michaela Garecht was one of them. She was kidnapped in broad daylight in Hayward, California, in 1988. Phil was residing in a halfway house nearby at the time. *(Yearbook photo)*

Michaela's mother, Sharon (second from left), went to Walnut Avenue when all the police activity was going on there in August and September 2009. Sharon had hopes that Michaela might still be alive, as Jaycee was. *(Author photo)*

A house next door to the Garrido home came under police investigation when they learned that Phil had been caretaker of that property for a period of time when no one lived there. *(Author photo)*

Police scent dogs were used by investigators on the neighbor's and Garrido's properties, searching for signs of human remains. *(Author photo)*

Hayward Police Department Lieutenant Christine Orrey gave progress reports to journalists about digging for remains in the properties' backyards. *(Author photo)*

Forensic bone specialist Bill Silva told reporters that even though human bone fragments were found on both properties, the bones were very old and might have come from a Native American burial site. *(Author photo)*

Phil and Nancy Garrido were arrested on multiple charges in El Dorado County, where the initial kidnapping of Jaycee Lee Dugard had taken place. Their court appearances were in Placerville, California, an old Gold Rush mining town originally known as Hangtown. *(Author photo)*

The DA's office in El Dorado County put together a team that compiled literally thousands of pages of documents on the case against Phil and Nancy Garrido. *(Author photo)*

Phil often stared off into space during court proceedings. *(Author photo)*

While Phil came into court with no emotion showing on his face,
Nancy generally looked distraught or embarrassed about being there.
(Author photo)

Nancy Garrido liked her first attorney, Gilbert Maines, but he got into trouble for allegedly making remarks about how he was going to make money from a film deal on the case. (Author photo)

Judge Phimister threw Maines off the case and appointed Stephen Tapson as Nancy's lawyer. Nancy was initially not pleased by this development. (Author photo)

Phil Garrido's lawyer, Susan Gellman, commiserated with Maines about this development. (Author photo)

When it snowed outside the courthouse, Phil Garrido's lawyer, Susan Gellman, bundled up and wore a cowboy hat. *(Author photo)*

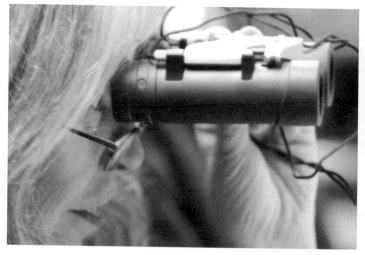

Veteran courtroom sketch artist Vicki Behringer took binoculars to court to capture every detail in exacting precision. *(Author photo)*

Katie Callaway Hall (first woman from left) was the woman Phil had raped in 1976. Katie came to all the court hearings in the Garrido case. She wanted him to know that she was there and sticking up for Jaycee and her daughters. Katie called Phil a monster. *(Author photo)*

Represented by famed lawyer Gloria Allred (photo above, third from left), Jaycee's biological father, Ken Slayton (also above, fourth from left), often went to court hearings. He sat next to Katie Callaway Hall in the gallery. *(Author photo)*

Judge Douglas Phimister had to rule on numerous decisions about points of law and media requests during pretrial hearings for Phil and Nancy Garrido. *(Author photo)*

Not unlike Walnut Avenue near Antioch, the Placerville courthouse became a beehive of reporters' activity after every major court hearing in the Garrido case. *(Author photo)*

CHAPTER 19

LIKE A HURRICANE

After the first news that Jaycee Lee Dugard was alive reached the outside world, reporters of all stripes hardly knew where to follow the story. There were so many angles, so many locations where events had taken place. They could go to Berkeley to try and talk to Lisa Campbell and Ally Jacobs. They could go to Lake Tahoe, where Jaycee had been kidnapped in 1991, or to Placerville, California, in El Dorado County, where Phil and Nancy Garrido were to be arraigned. Or they could go to Southern California where Terry Probyn and Carl Probyn both now lived, although Terry and Carl were separated.

Nowhere, however, became more of a magnet for journalists than Walnut Avenue, where Phil and Nancy Garrido had kept Jaycee, Angel, and Starlit as virtual prisoners for year after year. What started out as a trickle of local reporters turned into a flood as journalists from across the nation, and then the world, descended upon once-quiet Walnut Avenue. Even on Walnut Avenue, there were multiple angles to

report upon: the neighbors who had known Phil and
Nancy Garrido, the law enforcement officers who were
working the crime scene, the very house and grounds
themselves.

At first the scene was absolute chaos on Walnut
Avenue. Long lines of police vehicles from the Contra
Costa County Sheriff's Office, Antioch Police Department, Pittsburg Police Department (PPD), and even
FBI agents were parked every which way down the
narrow lane. Carloads of curious sightseers motored
by, and reporters' cars, vans, motor homes, and satellite trucks took up every free space they could find for
blocks around. Ground zero was, of course, the Garrido home and yard; and before long, law enforcement had strung yellow caution tape around the
surrounding perimeter of the Garrido property, trying
to keep journalists and the merely curious out.

Denied access to the Garrido property, journalists
spread out along Walnut Avenue talking to any resident they could lay their hands on. Sometimes there
was a surreal feeling to it all, as one resident who had
never so much as seen a newsman in person would be
surrounded by a local newspaper reporter, television
reporters from the Bay Area and Sacramento, journalists with national network television and print, and
video journalists from the UK, Germany, Australia, and
beyond. The *Contra Costa Times* noted, *More than a
dozen news trucks have carved out parking spaces on the
edges of the sidewalk-free country lane. Suited up and glued
to their cell phones, the on-air personalities shuffle through the
thick dust and fan themselves in the heat. All the major net-
works are here and some from overseas.*

One neighbor Phil had spoken with about his wild
ideas was Monica Adams. Monica's mother, Betty
Unpingco, lived on Walnut Avenue, and Adams told
journalists that on one occasion Phil set up speakers at

a party Monica was hosting at her parents' house. Phil stuck around and was annoying, even though he wasn't invited to the party. Monica finally kicked him out, stating, "Because he was acting weird and staring at all the women."

Monica added that later that same night, she was watching a program on television and discovered that anyone could look for sex offenders in their community. Monica got on her computer and found the name Phillip Garrido there, listed as a registered sex offender. Monica told the reporter, "We were irate, and we told our neighbors about it."

Monica said that she knew that some children seemed to be living on the Garrido property or were at least there a lot of the time. Monica said that she figured that law enforcement must know about the situation, since they were the ones who had listed Phil Garrido as a sex offender in the first place. Then Monica added, "He never bothered anyone. He kept to himself. What would we have done? You just watch your own."

Another neighbor, who would soon be very uncommunicative, initially spoke with journalists. This was Erika Pratt, twenty-five, who had lived directly next door to the Garridos with her boyfriend, Damon Robinson. Erika told a reporter, "Phil had little girls and a woman living in the backyard, and they all looked the same. They never talked, and they kept to themselves. I was always freaked out by Phil's behavior. The girls in the tent were about four years old, eleven years old, and another about twenty-five years old." Erika was speaking of an incident that had happened in 2006.

Erika was one of the very few who ever saw that tent compound that Phil had constructed behind the main yard, in which he had enclosed Jaycee Lee and her

198

198 *Robert Scott*

daughters. Erika said she had sneaked peeks through the chain-link fence that separated her yard from the Garridos' property. She described what she saw as a yard having tents, sheds, pit bulls, and water hoses from the main house to the tent area. She also told a reporter that on more than one occasion, Phil took water from her property to run a shower and fill a small plastic swimming pool.

On November 30, 2006, Erika had been so upset about this situation, she phoned the CCSO about what she had seen. A deputy came out to speak with her, and she told him about the young women living in squalor in the tent area. Erika now related to a journalist, "The deputy said he couldn't go inside Phil's home because he didn't have a search warrant. So he told me to just keep an eye on him."

Erika Pratt was one of the very, very few who knew that there was a secret compound in the Garrido's far backyard, and soon she wasn't talking to any reporters. Part of the reason may have been that law enforcement agencies were telling her not to divulge anything she had seen. Or she may have decided to keep mum about it on her own.

If Erika was silent, Damon Robinson, her former boyfriend, had plenty to say. Damon lived directly next door to the Garridos and he told numerous reporters about his interaction with Phil Garrido, and how Phil had become increasingly bizarre as time went by. Damon recounted to a *Los Angeles Times* reporter that Phil had once been a caretaker on the property Damon now rented. Damon said that Phil had changed locks on the doors so that people could be locked in rather than locked out.

Damon also said, "It took me a while to realize, but Phil had access to all of these buildings." (He meant all the sheds on the property.) "At first, I didn't even realize they were part of my land because there are wire fences splitting up the yard. When I moved over in one of the sheds, there was a music player, a couch, a mattress, and a VCR. He really wanted the VCR back when I found it."

Unbeknownst to Damon, this setup in the shed was eerily like the way the shed had been where Phil had taken Katie Callaway in Reno. And, of course, Phil had used that shed as a "porno palace" as Detective DeMaranville had described it.

Damon added that before he took rightful ownership of them, there had been times when Damon could hear music coming from the sheds in question. Damon said that he thought he had heard a girl's voice coming from one of those sheds, and Phil's voice as well. Damon related, "Maybe he was taking the girl over there for a change of scenery or something a little nicer than he had in his yard." It was never clear to Damon just who the girl was, or what relationship she had to Phil Garrido.

Unfortunately for Damon, he soon seemed to be embellishing what he was saying. Some reporters wondered if he was making up stories about Phil, just to make the man seem even more outlandish. And this embellishment was a constant threat to the validity of what reporters were hearing from people all up and down the street.

Ruth Laney, a *People* magazine stringer based in Louisiana, knew members of Damon's family. She learned that he had been asked by various national news agencies to appear live on their newscasts. She said, "One show was even going to fly him to New York. But he was like a deer in the headlights. There was all this unexpected commotion going on around him, and he didn't quite know how to react." Instead of going to New York, Damon hung around Walnut

Avenue, soaking up all the attention there. And then he started asking to be paid for all that attention.

This being paid for interviews was a real bone of contention with United States news agencies. They generally did not indulge in such practices. But several European agencies were used to doing things that way. Damon started charging news agencies to come into his yard and photograph across the fence into the Garrido's yard. And Damon got into trouble when he supposedly related some "exclusive" information to one agency, and then charged another agency for using the same information. The reporter for the first agency yelled at Damon, "Hey! That was supposed to be exclusive!" Damon's reliability began to taper off from that point forward with news agencies.

Laney related one more thing about Damon Robinson. Damon's uncle had come to visit him in the summer of 2009. While the uncle was there, Phil Garrido came out of his house and started talking to Damon, the uncle and some other people on the street in front of Phil's house. The uncle recalled Phil talking frantically about religion. Before long, the other people had left, but Damon's uncle stayed on, just to be polite.

"He was all wound up," the uncle told Laney. "He just wouldn't stop talking. Most of what he said didn't make much sense. I didn't know what he was talking about. It was about some kind of box he had with which he could talk to God and the angels. It all sounded pretty nuts to me. But I listened to him for about fifteen minutes and then I said I had to go. When I walked away, I thought to myself, 'This guy is like Charles Manson.'"

Another neighbor of the Garridos, Haydee Perry, told a *San Francisco Chronicle* reporter about a young blond girl she had seen clinging to Phil one day as Phil helped Haydee change a car battery. Haydee related, "The girl stayed close to him at all times. It wasn't normal behavior. She had a blank stare on her face. Now it seems like a cry for help." The little girl told Haydee at one point that she had an older sister named Alyssa.

Betty Unpingco, who lived a few houses down the street from the Garridos, and whose daughter was Monica Adams, told a reporter, "I once bought some of his business cards. We're all in shock. Scared it can happen just a few doors down." Unpingco also spoke about Phil and the party where he had brought speakers to the event. Betty said that Phil had been staring so much at the high-school girls there, he was asked to leave. She was so concerned for the girls, they were later escorted from the area by adults. Betty told a reporter for CNN, "It was so bizarre. I warned my children to stay away from him and to always walk in twos."

To a San Francisco television station, Betty added, "I was just in my neighbor's backyard last week. I looked through the three fences in the Garridos' backyard, and you couldn't see a thing (of the compound where Jaycee and her kids had been kept). There were always people at Phil's place, but you couldn't tell who lived there."

Angela Crabaugh, whose son lived across the street from the Garridos, had met Phil and thought he was a religious nut. She said, "I just always thought he was very bizarre."

Another person who lived on Walnut Avenue was Karen Walker. She told reporters about a woman who lived in the Garrido home, and it wasn't clear if she was speaking about Nancy or Pat. Karen said, "She looked kinda like she didn't have any medical attention. Like her teeth were not taken care of. And her hair wasn't brushed."

Then Walker told a Sacramento television reporter that Phil recently had a fire in his van. "When neighbors went to investigate, he shooed everyone away. I never saw the girl called Alyssa. But my nine-year-old grandson asked one day if one of the blond girls wanted to play. He and his friend asked if they could ride bikes with her. They were just being friendly. She said that she couldn't."

And to a Sacramento newspaper journalist, Karen talked about the high concentration of sex offenders in the area. "It was so close to home. We were thinking about moving before, but now there's no doubt about it."

Reporters were corralling every person they could possibly find in and around Walnut Avenue. Sam Kovisto, who lived down the block from the Garridos, told a *Los Angeles Times* journalist, "I never really expected what he had going on, but I expected something. You could just tell by his mannerisms and how he acted that he was trying to hide something. He came around to my place and he wanted to sing. It was always gospel singing and religious stuff. I told him to get lost and not come on my property. Since I first saw that guy, I knew there was something not right about him. He thought he was God. He was crazy."

Polly White, another neighbor, told a Sacramento television reporter, "It's extremely creepy to have someone back there, living close, and not know what they are doing."

Janice Deitrich, who lived in the area, said that Phil would visit and sometimes help feed an elderly neighbor, Dilbert Medeiros. It only came out later that Phil had been defrauding Medeiros and cashing and possibly even forging Medeiros's checks. Phil had generally behaved himself around Deitrich and not gone into his most outrageous modes.

Some people who lived in the area did not want to give their full names. One of these people would only give his name as Steve. Steve told a *Canadian Register* reporter, "As far as the girls went, I thought they were his nieces or something. It's kind of embarrassing to be here this long and not know what's going on under all our noses. When I first met him (Phil), I thought he was a nice guy. Now I'd just like to see him shot or hung."

At the nearby Bridgehead Café, journalists learned that Phil generally went there once a month to eat by himself. One waitress, Lusanne Bough, related, "Phil came here and he was always kind. He would always have a smile on his face. Very friendly."

Roger Lund, a patron of the café, said that he knew Phil, and Phil had never caused any problems at the café. "He behaved himself. He didn't preach here, or act crazy."

Café owner, Murray Sexton, added, "He was like a schoolteacher. Someone who just led an ordinary life, like the rest of us."

Now, of course, any aspect of Phil Garrido being "ordinary" was long gone. The café hummed with conversations at every table about "creepy Phil," who had lived only blocks away. And because Bridgehead Café was one of the few restaurants in the area, it soon became the local eating establishment for scores of reporters and investigators.

CHAPTER 20

"A VERY PRETTY YOUNG LADY."

Journalists were also speaking with people who Phil had done business with concerning his business card services. One business was J&M Enterprises in the nearby city of Pittsburg. Mary Thomas, an accountant for J&M, said that Phil had set up a revival tent on the business property and demonstrated his homemade device. She said, "He was always very professional and spoke the Word of God whenever he talked."

Cheyvonne Molino, co-owner of the business with her husband, Jim, related that just before all the news about Jaycee broke, Phil started dropping by J&M more often. Cheyvonne said, "Don't ask me why. He passed out water and quoted Bible Scripture."

Jim Molino added that Phil requested having a demonstration of his device in the parking lot, and Phil stated that eventually "millions of followers would come."

Employee Danielle LeBlue related that Phil was

doing all this religious activity, "As a way to give back for all he had done wrong." Of course, Phil made no mention of abducting Jaycee or having her father his children when she was only a child. Nor did he mention that Jaycee and her daughters were still virtual prisoners in his secret compound.

Danielle related that Phil shared his handwritten book about schizophrenia with them, and he told them that he'd recently given a copy to the FBI. Danielle said that the material in the book was "creepy." Then she said one more thing: Phil had recently brought Angel and Starlit to the shop and introduced them as "my girls." Danielle stressed, "He said, 'my girls,' not 'my daughters.'"

Of the girls who came with Phil Garrido to the shop, Cheyvonne added, "I don't think they realized anything was wrong or different, except they didn't go to schools with other kids. They were very shy. The older one was very clingy to her father." One of the girls spoke of having a church in the basement of their house.

Cheyvonne also spoke of a "Sweet Sixteen party" for her daughter on the Tuesday before Phil made his fateful trip to UC Berkeley with Angel and Starlit. Cheyvonne said, "He had never mentioned a wife or daughters before then, and we were kind of shocked when he said, 'Is it okay if my daughter comes to your daughter's birthday party?'"

Cheyvonne said it was okay, and Phil showed up with two young girls. Cheyvonne related, "He came, he brought his girls, and they stayed for a little bit. After a short while, Phil said, 'This isn't what they're used to. So we're going to go ahead and go.'"

Later, Cheyvonne told a San Francisco Bay Area reporter, "The media make it seem like these little girls were living like wolves or jungle kids in the backyard dungeon. Perhaps that's it, but they didn't give that visual to me. They were polite. They were well-mannered."

A woman who had met "Alyssa" was Melanie Dewey. Alyssa had designed brochures for Dewey's day spa. At the time, Alyssa had appeared to be very shy to Melanie. Dewey said that Alyssa wore "dingy clothes"and that her blond hair wasn't brushed. "She was kind of slumped over, with her head down, and looked really sad and withdrawn. I just thought that she was very insecure. When he (Phil) said, 'This is my daughter,' I just got the picture that this was her daddy telling her what to do. He's probably very strict and she does what she's told."

Tiffany Tran, who ran the Furniture Galley in Brentwood, also had business cards created by Phil Garrido. Tiffany told a reporter, "He seemed a little different, and he constantly talked religion and showed a device [that] he claimed he could control sound with his mind. Some people have a story behind their smile, some don't. He did. He was very happy-go-lucky, but you knew there was a story behind it."

Deepal Karunaratne, a Sri Lankan–born real estate agent in Antioch, purchased business cards and material from Phil over the years. Deepal believed Phil and Nancy when they told him that Alyssa was their daughter. Karunaratne related to a British *Sunday Times* reporter, "Alyssa was part of the family business, running the printing press in the backyard. I would see her in work overalls, covered in ink. I negotiated with her when she could not complete my order. She was always polite and professional. Sometimes she would be wearing jeans and a blouse, standing outside the house with Nancy, who did all the bookkeeping."

Deepal added that Phil would never let him see the printing press in the backyard sheds. Phil told him that his press was a trade secret. But Deepal did get glimpses of two young blond girls in the backyard area. And of these girls, Karunaratne said, they were allowed to go out and eat and even see movies with Phil. Deepal never saw the girls living in tents.

To a Sacramento news station journalist, Karunaratne said, "Alyssa always had a pretty smile on her face. When she came and talked to me, she was always smiling. A very pretty young lady."

Ben Daughdrill also attested to the good work done by Alyssa. Daughdrill told a reporter, "She was the design person. She did the artwork. She was the genius. I communicated with her by e-mail and phone." Ben had even gone out to the Garrido home and seen Alyssa there. It just seemed like a normal situation to him.

About Alyssa, Daughdrill told a television reporter, "Nothing stood out. Obviously, there was some brain-washing going on. That's all I can think. She had access to a phone and a computer, so obviously something went on that no one knows about."

Ben mentioned that one time when he went out to the Garrido residence to pick up material, Alyssa met him at his vehicle. "She came out, alone. She could have escaped if she wanted to. There is a reason she did not do anything."

Even entities like Kidnappedchildrenblogspot were doing investigative reporting. That site noted: At a hardware store that Garrido frequented, a receipt for a purchase he made on August 17, 2009, showed he paid $24.99 for a pressure switch. And he left a $2 donation. The receipt: The Children's Miracle Network, an organization dedicated to saving and improving the lives of kids.

Tim Allen, president of East County Glass and Window Company, was also one of Phil's business card clients. Like the others, Allen said that Phil brought his

device into the office and proclaimed that he had
channeled God's voice through the box. Tim added
that on one occasion, Phil brought two young
blond girls into the business. Allen described them as
"very clingy." As for Phil, Allen said, "I kind of felt sorry
for him at the time. I didn't know about his criminal
past. You never thought anything bad about the guy.
He was just kind of nutty."

Tim told a Sacramento television news station that
he had kept some of the business cards that had been
printed from Phil's business. And Tim was impressed
by the fact that Phil always hand-delivered the material
and promised to take any order back if there was a mis-
spelling or a problem with the color scheme. On one
of the visits to his place of business, Phil had brought
two young girls with him. Tim now said, "I walked
around the counter and actually met his two young
girls and shook their hands. I really felt almost sick to
my stomach when I realized what was going on following the arrest."

Because of his dealings with Phil Garrido, Tim Allen
became emblematic of the extreme demand by the
media to talk to anyone who had known Phil. In a
short period of time, Allen was on CNN's *Larry King
Live, Dr. Phil,* the BBC, and dozens of local television
and radio stations.

Steve Contreras, who owned a car repair business in
Antioch, talked to a United Kingdom *Telegraph* reporter. Contreras said that he'd purchased business
cards from Phil over the years and that Angel had
come in with Phil on occasion. She spent the time in
his auto shop playing with an imaginary friend.

Contreras stated, "She looked a lot smaller than her
age, and acted a lot younger as well. She kind of acted
like a five-year-old. She was talking to an imaginary
friend and speaking both sides. Phil used to come in

about every three months and he was really strange. He said the world was coming to an end. I thought he was a crank. Once, there was a mistake on my business cards. So I rang up and they were redone that day. Nobody does business cards that quick. I used to joke that he must have some slaves in the backyard doing them."

Maria Christenson, of Christenson Recycling Center in Pittsburg, said, "There was nothing weird with him in the beginning. But I noticed a year ago, he just went off the deep end. He came into my place and asked for a $2,000 advance. He came in with Nancy. They said they needed a new bathroom and had plans to start a backyard church."

Christenson told another reporter, "He started preaching and doing all this stuff. He was telling me about his voices. And then he said, 'You know, I've been to prison, and I don't masturbate anymore.' Out of the blue! Then he started crying, and she was crying. I was looking at them—thinking, 'What is this about?' I got freaked out."

Janice Gomes recounted to a *Los Angeles Times* reporter that she had been in a local beauty parlor, fifteen years in the past, when Phil Garrido had walked in the place, wanting to drum up clients for his printing business. Gomes was interested in printing for her business and she began talking with Phil. She recalled the year as being 1994 and Phil told her, "My wife just had a baby." By wife, he meant Jaycee, and the baby was, of course, Angel.

Gomes had worked for decades with criminals and gang members as a youth counselor and she said that her instincts were pretty good about people. But with Phil Garrido she related, "He had me fooled." It was Garrido who had printed flyers for her nonprofit work with the National Community Empowerment

Program. And, of course, Phil had told her, "Children should never go to a bus stop alone. They're no match for an adult."

And Janice had also heard Phil singing and playing some of the songs he said he had written. She said, "He would pull up a chair and burst into song. He'd just start singing. One of my daughters told me he sang Madonna songs and she felt one of his favorites was 'Like a Virgin.' He would sing very high and very off-key."

In relation to Phil's printing, Gomes did business with a young woman over the phone who called herself Alyssa. Gomes said, "She was very sweet. Very professional." In fact, Janice went by the Garrido home a few times to pick up business cards Phil had printed. Gomes told a reporter for the *Oakley News,* "The furniture in the house was old-fashioned. I did notice that there were no family pictures, no TV. Everything looked like a set." And then Janice added a strange comment that Phil made to her. "He said he had recovered from his past excesses, of prostitution, pornography, and masturbation. He never mentioned kidnapping."

More information about these songs of Phil's came from Marc Lister, who had run a glass shop in Antioch. Lister was interviewed by the *Today* show, and he said that he had some friends that were in the recording industry. Lister had told Phil about these friends, and one day Phil brought some CDs that he'd recorded into Lister's shop. Lister related that Phil had written the songs, sang the lyrics, and played instruments in the background. Phil wanted Lister to sell the songs in the music business.

Lister listened to the music and admitted that Phil did have a good voice. The songs were mainly in a rockabilly style. And Lister added, "I listened very closely to the lyrics and now realize he had written the songs about Jaycee and her daughters. It was absolutely horrifying. One of the lyrics went, 'For every little girl in the world, they want to be in love. You're just the same, go play a game, just tell me that you want me. C'mon, babe, I'm just insane, I'm crying out to you.'"

Marc reported to Phil later that there were no offers on the CDs. He wanted to give the CDs back to Phil, but Phil told him to keep them. Then Phil said, "Someday they will be worth millions." Only after the news came out about Jaycee did Lister and a friend take the CDs out of storage and listen to all the lyrics. The lyrics were haunting in light of what had just occurred. In one song, Phil crooned about a little girl that he adored. And he even sang about her "butt being cold," and adoring these types of little girls drove them wild.

To the *San Francisco Chronicle*, Lister related, "Phil told me that he wanted his music released to raise money for a religious program to let people hear the word of God in a way he interpreted it." And as far as Phil saying that someday the songs would be worth millions, Marc added, "I thought, well, Phil's just being weird again."

Marc said that he didn't want to make any money off the songs. If the music was ever released, he wanted the money to go to Jaycee Dugard's family or an abused women and children's center.

Lister also spoke with other reporters and said that he'd been to the Garrido home on Walnut Avenue several times. There he had met Alyssa, Starlit, and Angel. It was unclear to Lister at that time if Nancy or Alyssa was Phil's wife. Lister said, "Jaycee always looked healthy to me. There was absolutely nothing that I saw that would have raised suspicions." And he added that not once did Jaycee indicate that anything was wrong or that she needed help.

At least in the beginning, Phil's dad, Manuel Garrido,

was also talking to reporters. Manuel told a *San Francisco Chronicle* reporter that his son was now "absolutely out of his mind! His problems began when he had a bad motorcycle accident. He went from being a comical and funny boy to someone who fell in with the wrong crowd and took LSD. Tell those cops to treat him like a crazy person, because he is out of his mind. He's nuts! He's crazy! I hope they treat him like that!"

To a reporter from Australia, Manuel Garrido said, "After he started using drugs, he was gone. It ruined his life. He didn't want to go to school. We had a hell of a time getting him to graduate. We gave him a new blue Oldsmobile as a graduation present in 1969. Anything he wanted growing up, he got." Manuel mainly blamed Phil's mother for spoiling him. And Manuel added to a reporter from the *Sydney Morning Herald,* "He was a sex addict. That was his problem."

Phil's brother, Ron, agreed with that assessment. He'd had very little to do with Phil over the years, but in 2007, one of Ron and Phil's aunts told Ron, "I swear that the oldest girl (Angel) is his daughter. She's got his eyes." Phil had tried telling the aunt that Angel was a daughter of one of his neighbors.

CHAPTER 21

IN EVERY DIRECTION

Even though no reporter was supposed to go onto the Garrido property, things had become so super-heated in the quest for anything relating to Nancy and Phil Garrido that one journalist crossed the line. He was an Australian photojournalist and he sneaked into the Garrido yard, directly against police warnings. Soon the photojournalist's photos were circling the globe, via television and the Internet. The photos depicted a ramshackle set of tents, where Jaycee, Angel, and Starlit had lived. The photos also showed the incredible amount of items that had been stored in the compound, as well as a WELCOME sign above one of the tent enclosures.

The area of the compound was littered with broken toys, cardboard boxes, old furniture, and piles of discarded items that looked beyond use. One of the first law enforcement officers to later describe the scene was CCSO Sheriff Warren Rupf. He told reporters, "It was as if you were camping. The structures are no more than six feet high. All the sheds and tents had electricity furnished by electrical cords. There was a rudimentary outhouse and rudimentary shower."

Jaycee, Angel, and Starlit had been forced to live in a shed/tent area that contained an old sofa, old mattresses and faded worn-out carpet. A pile of dirty clothes was in one corner next to Barbie dolls. There were some books, puzzles, and games, obviously used by Angel and Starlit. Nearby was a shed that had been soundproofed by Phil Garrido, and in it were several guitars and recording equipment.

Incredibly, the investigators found an older model sedan still in the backyard area. It was the same type of sedan as first described by Carl Probyn so many years ago from which a woman had leaped out the door and snatched Jaycee. It seemed almost beyond belief that no one in all the intervening time had somehow made a connection between that car and the abduction of June 10, 1991.

News agencies were starting to learn more details about the compound in which Jaycee Lee Dugard and her daughters were forced to live. It was described as a series of outbuildings and tents, with locks on the outside of a fence so that the inhabitants could be locked in. There were sheds, tents, and water hoses snaking across the yard behind the tall wooden fence. The *San Francisco Chronicle* described the compound as *a messy campground with mattresses, small chairs, bikes, books, piles of toys, a trampoline, showers, an outhouse, swing set, and even a carved pumpkin.*

Of that compound, not much could be seen from the neighboring yards, but nearby resident, Diane Doty, recalled hearing the sound of a shower being used in the backyard area. From her deck, she could see tarps, but trees and foliage concealed most of the rest. There were sounds of children back there, but that sounded normal to her ears, as if the noise was of children playing.

Diane told the journalist, "I asked my husband, 'Why are they living in tents?' And he said, 'Maybe that's the way they like to live.'"

Another neighbor, Polly White, also spoke of hearing showers running in Phil Garrido's backyard. Polly related that she and her husband also heard young girls splashing around in a pool. "We used to hear children back there playing in the pool, and we thought they were just visiting Pat."

Polly had been tending to her garden one day near the back fence that bordered the Garridos' far backyard. Through a gap in the fence, she could see a young blond girl who was splashing around in the pool. White caught the girl's eye and asked her if she was having fun. The girl said that she was. Polly asked how old the girl was, and she answered that she was ten. But when Polly asked the girl's name, she wouldn't answer and ran away, instead. The next time Polly White went to that section of the backyard, she noticed that the gap in the fence had been boarded up by Phil Garrido.

Patrick McQuaid had been only five years old when he and his parents lived near the Garrido residence. One day, possibly in 1991 or 1992, McQuaid peeked through the chicken wire fence that separated his yard from the Garridos' yard. Patrick saw a young blond girl in the backyard. He recalled, "I thought she was pretty."

Then Patrick recounted, "I asked her if she was living there or visiting, and she said she was living there." But before Patrick could ask her any more questions, Phil Garrido came out and took the girl into the house. Patrick added, "At the time, I didn't think anything of it. I was young."

It was not long after this encounter that Phil built an eight-foot-high board fence that blocked the view from outside the property. McQuaid said he never saw the young blond girl after that. However, in the summer of 2009, McQuaid spotted two young blond girls riding in Phil Garrido's car. Patrick said he took note of them because by that time he knew that Phil was a registered sex offender. And these girls looked so much like the young girl he had seen in the Garrido yard in the early 1990s. Obviously the young girl he had seen then was Jaycee.

Heather McQuaid-Glace also had recollections about Phil Garrido. She told a *New York Times* reporter that she realized in later years that people in the neighborhood knew that Phil was a registered sex offender. They even saw two young blond girls over at the house, but nothing raised their suspicions because they figured law enforcement must know about the two girls. Heather said, "We never heard screaming. We never heard anyone crying for help."

Betty Unpingco's husband, Frank, also weighed in on this subject and told a journalist, "I knew Phil was a child molester, but I didn't bother him and he didn't bother me." In fact, most neighbors on Walnut Avenue followed Frank's example. They didn't bother Phil, and he didn't have much interaction with them. If Phil didn't have much interaction in that neighborhood, Nancy Garrido had almost none at all. Very few people on Walnut Avenue ever saw her outside of the house or her yard. Even a mail carrier who routinely delivered mail on Walnut Avenue said that she had only seen Nancy Garrido very few times. And she couldn't recall ever having heard the woman speak to her.

* * *

News agencies were sending their correspondents out in all directions by this point: Berkeley for a news conference, Walnut Avenue to the Garrido compound, South Lake Tahoe for reaction there, Southern California to speak with Jaycee's stepdad, Carl Probyn, and then on to Placerville, California. It was there that Phil and Nancy Garrido were due to be arraigned at the El Dorado County Superior Court.

Outside the courtroom, satellite trucks converged on the parking lot, as others had done on Walnut Avenue. In the courtroom gallery, journalists were packed shoulder to shoulder, with every available space taken up by news cameras. The arraignment was being presided over by Judge Douglas Phimister.

After a long breathless wait, suddenly there *they* were in the flesh—the subject of so much speculation and attention—Phil and Nancy Garrido. Ushered in by bailiffs, the Garridos wore orange jumpsuits and their wrists were shackled. Nancy looked embarrassed and forlorn, often sobbing and trying to cover her face with her long hair. Phil merely gazed off into space and sat quietly once he was in the courtroom. There were six felony counts concerning forcible rape, seven counts of forcible lewd acts on a child, with room open for more future counts.

Susan Gellman, a local attorney, was appointed as Phil Garrido's lawyer. Gellman had received her law degree from Temple University School of Law and her undergraduate degree from the University of Massachusetts. She began practicing law in Florida in 1989. Later, she moved to California and became a public defender in El Dorado County. Gilbert Maines was appointed as Nancy's lawyer. Both Garridos entered pleas of not guilty through their lawyers. Deputy District Attorney William "Bill" Clark asked for no bail, and Judge Phimister made a preliminary order of no bail for Phil and Nancy.

After the very brief hearing, DDA Clark and District Attorney Vern Pierson answered questions from a mob of reporters at the entrance of the courthouse. One question was about Nancy Garrido's role in all of this and the charges against her. Clark said, "She's legally charged with rape based on the theory she participated in it. We don't have to prove she physically did a rape. All we have to prove is that she aided and abetted with knowledge of the crime."

A reporter wanted to know how he felt about the general reaction in El Dorado County and especially about Terry Probyn and the incredible news that Jaycee Lee was alive. Clark responded, "People feel good about it, but there's another side of it. Jaycee has lived a whole other life. Terry Probyn was the mother of an eleven-year-old and never got her back. Now Terry has grandkids."

A question to El Dorado County sheriff Fred Kollar, who was standing nearby, was why had Jaycee Lee never tried to escape. Had she been brainwashed or a victim of the Stockholm syndrome? Kollar said, "All I know is there were no known attempts by her to outreach to anybody. It's way too early to conjecture on her part. She was in good health, but living in a backyard for eighteen years takes its toll."

It was also revealed that Jaycee and her daughters were now somewhere in the East San Francisco Bay Area with Terry Probyn in a hotel room. Just where they were was an intensely guarded secret.

Gilbert Maines had a few things to say about Nancy Garrido to the reporters. Maines related that when he was first introduced to her, she appeared to be in tears. Maines added, "She said to me, 'Thank you for being here.'"

* * *

One of the areas most interested in the unfolding story was of course the Lake Tahoe region where Jaycee Lee had been abducted on June 10, 1991. The fact that Jaycee was alive seemed almost like a miracle to the people of the area. At the Lake Tahoe Unified School District headquarters, employees huddled around television sets as the news broke about Jaycee. As the details were reported, Superintendent James Tarwater said out loud, "Oh, my God!"

Tarwater told a reporter for the *Washington Post*, "I think about all the students I've had and watched grow during the last eighteen years. You think of the potential that Jaycee had."

The principal of Meyers Elementary School, which Jaycee had attended, also spoke with the reporter. Karen Gillis-Tinlin said that when Jaycee Lee was kidnapped, Karen's four-year-old son said that he and a friend had come up with a way to find the missing girl. Of course, it was just a child's dream. But it showed that even four-year-olds were not immune to the story about the missing girl. Now the seemingly impossible had happened, and Jaycee was found alive.

Gillis-Tinlin related, "It affected all the children. There was an underlying fear because it could happen to anyone. A little garden was planted in Jaycee's memory near the multipurpose room. A plaque was placed there in her honor. She was always with us. All through the years, I would be contacted by new officers on Jaycee Lee's file. It never got dropped. It wasn't always at the forefront, but it was an ongoing case."

Gillis-Tinlin spoke to a reporter from the *Los Angeles Times* and said, "Jaycee never got to go to prom, to have that sweet first kiss, to have the opportunity to go to college. She has missed all that."

The *Los Angeles Times* reporter also spoke with Meghan Doris, who was one of Jaycee's classmates from 1991. Meghan stated, "I just wonder what Jaycee would have done. Would she have gone to college, or settled down and had kids?"

On this same theme, Laurie Ault, a mother of two, and friend of Terry Probyn, added, "I'm absolutely thrilled that she's been found, but you wonder about what long-term impact it will have on her, physically and mentally. She comes from a pretty strong family, so I'm hopeful."

Sue Prichette, who was a retired schoolteacher in Lake Tahoe, told a reporter, "I used to drive by that bus stop all the time. I'm absolutely ecstatic that she's been found."

Sue Bush had been Jaycee's fifth-grade teacher at the time Jaycee had been abducted. Bush related to a local journalist, "We're all happy she's back. But it's a life ruined. I hope in a few weeks, months, whatever it takes, I'll actually be able to talk to Jaycee and Terry. Terry never gave up hope."

Bush told a reporter for the *Tahoe Daily Tribune,* "I'm still in shock. I'm so glad she's okay. She was just a little sweetie in class. What happened to her scared the kids, and it scared them badly. The kids needed to talk about it. We tied a pink ribbon to her chair, and kept her desk the way she left it. What an incredible scary thing to have happen in a small town."

Just as they had done with many individuals from Walnut Avenue, national television news organizations wanted interviews of people from Lake Tahoe as well. CBS's *Early Show* contacted Sue Bush and interviewed her live on air. Bush said, "Jaycee was absolutely delightful. She was always happy. She had a smile on her face. Sparkly eyes. Well-liked by all the kids in the room."

Host Julie Chen asked Bush, "What do you remember

about that horrible day that she was kidnapped, and how did you learn about the kidnapping?"

Bush replied, "Well, you know, I actually learned about it after I arrived. I was at school already. I tended to go in early. And somewhere between eight and nine A.M., I got the call to come down to the office, and that's when I found out about Jaycee. And I just want to let you and everybody and Jaycee know that the entire community, her family, her friends, her classmates, her teacher, never ever forgot her or gave up the hope that she would come back someday."

Another area where journalists congregated was in Southern California, where Carl Probyn now lived. Carl told the Bay Area News Group about how he first learned the incredible news. Carl reiterated that he got a phone call from Terry, from whom he was now separated, and Terry told him, "They found Jaycee! She's alive!" Carl added, "We cried for about two minutes. Then Terry said that Jaycee remembered everything."

Carl let it be known that he had given up hope that Jaycee would be found alive and related, "I gave up hope for eighteen years, and just went into a recovery mode. I thought it would be nice just to recover her [remains] and capture the people and find out why they did this. Now I feel like I've just won the Lotto. It's just incredible!"

Carl recounted the events of eighteen years before and what had occurred on Washoan Boulevard where he had seen Jaycee Lee being shoved into a car. And also about his futile bike ride to try and rescue Jaycee. Carl said, "After eighteen years, you never think she'd be alive."

Carl told a reporter for the Fox Broadcasting station in Reno, "All of this broke up my marriage. I've gone through hell. I mean, I was a suspect up until yesterday." And as far as what had occurred to Jaycee in those eighteen intervening years, Carl said, "I don't know if she was brainwashed. I don't know if she was walking around on the street. I don't know if she was locked up under key for eighteen years. I have no idea."

Carl Probyn went on every national news show imaginable. He said on CBS's *Early Show* that Terry had told him, "Jaycee feels really guilty for bonding with this guy (Phil Garrido)."

Carl next went on NBC's *Today Show* and related, "She didn't try to get away. If she had been really spunky and fought and tried to escape, maybe she would have been killed."

Then it was on to ABC's *Good Morning America.* Carl told them, "My wife says that Jaycee looks good. She looks almost like when she was kidnapped. She looks very young. She doesn't look twenty-nine at all."

Carl later told an AP reporter about Jaycee's feelings toward Phil Garrido when he learned more of the circumstances about the confinement. Carl said, "Jaycee has strong feelings with this guy. She really feels it's almost like a marriage." Carl also said that Jaycee was a mellow, easygoing girl, who never got mad at anyone. And Carl related that was probably the reason Jaycee wasn't killed. Carl added, "She probably wouldn't climb a wall to escape. Her half sister, Shayna, would have climbed that wall every day, and probably not survived."

And the whole dynamics of the "bond" between Jaycee Lee Dugard and Phil and Nancy Garrido became a hot topic amongst journalists and news stations. Phil Garrido, after all, was the father of Jaycee's two daughters, Angel and Starlit, whom Jaycee adored. And CBS News posed the question, "Did Nancy Garrido deliver Jaycee Dugard's children?" CBS News noted that Nancy Garrido was a licensed nursing assistant in California between 1989 and 1995. Jaycee Lee's children had never been to a doctor. If Nancy hadn't help deliver those girls, then who had?

Nancy Garrido's attorney, Gilbert Maines, spoke about her for a news segment on *Good Morning America*. Maines said that Nancy was powerless to free Jaycee Lee because she was so far under Phil Garrido's control. Maines declared, "If she's being controlled, he doesn't have to be there physically. If she's being controlled, she's being controlled. I guess I would say she's a victim."

Maines added about his meeting with Nancy Garrido, "She was distraught. She was frightened. She seemed a little lost. She seemed to be like a ship without a rudder, but she understood why she was there."

This was important. If Nancy Garrido did not understand why she was jailed, she could not help in her defense. And in that case, she would have to be declared mentally incompetent and sent to a mental hospital before she could be tried.

One of Nancy's main problems now, of course, was the fact that Phil had been sent back to prison for six weeks in 1993 for violating his parole. During that time, Nancy did not help Jaycee escape. In fact, it could be postulated that she had kept Jaycee in confinement on Phil's instructions. Asked why Nancy didn't know that she was involved in criminal activity and free Jaycee at that point, Maines answered, "They acted like a family. It's sad, and there's a lot of collateral damage in this case. But she misses the girls very much. She loves them."

Maines added that Phil's mind control over Nancy was highlighted by an incident on August 26, 2009, when she, Phil, Jaycee, and the girls were at the parole office in Concord. A police officer had asked if they could search her home, and Nancy answered, "Whatever Phil wants. If Phillip says it's okay, it's okay." Maines said about all of this, "Phillip's brother apparently described her as a robot who did whatever Phillip wanted."

If things were going to be complicated in adjusting to a new life for Jaycee, how much more would that be true for Angel and Starlit? They had never known anything except that backyard compound. Writing for the *Contra Costa Times,* Suzanne Bohan asked various experts about this. Dr. Christian Ludke told her, "Most of all, trauma victims need appreciation." Dr. Ludke had worked with other kidnapping victims, hostages, and victims of bank robberies. The victims needed support from society to let them know they were not responsible for the things that had occurred to them. Ludke added, "They need quietness and distance from their painful experience, so that they can start their healing process."

Dr. Ludke said that for victims of those crimes, "They need rest and quiet more than the usual 'talking therapy.' Ludke related, "All studies of recovery from post-traumatic stress disorder show that talking is not very healing." If a person talked about the perpetrator and the situation, the incident stayed alive in the victim's mind. Ludke backed up his claims by showing a group of victims in Germany who had talked about the incident as opposed to some who had not. The people who had spoken about it, even in therapy, recovered less quickly than the ones who had not.

UC San Francisco professor Dr. Mardi Horowitz agreed that for most psychiatrists the things that Jaycee and her daughters had endured was unfamiliar territory. Horowitz said, "There's a big difference between simple post-traumatic stress disorders and complex syndromes." Until a victim was willing and ready to talk about the experience, it could do more harm to bring it up than to just leave it alone for the time being. And it was important for the victim to be around stable people in a nonstressful new environment.

Dr. Ludke had briefly counseled the father of an Austrian girl, Natascha Kampusch, whose kidnapping bore some resemblance to that of Jaycee Lee Dugard. Natascha had been held captive and sexually abused for eight years. She had been kept in the abductor's cellar. Natascha escaped one day while in his car when he was stuck in traffic. The man committed suicide hours later.

The one difference Dr. Ludke noted with Natascha was that she didn't have strong family support after her freedom, the way Jaycee did. Natascha had a tense relationship with her mother, and no longer spoke with her father. She was also thrust into the limelight after her freedom. Soon she was doing on-air interviews, and even hosted a television talk show. Donations poured in, until some started criticizing her for all the media attention and writing a book about her ordeal. Ultimately, all of this traumatized Natascha once again, and she became a recluse. From being a celebrity, Natascha retreated into a self-imposed reclusiveness.

Dr. Ludke foresaw better results for Jaycee Lee Dugard, who had strong family support, especially with her mom, Terry, stepdad, Carl, and half sister, Shayna, who all loved her. And Ludke noted with approval that law enforcement was doing everything it could to keep the throngs of journalists in the dark as to where Jaycee and her daughters were now located.

Dr. Ludke even saw hope for Jaycee's daughters. "What they need most is time, love, and tenderness. The best therapist in the world for a child and adolescent is their own mother."

CHAPTER 22

PHIL'S INTERVIEW

As if all of the other news wasn't enough, it was soon learned that Phil Garrido had given an exclusive interview from his jail cell to a reporter from Sacramento television news station KCRA. The interviewer, Walt Gray, began by saying, "So how are you doing? Can you tell me what happened? Are you doing okay?"

Phil replied, "Yes, I'm doing fine. In the end, this is going to be a powerful heartwarming story. One in which you're going to be really impressed. It's going to make world news. The first thing I would like to tell you, and the only thing I would like to tell you right now, of . . . Just because for some reason I didn't get to speak with you today and I asked to speak with you is this . . . contact, or go to the Federal Bureau of Investigation, fifteenth floor, in San Francisco, and ask for a copy of the documents that I left with them three days ago. This is for you, the mass media, that is left in your hands. There is something powerful in them. Once you get these documents, they have a (indecipherable word) in them. They have powerful witnesses concerning my situation. I would like to stop right there, so then we can sit across from each other and then you'll have that in your hands. Because what you're going to have in your hands will make world news immediately."

Gray asked if Phil could talk about the circumstances that happened back in 1991 in Lake Tahoe. Phil replied, "I haven't talked to my lawyers yet. So I can't do that. But I can tell you that those circumstances will begin to come to light as soon as you've seen those documents."

Gray wanted to know if this had anything to do with Phil Garrido's place of business.

Phil answered, "No. Place of business?"

So Gray clarified his remark. "Just in terms of listing your home. It is God's something—"

Phil interjected, "Oh, that. It's a church. The reason it is in the government's hands is so they will stay right in front of it. They have accepted it from me very happily."

Not to be put off about Jaycee Lee Dugard and the events of 1991, Gray asked again about what had occurred in Lake Tahoe that year. Phil responded, "I'm so sorry. As soon as I can sit down and do this correctly, because I have no desire to hold back in these things. . . . In fact, when this takes place, you're going to be really surprised of what has happened. It is a heartwarming story. If you would cooperate with me, you can make the decisions, and you get the information. I'm so sorry, because I don't want to disappoint you right now. I just know I have to do this in a cautionary fashion."

Gray said he fully understood Phil's line of reasoning and appreciated that he was talking to him at all. Then Gray asked what kind of situation Phil thought he was in at the moment.

Phil replied, "Well, I'm in a very serious situation.

But I can't speak to you about that. That will have to wait. I guarantee you, as time goes on, you will get the pieces of the story. When you get those documents in your hands, you are going to fall over."

Gray noted that two days previously, Phil had been at UC Berkeley, where he was contacted by some people in law enforcement. Gray wanted to know what happened there, and if Phil now felt somewhat relieved that they had found out about Jaycee.

Phil answered, "I feel much better now. It is a process that needed to take place. Please try and grab those documents, because they will do a lot for you. And then, like I said, they're going to be a part of the trial, because this is going to turn into a major trial."

Gray asked what Phil's hope was when the material in the documents was revealed. Phil said, "Well, let me tell you this. When I went to the San Francisco Bureau—and I'm not avoiding the question. I was accompanied by two children that are Jaycee Dugard's children that we had. So they sort of accompanied me elsewhere, to Berkeley. . . . Please get those documents. They will not disappoint you. I told you right away you are going to be in control of something that is going to take the world's attention."

Gray did not want to keep getting back to the documents, so he related that he knew Phil had spent some time in prison in the 1990s. After that, Phil had been out on his own, and the interviewer wanted to know how he had been employed.

Phil related, "The last several years, I completely turned my life around. And you're going to find the most powerful story coming from the witnesses and from the victim. If you take a step at a time, you will fall over backward, and in the end, you're going to find the most powerful heartwarming story revealing that something that used to be misunderstood. . . .

Well, that's as far as I can go. I really want to help you, but I also need to make sure that the media is also protected."

Gray wondered if most of the information Phil was talking about would be coming from Jaycee Dugard. Phil responded, "I guess she would also hand back the truth. Hmm, this is what we're going to do. We are going to try and make this . . . Well, wait till you read the document. My life has been . . . Wait till you read the story of what took place at this house, and you're going to be absolutely impressed. It's a disgusting thing that took place from the end to the beginning. But I turned my life completely around, and to be able to understand it, you have to start . . . I'm sorry, I want to help you further, but also I need to protect the sheriff's office and I need to protect the government. And I need to protect the rights of Jaycee Lee Dugard."

Gray tried another approach. "Can you at least share with me what you've told law enforcement?"

Phil said, "I haven't told them anything. But I will not speak to them until . . . Oh, well, what I shared with law enforcement . . . You'll have those documents. I didn't tell them anything else but what is in those documents—and they were really impressed."

Once again, the interviewer tried to get Phil to answer questions about the abduction in 1991 by saying, "Did you tell them that you did have a hand in taking Jaycee back in 1991?" All Phil would say was "Oh, no, no, no. It (the document) is going to explain something that humans have not understood well."

"I understand that, Phillip. I'm just saying you're mentioning that it is going to be a heartwarming story. Can you give me an overview as to it as a love story? Is it a story about children? What—"

Phil cut him off. "It is a story about turning a person's life around and having two children. Those two girls. Those two girls, they slept in my arms every single night." (And then Phil Garrido started crying.) "I never touched them. You just have to do what I ask you to, because I can't go any further. If I do, I'll go too far. People are going to be coming forward at this trial, and that's not all. I am going to leave them in a state of shock, when you see how many hundreds of thousands of people are going to come out and start testifying about something. Just do me a favor and follow the protocol that I asked you to follow because you make your own decisions from now and what you want to do. This is not for me. You will find out that this is not a play or a way of monopolizing anyone. It is a very well-constructed and powerful written disclosure. Please do that, and then we'll work from there."

Gray asked, "Let me ask you this before I go. Are the children okay, and everybody in the house okay?"

Phil replied, "Absolutely! The youngest one was born, and from that moment, everything turned around. People are going to testify to these things."

Gray said, "We were just somewhat concerned about the lack of medical attention for them."

Phil responded, "Absolutely. That is absolutely because we didn't have the finances and we were very concerned. You have to get into . . . The federal government was involved because they're being pursued by hundreds and hundreds of thousands of people who are suing them with lawsuits over, hmm . . . Just read the documents and we'll go from there. Thank you, sir. Thank you. God bless you for allowing me to talk to you."

Gray replied, "Phillip, thank you for the call."

Phil said, "I wanted to see you. You know. When it happened."

Gray responded, "I did not know you wanted to see me."

Phil ended by saying, "I am not going to play with the media. I am going to leave this with you because you are the first person here I was able to talk to, and I'm going to stop right there."

All Gray could think to add was "Have a good day."

One person not amused by Phil Garrido's rambling interview was his kidnapping and rape victim of 1976, Katie Callaway, who was now Katie Callaway Hall. Katie told reporters, "I want to scream from the depths of my soul! Scream because my fears turned out to be justified. I trembled for about four hours after I heard the news about him. I always knew he was capable of this, but he should not have been able to do it. When I saw his face on TV, I started screaming, 'Oh, my God! My God! He's the one who kidnapped me!'"

Speaking of the rape and its aftermath, Katie said, "I have lived in fear ever since. I knew he was hunting. I knew he was. I needed to disappear. I tried not to let it consume me, but it was always there. For years, I walked around like a zombie. Now I don't have to hide anymore. I don't have to live every day of my life wondering if he is looking for me. I am finally free from the fear I have lived with since the day I learned he was paroled. I can't imagine what Jaycee is going through. He had me for eight hours. He had her for eighteen years. I was an adult with instincts that helped me deal with the situation. She was a child."

CHAPTER 23

"WE ARE BEATING OURSELVES UP OVER THIS."

Because of Erika Pratt's revelation that she had called the Contra Costa County Sheriff's Office in November 2006 complaining about a young woman and two girls living in squalor on Walnut Avenue, CCSO sheriff Warren Rupf held a press conference on this issue and the issue of lax supervision of Phil Garrido. Rupf admitted that a sheriff's office deputy had gone to the Garrido's home and spoke with Phil for a half hour on the front porch. This deputy did not enter the house or go into the backyard, where Erika Pratt said she had seen the squalid conditions. All the deputy said to Phil was that people living in tents could be a code violation. The deputy at the time did not know that Phil was a registered sex offender, even though CCSO had that information. And if the deputy had spoken with any of Phil's neighbors, most of them had that information as well.

About Erika Pratt's call, Sheriff Rupf said, "The caller said Garrido was psychotic and had a sexual addiction. I'm the first in line to offer organizational criticism and to offer my apologies to the victims and accept responsibility for having missed an earlier opportunity. This is not an acceptable outcome. No one should have failed to recognize a sexual registrant, including law enforcement. Our work product should have resulted in a better outcome. We have a responsibility to report people living in a backyard."

Sheriff Rupf now told reporters, "I cannot change the course of events, but we are beating ourselves up over this and continue to do so. We should have been more inquisitive, more curious, and turned over a rock or two."

One person who always thought Phil Garrido was a dangerous man was former Washoe County deputy district attorney Michael Malloy. He now added his take to all of the tales and controversy surrounding Phil. Malloy said, "I think the Dugard case was somewhat predictable, given his behavior in 1976 for which he was convicted. There are certainly parallels. He had a place set up for the very purpose of raping someone. That's not usual at all. He had the place with carpeting on the walls, carpeting on the floor, carpeting hanging from the ceiling, and multicolored lights. And he was going to rape her (Katie Callaway), and said that it was her fault because she was attractive. Now he's saying what he said in 1977. That he was glad he got caught and that it would turn his life around. He blamed it all on drugs. That's precisely what he is saying now in the Dugard case. I think that's just amazing."

Detective DeMaranville, who had been the lead Reno Police Department detective on Phil's 1976 case, was now retired. But he remembered the case very well. DeMaranville said, "That case stuck out in my mind. He (Phil Garrido) was a sick puppy. He tried to seem remorseful, but I think it was mostly a put-on." One reason the case stuck out in DeMaranville's mind was because of the elaborate way Garrido had rigged up his unit in the warehouse. DeMaranville still referred to it as a porno palace.

About the same time, Leland Lufty, who had prosecuted Phil Garrido in Katie Callaway's federal case, weighed in on Garrido. Lufty told a reporter, "It was a horrendous crime. We had a tough judge. As far as we were concerned, he was locked up forever. How could they (the federal parole board) do that? Look at the record. Look at what guy did it! The case was premeditated as could be."

And then much of the reasoning of the federal parole board in the 1980s came out. The *San Francisco Chronicle* spoke with Dennis Curtis, a judiciary expert. Curtis told the reporter, "It would have been a routine decision by the (federal) Parole Commission to let him go at the ten year point. The guidelines back then for a kidnapper who did not hold her for ransom and had no serious criminal record were probably less than ten years in prison. You're looking at a much harsher sentence now."

By 2009, kidnapping with sexual exploitation and the use of restraints, as Garrido had done with Katie Callaway, carried a guidelines sentence of twenty-four to thirty years in federal prison. Under those circumstances, he could not have kidnapped Jaycee Dugard as he did in 1991.

By the end of August 2009, Contra Costa County Sheriff's Office spokesman Lieutenant Steve Simpkins told reporters that three law enforcement agencies were now searching the Garrido property for evidence on some of their old cases. These included CCSO, the APD, and the PPD. And then Simpkins dropped a bombshell. He said the law enforcement investigators were searching for clues to see if Phil Garrido had been involved in the murders of ten prostitutes in the 1990s that happened around Antioch and especially in Pittsburg. Several of the prostitutes' bodies had been dumped in an area off the Antioch-Pittsburg Highway, where Phil had once worked. Of the search, Simpkins said, "This could take a while."

And Contra Costa County spokesman Jimmy Lee added, "We will take a close look at if there are any links to open cases." About the next-door neighbors' property, rented by Damon Robinson, Lee said, "It looks like Garrido lived on the property in a shed."

A PPD investigator related, "Every law enforcement agency in sight is looking at this guy. It's safe to say that the closer you get to where he is or was, the more interest there is."

And CCSO captain Dan Terry reinforced this PPD angle by stating, "Pittsburg police, for whatever reason, decided Garrido was a person of interest." The particular reason was, according to Captain Terry, that in 1998 and 1999 the bodies of Valerie Schultz, twenty-seven, Rachael Cruise, thirty-two, and Jessica Frederick, twenty-four, had been found dumped in ditches near where Phil had once worked during that time period. They had been stabbed and strangled to death.

Now a big story got even bigger, and journalists were trying to find out everything they could about the murders that had occurred in the 1990s in eastern Contra Costa County.

CHAPTER 24

COLD CASES

One of the first cold cases being looked at by law enforcement concerning Phil Garrido didn't occur in Antioch, Pittsburg, or even Lake Tahoe. It concerned a case that had occurred in Reno, Nevada. In 1989, Reno children, Jennifer Chia, age six, and her brother, Charles Chia, age eight, were kidnapped at a school bus stop. It was only a short walk from their home to the bus stop, just as it had been for Jaycee Lee Dugard in Lake Tahoe. In the Chia children's case, they were seen getting off the school bus on the afternoon of October 18, 1989. They never made it home.

Their mother, Ann Chang, made an appeal to the public: "I never hurt people. I don't know why anybody would take my kids." Bloodhounds were used, door-to-door searches were made, and a helicopter search as well. Despite an intensive effort by law enforcement authorities, no clues turned up about the children.

By November, there were billboards with photos of the missing children all around the Reno area, and still no clues came in. Slowly, as in Jaycee's case, the amount of detective work dropped off. By the summer of 1990, only one Reno detective was actively working the case.

Then on July 25, 1990, a California Department of Transportation crew was doing roadwork in the Feather River Canyon, fifty miles northwest of Reno. While working along a road in Plumas County, between Quincy and Portola, the road crew stopped for lunch. One of the members of the crew gazed below an embankment and spotted a skull protruding from a mound of dirt.

The workers flagged down a passing highway patrol officer, who, in turn, stopped Plumas County Sheriff's Office (PCSO) sergeant Terry Bergstrand. The officers then went down to where the skull was and discovered the bones of two children. Bits of clothing had been scattered around the graves, apparently after an animal had been digging there. Both victims had dark brown hair still attached to their skulls.

Some clothing was intact, and a pair of jeans included the word "party" on it, while a white shirt had the word "Esprit." There was also a pair of Adidas athletic shoes. Four police agencies around the region responded to the PCSO, wondering if the bones were those of their cases. Because of the clothing matching the description of what the Chias had been wearing when last seen, the Plumas County Sheriff's Office contacted Reno PD.

Sergeant Bergstrand later told a reporter that lots of people used a dirt turnout near the graves to either take meal breaks or even sleep there in their cars. Truck drivers did not use the pullout because of its small amount of space. The turnout was at the tree line and was filled with oaks and pines, as opposed to the desert sagebrush in lower elevation.

The excavation of the graves was a slow process, as technicians photographed and videotaped everything that might be of evidential value. A Washoe County forensic team even sifted through gravel and dirt near the edge of the road, looking for clues. The bones weren't removed for two days from the graves.

Chang was at the Reno Police Department when she first learned about what had happened to her children. She went into shock and had to be transported by ambulance to a hospital. One of her neighbors told a reporter, "It's sad. So sad. But in a way, I'm glad they finally found out what happened. At least she now knows. She doesn't have to wonder anymore."

Another neighbor, Bylinda Rockson, had often chatted with young Charles Chia before he disappeared. When Rockson heard the latest news about the children, she said, "I couldn't believe that they were dead. The FBI had told me they were taken here right at the apartment complex. Right in front of my parking space. Charles was always chattering with me. He seemed so friendly. Maybe too friendly."

RPD lieutenant Mike Whan now said about Garrido, "There might not be any link between the cases and him. But we'd be crazy not to look at the possibility. Anything is possible with this guy. This guy would be a better suspect than others based on prior crimes he has committed."

Another case the Reno PD investigators were looking at in a possible connection with Phil Garrido was the abduction of seven-year-old Monica DaSilva. She had been snatched from her bedroom as she slept in 1990. Her remains were found three weeks later, east of Reno, but her killer was never caught.

Lieutenant Whan related, "During that time period, we had those child abduction cases, and since then, we haven't had any." Whan noted that Phil Garrido was out of prison during that time period, and, of course, he had abducted Jaycee Lee Dugard in June 1991.

Gail Powell, a Nevada Department of Public Safety spokesperson, said that all unsolved cases in the Lake Tahoe/Reno area were being looked at again in respect to Phil Garrido. And FBI spokesman David Staretz added that his agency was "currently looking at all unsolved female disappearances/kidnappings and a couple of homicides in the area."

The South Lake Tahoe PD was taking another look at the unsolved killing of a seventeen-year-old girl in 1976. That was the year Katie Callaway Hall had been abducted in South Lake Tahoe by Garrido and taken to Reno to be abused sexually. Agent Staretz told reporters, "We are attempting to track Garrido's activities while in Reno in 1976 and after his parole."

Closer to Antioch, the neighboring city of Pittsburg was looking into the possibility that Phil Garrido was connected to a string of murders in the 1990s. Several prostitutes had been murdered in an area where Garrido had once worked along the Antioch-Pittsburg Highway. On July 18, 1992, prostitute Sharon Mattos's body was found in a field near Pittsburg. On November 12 of that same year, prostitute Andrea Ingersoll's body was found in a field near Bay Point, then known as West Pittsburg.

One of the most compelling cases now being looked at in connection with Phil Garrido was that of fifteen-year-old Pittsburg High School sophomore Lisa Norrell. Lisa had been born in Mexico, and then adopted by Jesse and Minnie Norrell, of Pittsburg, California. Minnie always knew that she would tell Lisa about the adoption and her birth parents when the time was right. When Lisa was about six years old,

Minnie told Lisa a story about a man and a woman who were married and didn't have any children. Minnie said, "One day, they saw this beautiful little girl, with dark hair and big brown eyes. They loved her so much that they decided to adopt her. That meant she could live with them and be their daughter."

Lisa, in her typical headstrong fashion, replied, "That's a stupid story!" Then she rolled over and went to sleep. As far as she was concerned, Lisa knew exactly who her parents were—Jesse and Minnie Norrell.

Minnie later said of Lisa, "She was adorable. When she was a kid, she was happy-go-lucky. Then she became a teenager and was a brat. But she was a love-able brat."

Tony Quesada, Lisa's actual brother, was adopted by a family who lived close to the Norrells. Tony and Lisa saw each other on an almost daily basis. Minnie later said of this arrangement, "Lisa and Tony knew that they were brother and sister. Every time we went to the grocery store, she had to have something for her brother. And Tony's dad said the same thing. Every time Tony went somewhere, he had to buy something for Lisa."

Tony later said of Lisa, "We were close. We were always best friends. Brother and sister. I always went over to their house, and she always came over here. We were never apart. Something about her, she would always do—when we would have dinner, no matter how far away she put her drink, she would always spill it." Tony thought it was kind of funny.

Two friends of Lisa's who knew her very well were twin sisters, Lucretia and Patricia Smith of Pittsburg. The twins later spoke with journalist Lyssa Mudd about Lisa Norell. They said that they'd watched Lisa blossom from a shy girl to a gregarious teenager. They related that Lisa favored wearing sweatshirts and jeans, had boundless energy, and said hello to everyone on campus.

On November 6, 1998, Lisa had gone up to her brother, Tony, and asked him to accompany her to a dance rehearsal and be her partner. He said no, and has agonized about it ever since. Tony related, "Right then, I said no, because I'm not one for dancing. But if I had gone, I know she'd be here right now."

That evening, Lisa got ready to attend a friend's *quinceañera* in Antioch. A *quinceañera* was a rite of passage for a young female in the Hispanic community when she went from being a "girl" to a "woman." In preparation for the event, Lisa had her nails done and then bought a present for her friend. Lisa had also been practicing formal dance steps for the event for the previous two weeks.

Lisa wore casual clothes to the dance, but she brought her formal clothing with her. Apparently at the event, Lisa became angry when she could not learn the dance steps as quickly as the others. In a huff, she left the IDES Hall on Tenth Street in Antioch and began walking alone, back toward Pittsburg.

Lisa left the dance sometime between 10:30 and 11:00 P.M. She never made it home. At 3:00 A.M., Minnie Norrell called the Pittsburg Police Department to report her daughter missing.

The Antioch Police Department became involved as well, because Lisa had last been seen in their city. Captain Kitt Schwitters told a reporter, "She's been classified as a missing person with suspicious circumstances." APD began using ground units, a helicopter, and bloodhounds to try and trace the route Lisa might have taken back toward her home in Pittsburg. She most likely would have walked down Tenth Street in Antioch and out past L Street, where the area became less urbanized. From there, it was known as the Antioch-

Pittsburg Highway, with some businesses scattered here and there, but open fields as well. At night, almost all of this section was not lit.

When Lisa left the IDES Hall, she was last seen wearing a long gray sweatshirt, blue jeans, white socks and black Fila sandals. She had on three gold chains, one of which had her name imprinted upon it. She also wore numerous rings on her fingers.

Lisa had no history of being a runaway, and besides, when she had stormed out of the IDES Hall, she had left her wallet there, which contained her student ID and bank cards. The circumstances were so unusual that soon five FBI agents were also out looking for Lisa. The fact that the FBI was already involved testified to just how seriously they viewed the matter of the girl's disappearance.

Even though the Antioch-Pittsburg Highway was searched, no signs of Lisa turned up. Within two days the Pittsburg-Antioch shoreline, where the Sacramento and San Joaquin Rivers combined, was being searched as well. Police divers were even called in to search underwater. Lisa's mother, Minnie Norrell, told a reporter, "The police are doing a fabulous job, and the FBI is on top of everything." Minnie still had hope that Lisa would be found alive.

More than one hundred tips came in from around the area, and several people were given polygraph tests. Just how scary Lisa's walk might have been was portrayed by the *Contra Costa Times* in an article. The article related in part, *On her right, only the flickering lights of industry would have been visible across the void of the Delta marshlands. Another half mile west and the street lights end, and the only light would have been from cars roaring by.*

On November 14, 1998, the body of a young woman was discovered on the Nav-Land property on the Antioch-Pittsburg Highway after bloodhounds picked up Lisa's scent. Nav-Land was a business that sold rock and tanbark for landscaping. The body was found near a wall on the property.

A quarter mile away on the highway, Lisa's shoes were discovered, lying side by side. The news absolutely stunned Lisa's friends and schoolmates in Pittsburg. Manier Ahmed, a clerk at Abdul's Market and Deli on Harbor Street, said that Lisa had often frequented the market. Manier stated, "I thought they were going to find her alive. I was going through in my mind what I would say to her the next time I saw her. Everybody in the neighborhood came in here and said that they had found her body. It was shocking."

A neighbor of Lisa's related, "I look over at Lisa's house and I want to see her smiling face. She was just an innocent child, and it hurts. This just doesn't seem possible."

Felicia Killings, fifteen, who was a classmate of Lisa's at Pittsburg High School, told a reporter, "This is very upsetting that something like this could've happened. We never expected something like this to happen in our hometown."

Felicia's father, Henry Killings, who was the pastor of Pittsburg's Shilo Ranch, said a prayer for Lisa at a morning service and declared, "It's a heart-wrenching experience. You have to really feel for the youths who knew her and her family."

Lisa's mother and brother did not immediately speak to reporters about Lisa's death. They were too devastated. But a *Contra Costa Times* article of November 19 related that law enforcement authorities had spoken with Lisa's family members, and they agreed that the investigators could keep Lisa's body beyond the Saturday, November 21, funeral. The reason was for "investigative purposes."

Pittsburg lieutenant William Zbacnik told a reporter,

"We feel it's in the best interest of the investigation. There's a fear that the media would interview relatives or funeral home employees and find out how the girl was killed." Then Zbacnik indicated that this holding of Lisa's body would be more than a few days.

Terry Francke, a legal counselor for the California First Amendment Coalition, stated that this was highly unusual. Francke said, "I've never heard of a police department preventing the release of a body, because the press would somehow extract sensitive information from the family. The family will do whatever the police ask them to do." This lack of information only fueled rumors about how Lisa had died, and most of these rumors took on sinister overtones.

Some people were talking, however. Kurt Kuhn, whose father rented the property to Nav-Land, said that one area along a wall had been dusted for fingerprints by investigators. And someone at Nav-Land indicated that Lisa's body was found under some wooden pallets and boxes near that wall.

A few days later, a witness contacted police and said that on the night that Lisa disappeared, she was sure she spotted the young woman on the Antioch-Pittsburg Highway. The investigators even had a female officer dress the way Lisa had done and walk in that area at the same time of night, where the witness said she had seen Lisa. Lieutenant Zbacnik related, "The reenactment actually increased her confidence. This woman said that she had seen the girl carrying her formal dress and black shoes. Lisa's shoes were discovered several hundred yards east of where the witness had seen her. It was surmised by police that at the shoe site is where Lisa's attacker had first accosted her."

Kathy Russo, Lisa's aunt, began a Web site about the murder. Russo stated, "We don't believe Lisa was killed by somebody she knew. It's one of those things where she was in the wrong place at the wrong time."

It wasn't until the end of November that investigators confirmed that a pair of black shoes found on the Antioch-Pittsburg Highway had belonged to Lisa Norrell. This was done by DNA testing. A few days later, information was released that Lisa had died from asphyxiation.

CHAPTER 25

HELL'S HIGHWAY

Lisa Norrell's story was still very much in the news, when another young woman's body was discovered not far away. This occurred on December 5, 1998, near the Collins Auto Wrecking Yard on Industry Road. The victim was twenty-four-year-old Jessica Frederick. Jessica was an Antioch woman, the mother of two, with a history of drug arrests. Recently some people who knew her indicated that Jessica might have turned to prostitution to help pay for her drug habit.

Lieutenant Zbacnik said of this, "The area where her body was found is known as a place where prostitutes and their customers have sex. It's kind of where they go after they pick up their john. There's an indication she was probably dumped there."

Zbacnik related that Jessica's body had been on the ground for several hours by the time workers at Collins Auto Wrecking Yard discovered it at 11:30 A.M. on December 5. No one in the area had seen or heard anything unusual in the early-morning hours around the time of Jessica's death. As to whether Jessica's murder and that of Lisa Norrell were somehow connected, Lieutenant Zbacnik was being cautious. He told reporters, "We really don't have anything to show a connection." And the MO's were certainly different. Lisa had died of asphyxiation. Jessica had died of stab wounds.

Lisa and Jessica's lifestyles were also very different. Jessica's mother, Caroline, said that Jessica had experienced difficult years. Caroline said that Jessica was a good mom to her kids, and loved them very much. In fact, she was going to go to the school that her son attended and help him make a gingerbread house. Caroline also related, "She was a feisty, street-smart woman who was not afraid to stand up for herself. My daughter had a tough life. She ended up doing and being something other than what she desired in life. She wanted to be with her children, and she wanted help with her problems."

Jessica's former boyfriend, who now took care of the couple's sixteen-month-old daughter, said, "You know, when you have people who do drugs, they can still love life and be a good person. She was a good person. Her biggest enemy was drug abuse. She had been clean for almost three years until about five months ago. That's when she had arm surgery and began taking painkillers, which caused her to have a relapse. That's one of the reasons we broke up. When she began using drugs again, I didn't want that stuff around the baby."

Ten days went by, and then the unthinkable happened. Another young woman's body was found a half a mile away from where Lisa Norrell was discovered, and two miles away from Jessica Frederick's body. This victim was found around 11:00 A.M. in a ditch near an auto repair yard in the 1300 block of California Avenue. A man, whose truck had broken down, spotted the body.

Law enforcement soon related that no obvious wounds had been found on the young woman's body. Since there was no identification on her, fingerprints were taken. Adding to the mystery, there were no reports in the area of any woman missing in the previous twenty-four hours.

Naturally, the murders of three young women so close in time, and in the same general area, spurred fears that there was a serial killer on the loose. Addressing this possibility, a *Contra Costa Times* reporter spoke with San Francisco State professor Michael Rustigan, who taught police agencies about serial killers. Rustigan cautioned about the serial killer aspect, saying, "So far, no pattern appears to have emerged. The victims were all female, and their bodies were found in the same part of Pittsburg. But there, the similarities end. Is there a serial killer in the community? Maybe. But at this point, it's too early to tell."

Minnie Norrell, Lisa's mother, however, was more adamant that there was a serial killer in the area. Minnie said, "Some maniac is on the loose. I know that!" And Jessica Frederick's uncle Edward Steeves related that he thought copycat killers were on the loose. "It's allowed some people who wanted to do something like this to go out and do it," he said.

Plenty of citizens in Pittsburg and Antioch agreed with Minnie Norrell and Edward Steeves. Pittsburg councilwoman Lori Anzini stated, "I hate to be one of the first people to overreact, but my gut feeling tells me there's definitely a problem."

Reverend Ricardo Chavez, who had been Lisa

Norrell's parish priest, declared, "It may mean that more will continue to happen. If it's a trend, then this is going to go on until this person is apprehended."

Shelly Manuel, who shopped at a Home Depot, near where the third body was found, expressed her concerns as well. "I won't go out at night now without my fiancé with me." And Christine Alvarez, of Pittsburg, related, "I'm scared these days. When I was younger, I used to be able to sleep with the window open and walk to the corner store. Not anymore. What's the world coming to?"

By the next day, the Pittsburg police had an identity for this third victim. She was thirty-two-year-old Rachael Cruise. Her fingerprints were on file with the FBI because of some matter in Washington State. Lieutenant William Zbacnik said that it was unclear at that point why Rachael's fingerprints were on file in Washington State. And Zbacnik would not even say at that point if Cruise had been murdered. He did say there were no visible wounds on her body.

Rachael's family, not unlike that of Jessica Frederick's family, spoke of her as having drug problems, but she was also a mother who loved her children. Rachael's brother, Christian Cruise, said that Rachael "was making inroads with her children, and she was determined to find another job. Whatever she went through in life, she always loved her kids."

Rachael's mother added, "My daughter was a trusting type who overlooked the bad in people. She had a happy-go-lucky approach to life and was happiest when she was crocheting, hanging out with her kids, or singing along to her favorite tunes."

A few days later, police addressed the media about Rachael Cruise's case, and said that she had been strangled and smothered to death. And the police also said that contents of Rachael's purse had been found near Verne Roberts Circle, some distance away from where her body was discovered.

Adding to all of this mystery was the near-fatal beating of a prostitute in Bay Point near Pittsburg, on December 15. That woman was found in a portable toilet near a rest stop on Willow Pass Road. She remained in critical condition at John Muir Medical Center in Walnut Creek with a broken jaw, damaged eye socket, and facial cuts and bruises. This woman was later identified as thirty-eight-year-old Tammie Davis, of Bay Point.

One prostitute from the area, who only identified herself as "Gemini," told a reporter, "We're all talking about it and being more careful. The cops seem to be making a bigger effort to get a lot of prostitutes off the street, but it doesn't really matter. They can't always tell who is and who isn't a prostitute."

And then, incredibly, it happened again—on January 8, 1999. The body of Valerie Dawn "China" Schultz, twenty-seven, was found in a ditch along a barren stretch of Willow Pass Road, near Bay Point, not far from Pittsburg. Valerie had only lived in the area for a week before her body was found. She had grown up in Pleasant Hill in Contra Costa County, but had recently been living with her boyfriend in Kentucky. Her father, who lived in Minnesota, didn't even know his daughter had returned to Contra Costa County.

Lieutenant George Lawrence told reporters that CCSO didn't know yet if Valerie had been killed at the spot she was found, or dumped there. He also added that Valerie had a history of prostitution arrests in the Bay Point area from 1991 to 1994. She was a very pretty Chippewa young woman who got her adopted nickname of China from her exotic looks.

Several prostitutes, working the streets in Pittsburg, said that they knew China and added that she was too friendly and possibly not streetwise. Even with the recent murders of all the young women in the area, it's quite possible Valerie came into contact with the wrong man sometime during the late-night hours of January 7, 1999.

Valerie's father said, "She seemed quite happy being where she was in Kentucky. She talked about coming for a visit sometime in the next month. Over the past month, we had a lot of fun conversations. Kidding each other, talking about life. She was feeling pretty upbeat."

The *Contra Costa Times* contacted Professor Michael Rustigan again. Rustigan now said, "It looks to me probably like a thrill killer who's enjoying the publicity and thumbing his nose at the police. It's time to call the FBI. In a small community like Pittsburg, this is truly exceptional. It's beyond coincidence." He also noted that none of the victims had been shot. That was also the sign of a serial killer. Serial killers generally preferred a more intimate type of murder—by strangulation or stabbing their victims to death.

Acknowledging this aspect about a serial killer, James Fox, dean of the College of Criminal Justice at Northeastern University, related, "A gun distances the killer from his victim. It doesn't give the sense of superiority and satisfaction that they're after."

Law enforcement, however, still would not say that one killer had murdered all these women. PPD lieutenant Zbacnik stated, "Does that mean the killings are not connected? Absolutely not. We have to consider everything." As yet, however, there was no "signature" left by one killer. In other words, one particular thread in common to all the murders. The *Contra Costa Times* noted that there was no single factor of age or race on these victims. The only commonality was that all of them were murdered in an area where prostitutes worked. Lisa Norrell, who was not a prostitute, just happened to be in that area when she was murdered.

Making a match through DNA was also difficult, because a prostitute may have had sex with several different men on the same night that she was murdered. Or her killer may have worn a condom. Along with that, it was difficult to trace the last hours of some of these women. And other prostitutes, who knew them, would often not be cooperative with police.

With the death of Valerie Dawn Schultz, the string of murders came to an end in the Pittsburg area. The *Contra Costa Times* noted, *An uneasy calm has settled over Pittsburg and Bay Point.* It was uneasy, indeed. Linda Laney, of Pittsburg, told a reporter, "It's quiet, but you're still kind of nervous." Lisa Norrell's mother, Minnie, chimed in. She said, "I think people may be holding their breath. You just hope it doesn't happen again." Even Michael Rustigan admitted, "The intense media coverage and increased police work might have sent the killer or killers into hiding or made them flee the area."

In 2009, all of these cases were being closely examined by the Pittsburg Police Department to see if Phil Garrido was somehow connected to them. Adding to the speculation on this, a PPD spokesperson told reporters that a bone fragment had been found in the backyard of the Garrido home. PPD lieutenant Brian Addington said of this development, "A few items will require further forensic examination before they can be completely excluded."

A reporter for the *Contra Costa Times* spoke with Minnie Norrell about these latest developments.

Through tears, Minnie only said, "It makes me sad. There's not much more I can say." Adding fuel to the fire was the fact that Phil Garrido had done business with many establishments near the Antioch-Pittsburg Highway in 1998 and 1999. It was an area he knew well as he made his way from Walnut Avenue, through Antioch and over to Pittsburg.

Within a few days, the Pittsburg Police Department reported that nothing found on the Garrido property led them to believe that the Garridos were involved in the murders of Lisa Norrell, Jessica Frederick, Rachael Cruise, or all of the prostitutes near Pittsburg. On the late afternoon of September 4, investigators loaded an old Dodge van onto a flatbed truck and hauled it away from the Garrido property.

The *Contra Costa Times* ran a headline, FRENZY DISSIPATES, BUT SHOCK PALPABLE. One resident told the reporter, "*Twilight Zone* one week, and nobody home the next." All the news vans, reporters, helicopters, and law enforcement vehicles were quickly leaving the area.

Another resident, Lulu Pagnini, related, "It's just so overwhelming. Everybody recovers from everything, but this one . . . I think it touched everybody deeply. It's just so horrific."

And yet, as all the frenzied activity died down on Walnut Avenue, one small article in the *Contra Costa Times* presaged things to come. The article concerned seven-year-old Michaela Garecht, of Hayward, California, who had been abducted in 1988. As yet, few people took note of this possibility. But all that would change very soon.

CHAPTER 26

FACT AND FICTION

Along with information about Phil and Nancy Garrido, the compound, Jaycee and her daughters, there was also misinformation being dispensed by the media at an alarming rate. Part of the reason was the absolute frenzy of activity on Walnut Avenue and the fact that almost any story that anyone said was being taken at face value in the beginning. Because it was so amazing that Jaycee was alive at all, anything seemed possible.

One false account, which was initially being reported upon, was that Jaycee's daughters knew almost nothing about the world beyond Walnut Avenue. In fact, they were reported to be "starved for information," as if they had never been taught anything at all. And the youngest daughter was still having her name spelled as Starlet, Starlit, Starlite, and Starline.

This image of the girls being totally isolated from modern culture was soon dispelled by Tina Dugard, who said that they had seen things on the Internet. Tina also revealed that the girls were now playing the computer game Super Smash Bros. and a board game called Apples to Apples.

Tina also stated that one evening she and Jaycee watched a DVD movie of a Disney film, *Enchanted,* about a fairy-tale princess. Jaycee said that she wanted to see the Sandra Bullock romantic comedy *The Proposal.* And in the background the girls drew pictures and talked about their love of animals and climbing trees.

One thing that seemed to be true was when a detective told a reporter about the girls that "they are being given TV microwave dinners and their favorite meat loaf meals. They have never had fizzy drinks, so they get cooled water, which they are used to."

Leading the charge in news that could not be corroborated were tabloids like the *National Enquirer.* In one issue, they ran a headline, SEX PSYCHO DOSED JAYCEE AND HER KIDS WITH ILLICIT NARCOTICS. As to the validity of this comment, all the *National Enquirer* would relate was that it came from a "source close to the investigation." The article went on to note that Valium and other "highly addictive tranquilizers" had been found by authorities in the Garrido home. And the anonymous source supposedly said, "The narcotics were used to keep them from escaping. Garrido allegedly turned Jaycee into a sex slave, often keeping her in a drug-addled state, and police are investigating whether he gave the drugs to the daughters, too."

In a statement by another unnamed source, the person said that he had witnessed Phil Garrido force Jaycee to smoke marijuana. The exact statement in the article was: *"One night we were sitting around Phil's house when he lit a marijuana cigarette and shoved it into the hands of a young woman we knew as Allissa. He watched to make sure she inhaled. Phil said he wanted to make sure she did it right—but it was more than that. She was afraid, and he glared at her in anger. She tried to pass the joint back after a couple of hits, but Phil pushed her hand back and told her to keep inhaling."*

Even more startling was a comment by another un-named source. In this published quote, the person said, *"Phil wrote and recorded a creepy song about a man killing a woman and her young son, and laughing about it. And after he played the song, he said, 'That's me. I actually did it.'"* Backing up the *National Enquirer*'s claims of this incident, they cited a spokesman for the Contra Costa County Sheriff's Office agreeing that CCSO was investigating the CD in question and whether Phil Garrido actually had murdered a woman and her son. The CCSO was also looking into the possibility that Phil had secretly fathered a son with that woman, and then murdered them both.

By this point, just about anything seemed possible. One neighbor, Mike Rogers, had an account that no one else in the area corroborated. And yet, Rogers was adamant about his story. Rogers told a UK newspaper reporter that he'd seen wild parties occur at Phil Garrido's property. Rogers said that up to ten men would come over to the backyard and light bonfires, play loud music, shout, laugh, and curse into the early hours of the night.

Rogers stated, "Eight to ten men, mostly Mexican, would gather in a line in his garden, drinking beer, yelling and screaming and swearing. They normally had a bonfire and I saw them entering the tent, one by one. On a number of occasions, I saw them bobbing up and down through the window, and I thought, 'My God, there is something sexual going on in there.' They were drinking beer and smashing bottles on the ground. I thought they had a prostitute or something in there. I thought it might have been some kind of sex party or something."

Rogers added that when the men came out of the tent, they would give each other "high fives." Only later, when Rogers learned about Jaycee, Starlit, and Angel living in the tent, did he hope that Phil wasn't "pimping them out to these men." As to why he had never reported this activity, Rogers said he had discussed the matter with his brother. He took his brother's advice not to call the cops *unless* things really got out of hand.

Another person whose stories could not be corroborated was neighbor Dana Crandall. Crandall had lived in the area since she was young, and now worked at a local Save Mart. Crandall said that Phil shopped there and sometimes he took two young blond girls along with him.

Crandall told a UK tabloid, "Years ago, my brother heard someone in the backyard having sex. At the time, we just thought it was him (Phil) and his girl-friend. They had a hot tub back there. There were wooden shutters on the house that he would always put up, and he always locked the gate. I played back there as a little kid. Phil always peeked over the fence. He was real neighborly, but he never let anyone come onto his property. I never knew that it (the secret compound) existed back there."

Crandall also spoke of her meetings with Phil and the girls at the place where she worked. She said that Phil would come in and talk to her about religion and his recordings. She had met the two young blond girls on three occasions, and Phil introduced them as his daughters. Crandall said, "They were hanging on to his arms, and asking 'Can we get this? Can we buy this?' He just got milk and the bare necessities and always paid with cash."

* * *

Among all the so-called information that was making the rounds as facts were other stories that could not be pinned down as to whether they were true or not. One of these stories concerned an account of Phil and Nancy Garrido looking for a "cute blond girl on a child shopping trip to Lake Tahoe." This story was reported upon by the news source the UK *Telegraph*. The article stated: *Phillip Garrido selected the pretty blond girl with the gap-toothed grin as his prey during a child shopping trip because she looked so cute, his wife, Nancy, has told investigators in California. But the couple decided not to try and snatch the 11-year-old Jaycee Dugard that day in June 1991 because she was walking through South Lake Tahoe with a bunch of school friends. Instead they apparently trailed her home before returning the next morning to complete their horrific mission. . . . "That's the one I want," Garrido told her (Nancy) when he saw Jaycee in the resort town. "She's cute, but she's with the other kids. Let's come back later and get her."*

This story sounds quite plausible, but there were two things wrong with it. One was that Jaycee was abducted on a Monday, so she could not have been walking home with friends from school on the previous day. And a variation of this "walking home with friends" incident could not have happened as well. It was a story of Jaycee walking home with friends after the art fair on Sunday. An El Dorado Sheriff's Office detective who had been working the case for years emphatically stated that did not occur. Jaycee had returned home from the art fair in a vehicle with her father.

One of the most dramatic stories to come out of this period was one that detailed a late-night visit by investigators and Jaycee to the Garrido home after

August 26, 2009. According to the story, Jaycee led the investigators who carried flashlights, back into the compound where she had been a virtual prisoner for so many years. According to the tale, she showed the investigators where Phil Garrido had first raped her, and the spot where Angel and Starlit had been born.

The story went on to relate, "For the next several hours, police with flashlights led her around every shed and tent, asking her to describe in detail exactly where she had been imprisoned and what had happened where. Several times Jaycee broke down in tears, revisiting the scene of her nightmare."

It was all very dramatic, but an El Dorado County Sheriff's Office detective, who was absolutely familiar with Jaycee's case and the events of August 2009, said the story in his words was "garbage." He added that the investigators and Jaycee' roaming around the compound with flashlights, "Never happened. It's all fiction."

At least on September 6, 2009, there was some information that seemed to be correct about Phil and Nancy Garrido, but it was all filtered through Phil's elderly mother, Pat. And, of course, Pat had serious memory problems by that point.

A reporter for the UK's *Mirror* interviewed Pat, who was now residing in a nursing home for the elderly. Pat told the reporter that Phil had shown up one day in the 1990s with a young blond girl and said, "She's mine, Mom." Meaning that the blond girl was his daughter by a previous relationship that had nothing to do with Nancy.

Pat related that Phillip and Ron had been good boys, but she always wanted a daughter. "When Alyssa appeared one day, it was amazing. I was so pleased she was around. I was ill in bed. She was a real angel," Pat recounted.

Pat added that Alyssa was hardworking and helped Phil on his printing projects. And when two more young girls appeared on the scene, Angel and Starlit, Pat was thrilled. Phil introduced them as two more of his daughters by another relationship. Pat declared, "I've blocked out some of the memories, but I still remember the joy of having the children around. I saw all three girls as my granddaughters."

As far as Nancy went, Pat said that she had a "heart of gold." Nancy was always attentive and helpful with Pat and her medical needs. And over time, Alyssa also helped once in a while.

As far as Alyssa, Starlit, and Angel living in tents in the far backyard, Pat said that she had grown up during the Great Depression, and such living conditions were not out of place in her memory. Pat related that she was used to a lot of noise while growing up on a farm and spending a great deal of time outside, just like Alyssa, Starlit, and Angel.

Pat added that the girls had a trampoline to play on, and Starlit and Angel often played in the garden. They didn't have a lot of toys, but they did spend their time reading books and sitting with Alyssa. Alyssa mostly stayed in the garden in the daytime, but as the girls grew older, they spent more time in the main house. Pat said that the kids were messy, but Alyssa always tried to keep things tidy. Pat also said that Alyssa helped around the house and never complained.

Pat stated that Alyssa worked on the computer in regard to Phil's printing business. Alyssa even showed Starlit and Angel how she did it. And according to Pat, Phil in the last year had let the girls go on errands with him around the area. Pat also commented, "Nancy was always sweet to the girls, but sometimes Phil would shout at them."

As to how Jaycee's abduction, rape, and captivity—along with the advent of Starlit and Angel being right under her nose—had occurred, Pat said, "I was getting older then and was spending more and more time just in my room, in my bed, so some days I would just see Nancy and some days I would see Alyssa. I didn't know she was being kept there against her will. I was in my bed and all I knew was this smiley girl who came to see me."

Pat said she didn't want to talk about why Phil had done such a thing because it upset her. She did say that prison could be very hard on most people, but when Phil got out of prison, "He didn't have a scratch on him. It didn't seem to affect him at all."

Pat ended her interview by saying that she always thought that Alyssa, Starlit, and Angel were her grand-daughters. "I had no idea why he would do something like this. I don't know what's wrong with him, but he has made the family very sad."

Farther away, in Southern California, it was reported that Jaycee Lee's biological father, Ken Slayton, made known how he felt about Phil Garrido. Slayton told reporters, "When I think about what she went through, it's just horrible. I'd love to get my hands on Garrido and kill him. I hope he rots in jail."

Three hundred miles away from Southern California, there was a celebration taking place, and that celebration occurred where it had all begun back in 1991—Lake Tahoe.

CHAPTER 27

TEARS OF JOY

In the days before the next storm on Walnut Avenue, it was a time for happiness in Lake Tahoe. On Sunday, September 6, 2009, an estimated three thousand people attended a parade for Jaycee Lee Dugard in South Lake Tahoe. Many of them were clad in pink—Jaycee's favorite color when she was abducted—and many more carried pink balloons. Among the throng was South Lake Tahoe's mayor, Jerry Birdwell. He said he was there to show support for Jaycee and her family, just as the rest of the community was doing. "The innocence of the town was basically taken away that day," he said. Tahoe resident Sheryl Langstaff added, "The parade is a closure of a nightmare and the beginning of some peace and, hopefully, some happiness."

Car horns honked, people cheered, as young and old alike marched along the route. Most had never known Jaycee Lee or her family personally, but there were some marchers in the parade who had. One of those was Meghan Doris, who had been a classmate of Jaycee's. Since then, Meghan had stayed in touch with many of her classmates, who had been traumatized by the events of June 10, 1991, and Meghan said that she had attended some of their weddings. Like Jaycee, Meghan had been a blond-haired, blue-eyed pretty girl. When Meghan's mother had first heard the description of the kidnapped girl, she feared that it had been her own daughter who had been abducted. Like many others, Meghan expressed a common refrain: "We were robbed of the safety of the community. Even in high school, our yearbook did a dedication to her. We never forgot her. Hearing the news of Jaycee's discovery has brought back all of the memories."

Meghan also spoke to a reporter from CBS news. Meghan related, "It really haunted us over the years. I'm just excited to get her back. Putting myself in her place, I can't imagine what she went through. I wish her the best in the healing process and hope she can lead a normal life."

CBS also spoke to Jillian Broadfoot, who had attended Meyers Elementary School in 1991 when Jaycee had been kidnapped. Broadfoot said, "We just want her to know that we love and support her. I think Tahoe lost its innocence with the kidnapping, and, hopefully, her return restores a little faith here."

Jaycee's school principal, Karen Gillis-Tinlin, told the CBS television news reporter, "All I want to do is cry right now. I feel overwhelming joy and happiness. Obviously, Jaycee hasn't been forgotten. She has remained in our minds and hearts all these years. She could have been anyone's child, and that's why you personalize it. You think, 'It could have been my child who was kidnapped.'"

Another marcher, Roxie Upton, had a daughter in the school system who was eleven years old in 1991, the same age as Jaycee. Upton said, "There was not a soul in this town who didn't know what happened to Jaycee." Another woman, Jackie Hardie, recalled how her daughter had wanted to walk to the school bus stop alone, and she wouldn't let her. When Hardie finally allowed her daughter to walk by herself, she followed close behind her in a car. In the parade, Hardie now rode a bicycle with a large handmade sign on it, WELCOME HOME JAYCEE.

Not only were friends of Jaycee in the parade, but police officers who had initially worked on the case as well. One of those was veteran officer Larry Hennick, of the El Dorado County Sheriff's Office. Hennick said of the kidnapping, "It was really hard. It was something we all lived with. We all had those missing person posters in our cars. There wasn't a day we didn't look for the abduction vehicle."

On the day of the parade, many of the missing person posters from when Jaycee was eleven years old were put back up on the parade route. People on the sidewalk, people in restaurants, people driving by in their cars, all shouted and waved as the parade wound by. South Lake Tahoe police chief Terry Daniels said of the throng of marchers, "I'm not surprised. The community has been very supportive. Everyone was excited and anticipating this day."

Off on the sidelines, Carl Probyn watched the marchers from the seat of an SUV, surrounded by a film crew from Australia. Carl stated about the march, "I wanted to be here, but I didn't want to be the center of attention. I didn't want it to be about me."

The Soroptimist Club, which had sponsored Jaycee's family all through the years, put on the event, and Soroptimist Sue Novasel said, "The parade signifies a full circle." People came from all over the area to be in it, including Kelly Tousey, of Fair Oaks, California, a city about one hundred miles away. Tousey was there with her husband and three children, ages five, fourteen, and sixteen. Tousey told a reporter, "We wanted to celebrate and rejoice. We wanted to show our support for Jaycee and her family."

The culmination of the parade was at Meyers Elementary School—the place where Jaycee Lee had been going on the morning that she was kidnapped eighteen years before. At the school, the Soroptimist Club handed out pink-frosted cupcakes and pink T-shirts emblazoned with TAHOE LOVES JAYCEE. A party atmosphere took over the grounds, with people Hula-hooping, blowing bubbles, displaying homemade signs, and cheering. And the crowd really cheered when a pair of loudspeakers began playing the song by Sister Sledge, "We Are Family."

Later, El Dorado County Sheriff's Office lieutenant Les Lovell told the crowd, "I was expecting that we would never see her again. Her story shows that anytime there's hope, we need to keep hope alive." Then Lovell told the children in the crowd, if ever faced with the same situation as Jaycee, "Fight! Fight your way out of it. Don't be complacent."

South Lake Tahoe police officer Rebecca Inman told reporters that since Jaycee was abducted, three thousand children had taken part in the Fighting Chance program. It taught them how to fight back against an abductor. And then Inman told the crowd, "My heart is just overflowing with joy." Inman raised her fist in the air in celebration.

A few days later, in Brentwood, California, UC Berkeley police officer Ally Jacobs was honored in the town where she lived. A crowd packed City Hall as the mayor and the entire city council presented Ally with a key to the city. She was only the second person in Brentwood's history to receive such an award. Mayor Bob Taylor said of Ally, "I think what she did is remarkable." Even a United States representative's aide was there to let the gathering know that Congressman Jerry McNerney had entered into the House record, "Had it not been for Officer Jacobs's outstanding performance of her duties, the abuse of Jaycee and her daughters would have continued indefinitely."

Ally Jacobs was escorted into City Hall by members of the local Warriors' Watch Riders and American Legion Post 202. When Ally was presented with the key to the city and a dozen roses, she tried not to cry, but she brushed back tears from her eyes, anyway. She told the gathering, "I'm completely humbled and honored for what I feel was me just doing my job."

Over in Antioch, there was less of a celebratory mood. Antioch had gotten a black eye in the press, around the world, for something the citizens, and especially the mayor of Antioch, thought was not their fault. Walnut Avenue, where the Garridos had lived, wasn't even within the city limits. Many citizens of Antioch believed they were being unfairly painted with a broad brush for things that only Phil and Nancy Garrido had done.

Even the *Contra Costa Times* ran an article that Antioch was being unfairly tainted. The article's headline was ANTIOCH'S INFAMY UNFOUNDED. The article related, *It's a juicy nugget for the worldwide press, tripping alarms on the cable news fear-o-meter. Anderson Cooper of CNN has the graphics to prove it and a roster of experts to explain how the local area where police say Jaycee Dugard was held in sexual bondage for eighteen years has fast become a dense haven for registered sex offenders.* The article went on to say that the media was frightening the locals with unfounded reports.

The article proved, in fact, that Antioch was well below dozens of other Bay Area cities as far as a ratio of registered sex offenders per capita. And it barely made the top ten of Contra Costa County cities in that regard.

The article quoted Antioch police chief Jim Hyde saying that Antioch was taking flak from reporters using "high-school journalism." Hyde also said, "Many Antioch residents are mad because they feel their town has been defamed." And Antioch councilman Brian Kalinowski stated, "From my perspective, one individual who's sick in the head doesn't define a community."

One angry resident declared, to a different news source, "If we're going to be defined by Phil Garrido, then Londoners should be defined by Jack the Ripper, and Berliners by Adolf Hitler. When you start making wrong assumptions, you can say all sorts of stupid things. Some of the worst are the foreign journalists!"

Blame, censure, and chaos spread in all directions as the "Jaycee Lee Dugard story" continued to be a hot commodity. The Telegraph.co.UK reported, Given this interest in the case, one British paparazzi agency has suggested that a deal for an exclusive interview and pictures (of Jaycee Lee and daughters) would stretch into several hundred thousand pounds, and could easily top 500,000 pounds. However, they speculated that it was more likely that an American television company would secure the rights to hear Dugard's story for an even greater fee.

The site posited that the reason that no photos of Jaycee Lee or her girls had yet come to light was because law enforcement and mental-health professionals might have blocked the release of any photos. Then it related the story about Austrian victim Natascha

Kampusch. It also related how far the paparazzi were willing to go to obtain photos and stories like these. When it was learned that Josef Fritzl had kept his daughter captive in what amounted to a basement dungeon, one British photographer broke into the kitchen of her hideaway home in an attempt to secure photographs.

Law enforcement, and especially the FBI, wanted none of that taking place with regard to Jaycee Lee and her daughters. When law enforcement learned that Cheyvonne and Jim Molino had allegedly made some kind of deal with the media about videotapes showing Angel and Starlit at their daughter's recent Sweet Sixteen party, law enforcement cracked down hard.

Cheyvonne related later, "They came in and up-ended drawers and mattresses, looking for authentic photos of Phil's girls. I never videotaped the girls. I need to let people know what really went on and clear my name."

Cheyvonne added, "I had no idea what Phil had done to Jaycee Lee or anything about that. As for those girls, they behaved like normal kids on the day that photo was taken. He left the girls unattended at the party. He dropped them off. He picked them up. The girls did not attempt to flee."

There was one photo in particular of Angel and Starlit at that party that was now starting to come to light on the Internet and on television. And law enforcement must have put the fear of God into any news agency that ran those photos unaltered. Several media sources depicted the girls with their faces blurred out. The depictions showed two young girls, dressed in party dresses, walking into a room where a party is taking place in the background.

* * *

Amidst all the media frenzy and finger-pointing, there was almost a calm at the eye of the storm now for Phil and Nancy Garrido as they sat in their cells in Placerville. The two suspects certainly weren't going anywhere. There was one report in the *Herald Sun* that both Phil and Nancy Garrido were being protected from other prisoners while in jail. According to the *Herald Sun,* there had been a stream of death threats upon Phil and Nancy ever since the story had broken.

CBS News.com also reported about this aspect: **Fellow prisoners are warning that they'll rape or murder Nancy Garrido. She's spending her time reading the Bible, sources say.**

Former San Francisco prosecutor Michael Cardoza told CBS News, "In a prison system, there is a certain code of morality, and this type of crime ranks at the very, very bottom. So it doesn't shock me that either one of them has been threatened with death or the rape. The sheriffs in the jail there have to keep them from the rest. And even when and if they go to prison, they will have to be kept in isolation, because there will be the big worry that someone will try to murder them."

As far as the present concerns of the Garridos' safety in the El Dorado County Jail, DA Vern Pierson commented, "Every effort is being made to ensure their safety while they are held in the county."

The Garridos' fellow inmates in the El Dorado County Jail weren't the only ones who wished they could get their hands on them. Ken Slayton, Jaycee's biological father, told reporters, "I think they should live as long as they possibly can, and someone should torment them as much as they did Jaycee and those little girls. In fact, that's too good for them. I'd skin him."

And in all of this, Nancy Garrido was indeed the

mystery woman. It seemed that almost no one knew much about her, even people who had lived next to her for years on Walnut Avenue. Damon Robinson had told one reporter, "The wife (Nancy) was like a hermit. She looked like she had no spirit." In fact, people who received business cards from Phil had seen more of Jaycee than they had of Nancy Garrido.

Trying to plumb the depths of the mystery woman, the *Contra Costa Times* ran an article, WHO IS NANCY GARRIDO? The article began by stating that Nancy had worked as a state-licensed aide for a respected non-profit agency that served a thousand adults and children with disabilities. She worked full-time for the Contra Costa County ARC from December 1994 until March 1998. The agency's executive director, Barbara Maizie, said that Nancy was accepted because "she had a stellar reference as a nursing aide and physical therapy aide. The people who received services through her liked her very much. She was a good employee and she was well-liked by the people she worked with. They cannot believe this is possible. They're totally shocked."

Maizie went on to say that Nancy Garrido worked with adults only. Nancy's credentials and references dated back to 1981, the same year she married Phil Garrido in Leavenworth Penitentiary. And, of course, Nancy had followed Phil to California after his release from Leavenworth, Kansas, and his stint in a Nevada prison.

The *Contra Costa Times* article noted that when Nancy Garrido first came to work at the Martinez-based agency, Jaycee Lee was already a teenager and having the first of her two babies. Even though there was a great deal of speculation that Nancy had helped in the birth of Angel and Starlit, Ken August, a spokesman for the Department of Public Health, said that Nancy did not have training in assisting with childbirth. This, of course, might not have stopped her, since of all the members of the household on Walnut Avenue, Nancy had the most medical training.

Nancy's family, in Denver, Colorado, became a magnet for media outlets. The UK *Telegraph* sent a reporter there to try and speak with family members. The journalist did talk to brother David, reporting, *The 46-year-old looked bleary-eyed and exhausted when he opened his front door in a Denver suburb.* "My mother looks even worse," he said.

When asked about Nancy, David replied, *"I've got nothing bad to say about my sister. He (Phil Garrido) turned her into that. She was normal until she hooked up with that guy."* Then David spoke of the sister he had known who used to go fishing, canoeing, and other fun activities.

Inside Edition's Diane McInerney also spoke with Nancy's brothers, David and Ray Bocanegra. McInerney asked, "What happened to your sister?" Ray answered angrily, "Phil Garrido! That's what happened to my sister! She was a normal kid. A teenager going out with friends, working, having a good time."

"She never did drugs?" McInerney asked.

"No."

"Any prior arrests?"

"None. I don't think she even had a speeding ticket. Not even a parking ticket."

David related, "Once she met Phillip, that was it. It was like she was no longer around." Then David added that the family was deeply concerned when Nancy married Phil in a prison ceremony in 1981. They wondered what kind of life she could hope for with a convicted sex offender.

When David and Ray first saw photos of what kind of living conditions Nancy had been living in on Walnut Avenue, Ray said, "That's not the way we grew up." And David said that when he'd had his last phone conversation with Nancy, three years previously, she was saying whatever Phil wanted her to say.

David stated that Phil had spoken to him and brought up the situation with his "magical black box," with which he could talk to God. David said, "It was just really off-the-wall when he talked about that. I couldn't believe my sister was with this guy. That was just nuts!"

David and Ray were very disturbed by the fact that it might have been Nancy who actually grabbed Jaycee off the street and forced her into the car in 1991. Ray said, "I think Nancy was a victim, too. Just like everybody else was a victim of Phillip Garrido. She was scared, brainwashed."

Despite the fact that David and Ray thought that Nancy had been brainwashed, they didn't make excuses for what she had done. David said, "She took someone's life away. I apologize to you (Jaycee) and your family for what my sister did. I hope you're doing better, you and your kids. God bless you."

Even Ron Garrido, Phil's brother, thought that Nancy had been brainwashed. Ron told a reporter for the *Sunday Times,* "She was a robot. She would do anything he asked. I told my wife, 'It's no different from Charles Manson and those girls.'"

An article in the *First Post,* entitled MADNESS OF WANTING TO BE NORMAL: *Nancy Garrido's Make-Believe Family,* related that a woman often joined forces with an abuser in order to feel loved. The couple didn't have to live in the real world; they could create a parallel one that masked their inadequacies.

One thing seemed clear regarding Nancy's role in the initial abduction of Jaycee on June 10, 1991. It was a dark-haired woman whom Carl Probyn had seen throwing Jaycee into the kidnapper's car. A woman who matched Nancy Garrido's looks of that period.

And Gilbert Maines was going to have a tough sell with this factor. Nonetheless, it appeared that he was doing his best. On NBC's *Today* show, Maines said that Nancy was a victim of her husband's suppressive control. Maines declared, "The crux of the matter, the argument, I think, goes to maybe her mental condition at the time, and not so much what physically happened." And Maines went on to reiterate how Nancy felt about Jaycee, Angel, and Starlit. "What she said that I can tell you about is—there came a time that when she felt that they were a family and that she loves the girls very much and loved Jaycee very much, and that seems a little strange, given the circumstances, but that's what she told me."

Maines also noted that Nancy had waited patiently for seven years, from the time she and Phil were married, to the time he was released and they could finally live together. Even during that long period, she seemed to be under his spell. So much under his spell, in fact, that in 1993, even when he was sent back to prison for a parole violation, she still obeyed his orders to keep Jaycee in the hidden compound.

CHAPTER 28

MIND CONTROL

As to the possible "mind control defense" for Nancy Garrido, Alan Scheflin, professor of law and psychiatry at Santa Clara Law School, and author of *The Mind Manipulators*, stressed how hard it was to convince a jury in that regard. Scheflin told a reporter, "The courts are very reluctant to open up to the idea of a mind-control defense. It certainly is, to say the least, a last-ditch defense."

Bay Area television station KTVU also took up this issue of "mental state," not only concerning Nancy Garrido, but Phil Garrido as well. KTVU reported that in the days before the arrest, there were already cracks appearing in Phil Garrido's elaborately constructed façade.

The report went on to tell of the most glaring of these "cracks" in his façade. He had taken Angel and Starlit to UC Berkeley with him, and he had actually gone with them to see a parole officer in Concord on the day he was arrested, instead of going on the run. The report noted, *Whether rooted in bravado, mental illness or both, his actions in the years, days and hours before his secret life was exposed raise questions about whether he subconsciously wanted to be caught.* The report went on to state that in the days ahead, Phil's behavior would become increasingly relevant as prosecutors prepared their case and law enforcement agencies looked at possible connections to other unsolved crimes in their jurisdictions.

Ken Lanning, a consultant and former FBI agent, weighed in on this topic, as well, and said that it wasn't unusual for sex offenders to have their defenses eventually break down. Lanning related, "Some try to justify their deeds by arguing that their victims cared for them or somehow benefited from the abuse. Deep down, this guy knows he kidnapped this girl eighteen years ago, but he is not thinking of this every day. He probably wanted to convince himself that he had changed. 'I was bad at one time and this is the proof that I am a different person now.' His need to validate that belief system is a far more likely explanation than that he was crying for help."

And Phil's document about schizophrenia obviously raised questions about his mental state and possibility of increasing mental illness. Michael McGrath, a forensic psychiatrist in Rochester, New York, told the media, "These things he is writing would lead one to question his sanity or at least his grasp on reality. Going and proselytizing it in a public place, needing to get a permit and then he brings the two kids and blurts out his criminal record—it's very possible on some level, unconsciously, he wanted to put an end to it and didn't know how to do it."

And then an issue was brought up that had pertained to the Elizabeth Smart case in Salt Lake City, Utah. Fourteen-year-old Elizabeth Smart had been kidnapped by a religious zealot, Brian David Mitchell and his wife, Wanda Barzee. Nine months later, these two were caught, and Elizabeth was released to freedom. However, since then, the Mitchells had not been brought to trial because they were deemed to be too mentally incompetent to participate in their defense. Under United States law, a defendant must be competent enough to understand what is going on in the courtroom and be able to assist their attorney. Brian Mitchell did not reach this standard of competency until the autumn of 2010. He was not found guilty of the crime until December 2010.

At the end of the news report about Phil Garrido and Jaycee Dugard, Ken Lanning added another insightful comment: "None of the actions by Jaycee Dugard should be second-guessed about why she didn't run away. If you are alive after eighteen years, you did the right thing. I don't care what you did, it was the right thing."

Things moved from the realm of speculation to reality in the El Dorado County Superior Court on September 14, 2009, in another hearing. Phil Garrido entered the courtroom with a bandage on his nose and a newly grown gray beard. Phil had a vacant stare on his face; while Nancy once again looked embarrassed and avoided eye contact with the gathered media. She tried hiding her face with her hair as still cameras clicked incessantly in the courtroom and film cameras whirred. Neither Phil nor Nancy looked at each other except for one brief glance at the beginning of the hearing.

In a brief court hearing, Susan Gellman, Phil's attorney, asked Judge Douglas Phimister for a psychiatric evaluation of her client. This was granted by the judge. Nancy Garrido's attorney, Gilbert Maines, reserved the right to request an evaluation at a later date for Nancy. Asked how they were pleading, both Phil and Nancy pleaded not guilty to all twenty-nine charges. And both waived their rights to a speedy trial.

Susan Gellman brought up the fact that several law enforcement agencies wanted to speak with Phil about unsolved cases in their jurisdictions. Gellman stated to the judge, "He does not consent to be questioned for any purpose."

Then the issue of bail amounts on Phil and Nancy Garrido came up. Phil's bail was set at $30 million and Nancy received no bail. This was somewhat unexpected, except for the fact that she might have been the one who actually snatched Jaycee Lee off a street as Jaycee walked to the bus stop. It was, of course, very unlikely that Phil was going to be able to raise such a huge bail amount.

Once the proceedings were over, there was the usual crush of media outside the courtroom, badgering DA Vern Pierson with dozens of questions. Pierson said that more charges might be leveled against the Garridos as time went on. And then Pierson stated that Jaycee Dugard would likely have to take the witness stand when it was time for a trial.

As far as Jaycee Lee Dugard and her family went at present, Pierson exhorted the media to respect their privacy. He said the family needed a time of quiet so that they could heal. With scorn, Pierson declared, "I've heard comments referring to this family as a piece of property to be had. I think they need to be left alone! If you look at this family, they have a lot to deal with right now. Basic human decency mandates honoring the family's request for privacy."

Asked if he had ever prosecuted a case like the present one, Pierson responded, "I don't think anyone has handled a case quite like this one."

DDA Trish Kelliher had one more interesting thing to add that had not come up before. She let it be known that a stun gun was used to subdue Jaycee Lee Dugard on the day she was kidnapped. This information must have come from Jaycee herself.

Lieutenant Pamela "Pam" Lane, of the El Dorado Sheriff's Office, who had control over the county jail, told reporters that both Phil and Nancy Garrido were receiving three meals a day and could shower every other day. They couldn't watch television, but they had access to newspapers and magazines. They were, of course, in a high-security area because of death threats.

And the issue of threats also came up as a topic with Vern Pierson. He said he had recently learned that a parole agent and his family had received threats because of the missed opportunities concerning Jaycee. Pierson said, "There's probably some very legitimate criticism in terms of this historically. But after a tip, Parole Agent Eddie Santos successfully broke through an elaborate well-planned cover story that was eighteen years in the making." Pierson told people to leave Santos and his family alone.

Gilbert Maines was fairly closemouthed about Nancy Garrido after the court hearing except to say, "She is very closed down right now." And Susan Gellman, when asked about the bandage on Phil Garrido's nose and whether he'd had some minor surgery, replied, "I think so." Both attorneys noted that they were seeking to meet with their clients in a room rather than behind a wall of glass as they were doing at present. Other than that, Maines and Gellman said very little.

There was always information and misinformation bubbling to the surface on such a big case. One bit of misinformation was reported by Britain's *Daily Mirror.* It ran an article stating, *Dugard will appear on* The

Oprah Winfrey Show *in December, and she will receive $1 million for the appearance.* Soon thereafter, a spokesperson for Oprah Winfrey's show denied this contention, and said, "We don't pay for interviews."

Things seemed to be settling down into a more quiet routine by now. But all of that was about to change in an instant. Law enforcement revealed that a bone recovered from the Garrido property was a human bone. And two police agencies were interested about kidnapped children in the Bay Area. A second tidal wave of reporters, satellite trucks, police vehicles, and investigators was about to descend on Walnut Avenue. And this wave, in some respects, was even larger than the first.

CHAPTER 29

THE SECOND WAVE

Jimmy Lee, who was a spokesman for the Contra Costa County Sheriff's Office, informed the media from time to time on new developments on Walnut Avenue. One small item in the newspapers coming from Lee cropped up earlier about a bone fragment that had been discovered. In an e-mail to the media, Lee cautioned that it might be a very old bone. "The bone is human, but it is not uncommon to find Native American remains in Contra Costa County." Lee also said that the bone fragment was being tested at a Bay Area facility to make sure that it was human and to try to judge how old it was.

The interesting thing about this bone was that it had been found on next-door neighbor Damon Robinson's property. But Lee let it be known that for a period of time that house had been vacant and Phil Garrido had been the "caretaker" there. This story died down for a few days until September 16, when it was learned that more human bones had been discovered on Damon Robinson's property and on the

Garridos' property as well. The media blitz that had come and gone from Walnut Avenue went into its second stage.

Once again, reporters poured in, news vehicles lined the street, satellite trucks sent up their antennas and dishes, and helicopters buzzed overhead. And more than that, a swarm of law enforcement officers descended on the Garrido house and property. Soon law enforcement alone had brought in ventilation units, a large generator, a Bobcat tractor, tents, Porta-Potties, and large mobile home–type command vehicles. The street began to look more like an RV campground than a regular street.

Three truckloads of debris, weeds, and small items were trucked out of the yard on the first day of renewed work. Other items of evidentiary value were carted off to large vans and trailers parked along the street. And to make matters even more interesting to the press, it became apparent that the Hayward Police Department (HPD) was looking for clues to see if Phil Garrido had snatched Michaela Garecht, of Hayward, on November 19, 1988. And the Dublin Police Department (DPD) was also there to try and find out if Garrido had been responsible for the disappearance of thirteen-year-old Ilene Misheloff, of Dublin, in 1989. It was a major operation. Sixty investigators from five agencies were scouring the yard and house for clues. And as time went on, more bones kept turning up in the yards.

As far back as September 2, the *San Jose Mercury News* gave a hint about what was coming. In an article they reported, *Police see similarities between Dugard, Garecht cases. With long blond hair, blue eyes and a friendly big-toothed grin, Michaela could pass for Dugard's sister.*

Of Michaela, her mother, Sharon, later said, "She was my first child, the desire of my heart for over five years before she was born, finally conceived only with the assistance of prescription fertility pills. She was the first person to curl her little tiny hand around my fingers, and around my heart, the first one to call me Mommy. Beautiful beyond measure, tenderhearted and compassionate, she was a living light in the world."

On November 19, 1988, Michaela and her friend Trina wanted to go to the Rainbow Market to buy some candy and sodas. Michaela had been there before in the company of teenage girls, but not with someone who was just her age. Even though the market was only two blocks away, Sharon did not want her to go with eleven-year-old Trina. But Michaela begged and begged, and finally Sharon let the girls go. The girls jumped on their scooters and headed to the Rainbow Market. Sharon watched them go, and then went back to her kitchen to wash the breakfast dishes.

Michaela and Trina left their scooters by the side door of the market and then went inside where they bought candy, sodas, and beef jerky. They left the market with their purchases and began walking home, when they suddenly realized they had left their scooters by the side of the market. The girls returned and discovered that one of the scooters had been moved next to a parked vehicle about three spaces down from the market door. Michaela spotted it and began to walk over to retrieve it.

As Trina watched, a man suddenly jumped out of the car and threw Michaela, screaming, into the car. The man jumped into the driver's seat, peeled out of the parking space, and took off at a high rate of speed on Mission Boulevard.

Within moments, Trina ran into the store for help. The police were called, and Trina phoned her father, who then drove over to Michaela's house. Michaela's father, Rod, was working on his car in the driveway when he got the news. Within seconds, he ran into the house and declared to Sharon, "Somebody snatched Michaela up at the market!"

Sharon couldn't believe what she was hearing. In a daze, she phoned 911. She was stunned to learn that the dispatcher already knew Michaela's name. The dispatcher asked Sharon a few questions and told her to wait at her house. Sharon said later, "I hung up the phone and began waiting, began a lifetime of waiting."

As the investigation would go for Jaycee Lee Dugard three years later, there were hundreds of tips, numerous possible sightings, and nothing that led to Michaela Garecht's whereabouts. For many years, Sharon gave up hope that Michaela could still be alive. And then one day, around 2007, Sharon received a tip about a young woman who lived in another state. The woman, who pronounced her name as Ma-kay-la, the same way Michaela Garecht did, had amnesia about her younger years. In the end, it turned out that the young woman was not Michaela Garecht, but it gave Sharon new hope that Michaela might still be alive. As Sharon later said, "Many kids who run away (or are kidnapped) end up feeling so ashamed of the way they have been living that they are afraid to go home. They are afraid they will no longer be loved because of who they have become."

And then on August 26, 2009, came the astonishing news that Jaycee Lee Dugard had been found alive. Sharon related that her first thoughts were that Michaela would be found in the same secret compound where Jaycee and her girls had been found. Sharon agreed with many in law enforcement that the mode of abduction and the vehicle used in Michaela's case were very similar to the mode and vehicle in Jaycee's case.

As it turned out, Michaela was not found alive in the secret compound on Walnut Avenue. And when human bones started turning up in the Garridos' backyard and neighboring yard, Sharon had to brace herself for a more grim possibility in Michaela's case.

As more and more bones turned up, HPD lieutenant Christine "Chris" Orrey told reporters, "We need to send the bones to a lab for testing to determine if they are human or an animal, and if they are possibly connected to the cases of the missing girls." (She meant Michaela Garecht and Ilene Misheloff.) "We're trying to be cautious. Finding them is the first step of the process, now we have to find out what they might mean. We haven't found anything that breaks our case, but there's certainly some stuff worth taking a look at."

One thing that made the Garrido angle so compelling was the fact that Phil Garrido at the time of Michaela's disappearance was in a halfway house in Oakland, not far from the crime scene in Hayward. Of that matter, Orrey said, "The fact both kidnappings happened in broad daylight, the similarity of the car, the area, the fact he was released from prison a few months before Michaela was taken, it's all compelling evidence. And if you look at the picture of Jaycee and Michaela, they could be sisters. We're looking for any physical evidence that ties Phillip or Nancy Garrido to Michaela's case."

Then Orrey said that in the pursuit of their search, they had come across photos of Jaycee and her girls amidst all the clutter and debris in the Garrido home. Those photos had been taken and were being safeguarded by authorities.

Sharon, Michaela Garecht's mom, was, of course, transfixed by the search transpiring on Walnut Avenue. She told a reporter, "I have a little fantasy about how the search will go. There will be some kind of false room, and Michaela will be inside. Ever since I heard the description of Jaycee reuniting with her family, I've just had such a longing for that to happen."

Lieutenant Orrey added at a later press conference, "We've made a lot of progress, but we haven't found anything earth-shattering at this point. Each agency has its own focus, and we're looking for specific things. Officers are looking for particular items that El Dorado County and Pittsburg authorities involved in the Jaycee Dugard case may not have been interested in during their searches. Those items include a pair of pearl-colored earrings that resemble feathers, a white T-shirt with *Metro* across the front, denim pants, flesh-colored nylons, and black shoes. That's what Michaela was wearing when she vanished.

"We are also looking for disturbed soil that could indicate a grave site. We are going to bring in a magnetometer, which could locate fillings from teeth, as well as ground-penetrating radar. It's probably the most intensive search Hayward has been involved in. We are considering dismantling the interior of the Garridos' home. If we feel that's important to do a thorough search, then we'll pursue that. We are very interested in what is under the flooring, under the ground, so that is a possibility. The FBI, Contra Costa County Sheriff's Office, Alameda County Sheriff's Office, and Alameda County Crime Lab are all aiding in the searches and examinations. Our aim is to methodically, systematically, and very thoroughly search the property with our own case in mind."

* * *

Dublin police lieutenant Kurt von Savoye was also there, and at the press conference, he told the gathered media, "We are attempting to locate any possible evidence that connects the Garridos to Ilene Misheloff. We have a sedan [that] is similar in description to what a witness observed Ilene getting into on the day she went missing."

On January 30, 1989, thirteen-year-old Ilene Misheloff had been walking home from Wells Middle School to her skating practice. It was 3:00 P.M. and she was to meet her ice-skating coach at the woman's home on Alegre Drive in Dublin. Misheloff's usual route took her from the school, down Amador Valley Boulevard, toward Mape Park. Someone saw her pass the Fosters Freeze around 3:10 P.M. Then she moved off toward a ditch that ran along the edge of Mape Park, out of the witness's line of sight. Somewhere in the maze of ditches, she passed out of sight and simply disappeared.

By 6:00 P.M., Ilene Misheloff's mother was frantic and phoned the Dublin Police Department. It was not like Ilene to miss an appointment and not tell anyone where she was. There was little hesitation between the phone call and response. Michaela Garecht, who had been kidnapped in nearby Hayward, was still very fresh in all local police departments' minds. Before long, Dublin patrol units were enhanced by units from the Alameda County Sheriff's Office (ACSO). Officers spread out, in patrol cars and on foot, to look for the missing girl. And as in the Jaycee Lee Dugard case, two years later, mounted sheriff's patrol set off on horseback to scour the hills behind Dublin.

Ilene Misheloff's father, just like Ilene's mother, was frantic with worry. He soon told a *Tri-Valley Herald* reporter, "I searched the creek behind the house. I kept it up until the batteries in the flashlight were completely discharged. I was just frantic afterward and it's been a long, frightening night."

There were many more long, frightening nights to follow. As in Michaela Garecht's case, all the leads and tips went nowhere. Months turned into years, and by 2009, Ilene Misheloff still had not been found.

Regarding the present search of the Garrido and Damon Robinson properties, Detective von Savoye said, "It's a very large piece of property. There are a lot of things on the property to go through. It is equivalent to looking for evidence in a landfill."

Asked if the Garridos were "suspects" in the case, von Savoye replied, "We've not been able to eliminate them as suspects."

Soon Michaela Garecht's mother, Sharon, was on the scene. She couldn't stay away with even the slim possibility of Michaela being found alive. Sharon related, "If my daughter comes home, she will be able to see in so many places that we love her. We've been looking for her so many years now, and she'll be able to see on my Web page, on my blog, very clearly that we never stopped loving her."

Michaela's father, Rod, couldn't stand going to Walnut Avenue, however. Instead, he contacted a reporter and said, "I have a hard time putting it into words. I'd like closure one way or the other. Whether my daughter is dead or alive, whether he did it or not, at least this is getting publicity out on my daughter's case."

The next day, the search on the properties was just as intense, if not more so. Reporters watched a stream of investigators coming and going from the two properties as they sought any shade they could find on a very hot day. Some reporters spent the time between press conferences talking to the Garridos' neighbors who were still willing to talk to them. By this point, there were many on Walnut Avenue who only wanted the media circus and police presence to end.

At least this time, there was not a stream of curious sightseers going up and down the street. No one got onto Walnut Avenue from Viera Lane without a press pass, law enforcement identification, or proof that they lived on Walnut Avenue. Every press conference, usually two per day, brought a throng of reporters to the edge of the yellow tape that sealed them off from the Garrido home and Robinson property. And a great deal of their interest focused on scent dogs, which had been brought in by the ACSO. Reporters watched from a distance as a cadaver dog and a "bone-sniffing dog" went up and down and all through the Garridos' yard and Damon Robinson's yard. ACSO spokesman J. D. Nelson told reporters, "Each dog works independently of the other. The first dog gave some tentative indications at one spot. The second dog indicated there very quickly. It showed interest there almost immediately, and was forceful." Sergeant Nelson said that particular location would soon be searched more thoroughly by investigators.

Other activity that day included the tearing down of a shed and the hauling away of one truckload of debris from the property after another. Lieutenant Chris Orrey related, "There are concrete slabs on both properties and they have been randomly placed. They have piqued our interest." And Lieutenant Kurt von Savoye added that his department had received dozens of new leads from people about Ilene Misheloff's disappearance since all the work began on Walnut Avenue.

One of the main points of interest for the media that day were photos taken by the Contra Costa County

Building Inspection Department (CCCBID). In fact, CCCBID had taken 102 images of inside the Garrido home, and the photos revealed the incredible clutter inside the house. In some rooms, it barely seemed possible that a person could move around amidst all the piles of stuff. There were dishes stacked alongside a sink, piles of boxes everywhere, mattresses and magazines and unidentifiable clutter. Almost every chair and couch had items stacked upon them. A can of pinto beans, a jar of peanut butter, and a box of crackers were placed on a microwave oven stand.

In one room, a projection screen dominated one wall, and above a computer was a sign taped to a wall proclaiming: FAITH and TRUTH. There was a photograph of Phil and Nancy in their younger years stacked against the leg of a table, surrounded by incredible clutter. This appeared to be the photo of Phil and Nancy when they got married in Leavenworth Penitentiary. And there was a painting on one wall of a young blond girl. To many, it seemed like an idealized rendition of what Jaycee might have looked like at one time.

Outside in the backyard, there were more piles of boxes and scatterd items, which included a child's bicycle, a plastic white toilet, Barbie dolls, and a stuffed panda. Electrical wires snaked across the backyard and over the tall wooden fence to the secret compound beyond. So did a garden hose, amidst tall grass, weeds, and abandoned piles of junk.

The building inspectors wrote up a list of violations on the property: *Hazardous wiring used for occupancy, piles of garbage, refuse, discarded furniture, discarded appliances, yard cuttings, cardboard boxes and barrels, improperly stored non-operational vehicles parts, tarps, plastic and metal buckets, open septic hole and outside toilet that is not connected to a sewer or septic system.* The building inspectors slapped an UNINHABITABLE red tag on the front of the house.

Meanwhile, investigators kept hauling more and more trash out of the house and yard. Lieutenant Orrey said that ten truckloads of debris and items had been taken out in one day, after everything was looked at carefully for evidentiary value. Late in the day, Lieutenant Orrey added that the search in the interior of the Garrido home was finished, but there was still plenty to be looked for on the Garrido property and next door.

On Friday, September 18, several concrete slabs were removed from the properties. Lieutenant Orrey told reporters that as far as the Garrido house went, "We know that we may have to pull down some sheetrock and pull up some flooring. But we will probably not be tearing the entire house down." And Lieutenant von Savoye said that on Ilene Misheloff's case, "We found several items that we'd like to examine. At this point, we're unable to determine if they are directly related or not."

Ground-penetrating radar (GPR) equipment was brought in by forensic archaeologist Bill A. Silva, of BA Silva Sensing Systems. He and his crew began running the equipment over the yards, especially where the scent dogs had indicated anomalies. After working with his crews, Silva later told reporters on the street, "We did pick up an anomaly that's denser than the surrounding soil. I know that the land was an almond orchard many years ago, and what the radar was picking up could be the remains of trees."

Lieutenant Orrey also cautioned about the anomalies in the ground. She related, "Obviously they are of interest to us, but it could be nothing. There's a lot of things it could possibly be." And then Orrey said that another bone had been found on the Garrido property, but it was too early to tell if it was human or animal.

CHAPTER 30

"MY HOPE IS STILL ALIVE."

Of course, one of the people most interested and concerned about the bones was Michaela Garecht's mother, Sharon. She said at a press conference on Walnut Avenue, "As much as I hope, as much as I believe, I do realize . . ." Then her voice trailed off. When she began again, Sharon said, "For her to be found alive and come home would be so good. It would be too good to be true." Sharon also said that it alarmed her that Michaela might have been killed recently enough so that a cadaver dog could have picked up her scent. "I guess I always thought that if Michaela had died, it would have happened soon after she was taken. She would've spent the last twenty years in peace."

Peace of mind was hard for anyone to get on the Michaela Garecht case, and that included her friend Katrina "Trina" Rodriguez. Katrina, of course, had been at the store with Michaela on November 19, 1988, and witnessed Michaela being kidnapped. Even now the memory was still raw and painful for Katrina.

She told a reporter for the *San Francisco Chronicle,* "I looked up when I heard her scream. I saw a man putting her into his car. She was still screaming. I just stood there and watched, frozen and in shock."

Katrina was now also on Walnut Avenue, watching all the investigators' activity. She said that she had looked at photos of Phil Garrido from that era, and said there was a similarity to the man she had seen kidnapping her friend Michaela. Katrina related, "Michaela's abductor was tall and slender, like Garrido. He drove a car that was similar in shape, though different in color. I really thought that of all the pictures I've seen, at least recently, he looks more like the kidnapper than anyone else. I think there's good cause to look at him as a suspect."

Katrina spoke to the reporter about how the kidnapping had made a major impact on her life. Her parents stopped allowing her to be home alone as a child in the afternoon, instead putting her into after-school care. Three years later, her parents divorced, in part from the trauma in the wake of the kidnapping. Katrina eventually became a youth minister at a church, to try and help children with problems. She said that she couldn't watch any movies about kidnappings or psychopaths. She was very emotional all the time, and cried easily. "All of this made me grow up faster, and left a hole in my heart. I feel so sad that Michaela hasn't had the experiences I've been able to have. I was able to go to college, get married, have kids, have a normal life. I'm always going to be more overprotective than other moms, and a little more afraid of the dark. But compared to what Michaela had, I'm blessed."

The parents of Ilene Misheloff were also very interested in all the activity of investigators on Walnut Avenue. About Jaycee, Ilene's father, Mike, said, "It just goes to show that good things can happen. Miracles do happen." And Mike pointed out a report by the

National Center for Missing & Exploited Children. "About sixty percent of the children who are abducted the way Jaycee, Ilene, and Michaela were—stereotypical kidnappings by strangers who do not plan to return them—are found alive." These were scenarios where kidnappers planned to raise the children as their own, not to murder them right away. Of course, this was using a premise that Michaela Garecht and Ilene Misheloff fell into the same category as Jaycee Dugard.

Not only debris was removed from the Garrido property, but a number of animals were taken away as well. These included five shorthair cats, a Labrador mix, a Rottweiler mix, three cockatiels, a pigeon, and a mouse. All of the animals had been part of Jaycee, Angel, and Starlit's lives. Animal services lieutenant Nancy Anderson said that all the animals were in good health. "They are doing really well. Really friendly and well-taken care of. The cats are really sweet."

And Anderson said that Jaycee and her daughters would like to have the animals back. For Jaycee's daughters, especially, it would help link them to a life they were used to and lessen the impact of being uprooted. For the daughters, the backyard compound was the only life they had ever known.

By now, there were seventy law enforcement investigators going over the two properties. More ground was being cleared to help scent dogs when they returned for another round of sniffing for evidence. And it was reported that one more human bone had been found on the Garrido property when debris was being cleared away. The proceedings were intense on Friday, since most of the investigators were going to be given the weekend off. It was a chance to give them some rest and also cut down on the huge expenses that were being incurred from all the overtime pay. ACSO sergeant J. D. Nelson said that only a skeleton crew would be working on the properties over the weekend.

Lieutenant Orrey added, "It's not just about the money. We have a lot of worn-out people who have really worked hard for four days in a row under really hot, dirty, dusty, labor-intensive conditions. On Monday, they can come back fresh and do this better."

There wasn't much activity on the properties over the weekend, and little news as well. But archeologist Bill A. Silva did relate, "I was up until one-thirty last night processing the data. There's a set way of doing it. I'm using three-dimensional software called GPR slides that will allow me to create 3-D images and then slice down into it so that I can look layer by layer to determine exactly what it is. One of the things I stress is the use of multiple technologies. They see similar things, but different aspects of those things."

Silva added that a magnetometer recorded a location and looked for organic material that filled a pit. If something of interest showed up there, then scent dogs would be brought back to that location. Silva related that scent dogs were best for that type of work instead of electronic and mechanical devices. He also said that there was still a lot of ground to cover on both properties.

During the "downtime," Lisa Campbell was honored in her own ceremony in San Ramon, where she lived. Attended by police officers, UC Berkeley PD personnel, and city council members, Congressman Jerry McNerney told the gathering, "This is a true occasion of heroism. It just took the intuition of one officer to recognize that something didn't look right. That's the essence of good police work, in my opinion."

Contra Costa County supervisor Mary Piepho called Campbell's contribution to Jaycee's discovery "profound."

"That little voice in the back of your head—you acted upon it. And because of it, so many lives have been changed forever. Just that little action changed the world forever."

San Ramon mayor H. Abram Wilson presented Lisa with flowers and a plaque. Wilson said, "We're just so happy that you chose San Ramon as your home."

Obviously touched by all the attention, Campbell replied, "It was a collaboration of great police work that enabled us to accomplish something [that] we had no idea would be so monumental."

Also over the weekend, reporters learned from Lieutenant Orrey that investigators from Hayward and Dublin had not directly spoken with Jaycee Dugard about their cases. Orrey related, "She's not saying anything that helps us solve our case. I just know that there's nothing definitive in our case."

Also, over the weekend, Kevin Fagan, a reporter for the *San Francisco Chronicle,* spoke once again with Kathy Russo, who lived a few doors down from the Garrido home. It was Russo's niece, fifteen-year-old Lisa Norrell, who had been a focus of the initial round of investigation into possible links with Phillip Garrido. Fagan wanted to know what Russo's reaction had been to the second round of frenzied activity on Walnut Avenue. During the first round, reporters had constantly been seeking interviews with Russo. That was not the case now.

Russo told Fagan that as awful as it would have been, had Phil Garrido been tied to the murder of Lisa, it would have been preferable to the situation as it stood. Russo said, "People just can't realize how hard it is never knowing. The pain never goes away. We've always hoped for something, but after all those years you just kind of give up. Then two weeks ago, it was hopeful, but hard when all this came up. Now, it's back to square one."

Russo and her family were very happy for Jaycee and her family, but she added, "We would just like to have some resolution of our own, too." Then she gazed at a photo of Lisa and said, "She was such a wonderful girl. It's such a shame. Such a shame."

As a reminder to reporters about Lisa, Russo kept a sign on her front yard's chain-link fence. The sign stated that there was a reward for $60,000 in Lisa's case if her killer was arrested and convicted. Most of the reporters passed by with barely a glance at the sign. All the attention was now on the Michaela Garecht and Ilene Misheloff cases.

Down the street at the Garrido property over the weekend, the Contra Costa County Fire Protection District poured 3,600 gallons of water to help the scent dogs when they came back and also to keep the dust down for the work crews. There was some GPR scanning and a skeleton crew cleaned more debris from the area. However, compared to the frenzied activity of seventy investigators and officers earlier in the week, it was quiet and calm by comparison.

When the investigators did come back to the properties on Walnut Avenue on Monday, September 21, Lieutenant Orrey said that they would be concentrating on one particular area. Orrey stated, "One of the search dogs did alert to an area where another search dog alerted previously. Now we basically have to see what they're alerting to. Today we're going to be briefed by Bill Silva from his analysis over the weekend. There's a small section where he needs to finish the GPR scanning, and by the afternoon, we estimate we will begin digging the one area of interest."

Asked when the investigation on Walnut Avenue could end, Orrey said that Monday's search was crucial. "It really depends on what we find when we start digging today. If we don't find anything of significance, we hope to wrap up the operation tomorrow. The goal is to search the property as thoroughly as possible."

Later in the day, Orrey reported that some bones were found, but they were very, very old, and probably animal bones. And Orrey added, "No evidence has yet turned up about either Michaela Garecht or Ilene Misheloff. We're really at a tough point, where if we do find something, it will be some type of tragic ending."

During all the digging and searching on Monday, Michaela Garecht's mother came out to the area once again. She presented the investigators with a hand-made thank-you note. Then Sharon said to the media, "I'm just hoping someone will give us the answers we need to end this. I felt nauseous at one point, because I thought of what might be found. A friend asked if I was nervous about going there if authorities found something. I said they didn't have to worry. I have plenty of loving arms around me."

In the end, after all the renewed frenzied activity on the Garrido and Robinson properties, no new significant clues about Michaela Garecht or Ilene Misheloff surfaced. At Tuesday's noon news conference, Lieutenant Orrey told reporters that another bone had been discovered, but it was very old. Some teeth were also found, but the teeth were determined to be from an animal.

Orrey related that search crews were now packing up and about ready to leave. She stated, "We will walk away from these properties knowing we left no stone unturned." Both Orrey and von Savoye added that now it was time to sift through all the items that had been taken from the properties to see if there was anything significant to their cases. They also said at that point that Phil and Nancy Garrido had not been eliminated as suspects in their cases.

For Michaela Garecht's mother, it was a bittersweet moment. She thanked police agencies for their efforts, but said she was glad they had been unsuccessful in finding Michaela's remains. Sharon told reporters, "My hope is still alive. I can't help but feel relieved they didn't find anything here. I'm still hoping to find Michaela alive."

In the end, after a week of intense searching, the investigators did not find any evidence linked to Michaela Garecht, Ilene Misheloff, or any other missing girl. The discovered bones were either very old human bones or animal bones. Most of the ground anomalies were only holes filled with concrete or chunks of debris. Damon Robinson was allowed to return to his home, and the mob of reporters once again disappeared from Walnut Avenue. The residents of the area heaved a collective sigh of relief. They had weathered a "second invasion," and it was finally over. Most of the activity surrounding the Garridos was now shifting to Placerville and the arena of the court.

And not unlike the scene at Walnut Avenue, there were still plenty of new twists and turns in the drama that surrounded the case. Now it was learned that Jaycee Lee Dugard's biological father was trying to become part of her life, and he had just retained one of America's most famous lawyers to represent him in that quest: Gloria Allred.

CHAPTER 31

"I'M SO HAPPY!"

As early as August 27, 2009, there had been reports that Ken Slayton, sixty-three, was the biological father of Jaycee Lee Dugard. Then on September 25, 2009, there was no doubt about it. Slayton sat down with his lawyer, Gloria Allred, and held a video news conference. Slayton said that he, his wife, and his children were ready to add Jaycee and her daughters to their family. Ken admitted that he had dated Terry Probyn in 1979, and she became pregnant. He claimed that after that, he lost track of her when a baby was born, who turned out to be Jaycee.

Slayton stated that he had been informed by the FBI in 1991 that a daughter he had never met had been kidnapped, and she was named Jaycee Lee Dugard. Ken said, "I've had nightmares over the years wishing there was more I could have done to help Terry and Jaycee. Now that Jaycee has been found, I want her to know that our hearts are open to her, and we long to be the loving, supportive, and normal family to her and her children that she has not had for eighteen years. We love you, Jaycee, and wait for your call. And we would like to meet you in person, hopefully very soon."

This latest twist in the dynamics of all these family relations had many people puzzled and others skeptical. In a poll of viewers, Bay Area KRON television station posted some of their comments. One person stated, "Please give this girl some space. She needs to get her mental state in order for herself and her family first." Another person commented, "It is unfortunate Mr. Slayton went in front of television cameras with Gloria Allred. His motives may be pure, but given the manner that he made his request public, he seems like a guy who wants his fifteen minutes of fame in the spotlight. He could have contacted the family privately and without Allred—who is also in search of a TV camera."

The most important comment came from Erika Schulte, who was by now spokeswoman for the Dugard family. Schulte said that Slayton's remarks "came as a big surprise." Schulte added that neither Ken Slayton nor Gloria Allred had invited Jaycee or her family to the press conference or provided them with copies of their statements. Schulte said that the Dugards were in seclusion without a television, and may not have been aware of this latest turn of events.

Whatever Ken Slayton's motives, more interest was shown by the media about Jaycee and her daughters when McGregor Scott, a former U.S. attorney from Sacramento, gave out the first details of what life was like for them since they resurfaced from the Garrido compound. Scott and his law firm had agreed to donate their services to Dugard to help with a myriad of issues including how to handle all the media attention. McGregor Scott had been a DDA in Contra Costa County from 1989 to 1997. From 1997 to 2003, he had been the DA of Shasta County. And from 2003 to

2009, he was the U.S. attorney for the Eastern District of California. Now he was in private practice in Sacramento, and mainly focused on white-collar crime and corporate investigations.

In a press conference on September 24, 2009, Scott related that he had recently met twice with Jaycee, her daughters, and Jaycee's mom, Terry. Scott said that Jaycee and daughters were receiving top-notch medical care and therapy. They were also taking care of practical matters, such as obtaining birth certificates for the girls and setting up a trust fund for donations that were coming in.

Scott said, "They're doing remarkably well, under the circumstances. When I met with them last week, I was very pleasantly surprised by what I saw. And when I saw them this week, it was even better. It's a very encouraging set of circumstances. The girls are getting tutoring and Jaycee's observing that. You have to remember that Jaycee only has a fifth-grade formal education. She very much has a brain she wants to develop."

Scott added, "Jaycee has conflicting emotions about the arrest of her alleged captors, Phillip and Nancy Garrido. There's no question she knows terrible and wrong things were done to her, and that the people who did those things must be held accountable by the authorities. Therefore, she is cooperating fully with law enforcement in their investigation. She understands and appreciates that she will testify at a trial." Then Scott added, "It's a very sordid tale."

As far as keeping Jaycee and her daughters secluded, Scott related, "There are a lot of people in law enforcement and elsewhere who've been working very hard to maintain that privacy, and it continues as we speak. They just need to be left alone right now, but it's a struggle. So far, law enforcement have done a very nice job of balancing the demands of their investigation with Jaycee's need for space and privacy."

As to law enforcement and the courts having failed Jaycee for so many years, Scott said, "I've spent two decades of my life in law enforcement in this state and we failed Jaycee Dugard and her family." And Scott added that a miracle had happened, and Jaycee and Terry wanted the focus to be on helping other families with missing children. Terry had a written statement thanking everyone for their well wishes for Jaycee and the girls. Asked about Ken Slayton wanting to meet with Jaycee, her daughters, and Terry, Scott would not comment about that at all.

In the arena of court proceedings, Phil Garrido's lawyer, Susan Gellman, showed just how seriously she took her job. In an "Informal Request for Discovery," Gellman addressed the judge by stating she wanted the names and addresses of people the prosecutor intended to call as witnesses. She also wanted all relevant statements made by the defendant. In addition, she wanted all relevant documents on any items seized concerning Phil Garrido and "the existence of a felony or moral turpitude" of any material witness. Other items included all photos taken by law enforcement; statements made by Phil Garrido regarding the case; any documents relating to physical examinations of Phil; and any reports about substances taken from him, including blood, hair, tissue, and urine. In fact, the list went on and on, up to thirty-seven different topics.

Stories about Jaycee Lee Dugard continued to make news that autumn, even when all the frenzied activity on Walnut Avenue had ceased. The *National Enquirer* supposedly scooped everyone else when they ran a photo purportedly to be that of an adult Jaycee Dugard on their front cover. The *Enquirer* had surmised that a photo of a blond young woman on one of Phil Garrido's business cards was that of Jaycee. The photo depicted a very pretty blond woman in her twenties, wearing a jean jacket. The *Enquirer* caption stated, *The striking blonde pictured on the back of it was introduced to barber Thompson as Garrido's daughter Alissa.* Thompson was Wayne Thompson, owner of Wayne's Barbershop in Pittsburg.

Thompson's own comments were that "I gave the card to the *Enquirer* for free. I was told it was her (Jaycee/Alyssa) by Phillip. He said he put his daughter's picture on the card to show what he could do with photos."

The photo definitely appeared to be what Jaycee might look like as a woman in her middle twenties. But family spokesperson Erika Schulte remarked, "Either it's inaccurate or, if it was her, you'd be identifying a victim of a sex crime against her wishes. I think it's horrendously irresponsible to run something like that."

And Ben Daughdrill, of Oakley, who had been a customer of Phil's business card establishment said about the photo being Jaycee/Alyssa: "It's not even close! I'm positive that's not her. No way!"

In the end, Daughdrill was proven to be right. Within a short period of time, *People* magazine had a photo of the "real" adult Jaycee Lee Dugard on its front cover, and she looked nothing like the blonde on the business card. In fact, Jaycee was now a very pretty brunette with the same smile she had shown as an eleven-year-old girl. Along with the front cover photo were more photos in the magazine and an extensive article about Jaycee and her new family life. In large letters on the magazine cover was a quote by Jaycee: "I'm so happy to be back."

The article began by stating: *At age 29, most young women are happy to be out on their own, free of their parents. Jaycee Dugard and her mother, Terry Probyn, see things a little differently.* Jaycee related that she wanted to live with Terry for the foreseeable future, and Terry was thrilled with that. Terry still had to pinch herself, as if all of this was a dream from which she might wake up.

The *People* magazine photographer apparently did not interview Terry, Jaycee, and Jaycee's half sister, Shayna. Instead, Jaycee gave a written statement to be published. In it, she wrote, *I'm so happy to be back with my family. Nothing is more important than the unconditional love and support I have from them.*

The article noted that no one knew how long and hard the recovery for Jaycee would be. But it related that the photos of a smiling, healthy Jaycee was testament of a good start. No photos were taken of Angel or Starlit, but family spokesperson Erika Schulte said, "They're focused on being a family." And as to the Northern California location where they were staying, Schulte said, "It's a very secluded existence right now by design. They're not hiding. They're enjoying their privacy. They occupy their time with catching up, reading, and cooking."

Terry did pass on that Jaycee made salsa, beans and rice, and the dish was very good. And under the circumstances, Terry said that life was moving along in a very "normal" fashion. And Terry's stepmother, Joan Curry, related that Terry, Jaycee, and Shayna all knew of the struggles that lay in the future. Obviously, Jaycee had been impregnated at a very young age by her captor, and Phil Garrido was the father of her children, Angel and Starlit. Curry related, "Jaycee is realistic." McGregor Scott added, "She knows this is not going to be the easiest road that she's ever traveled, but she is just very upbeat, giddy that's she's with her family. She smiles a lot."

Another revelation was that Jaycee's therapy included horseback riding, which she loved. Jaycee, Shayna, their mom, and the therapist all went for horseback rides in the secluded locale where Jaycee was staying. Of this, Schulte said, "Horse therapy is part of the reunification therapy they're going through. Jaycee and the girls really love riding horses."

From the photos, it could be determined that Jaycee and her daughters were now in a semirural area, somewhat like the landscape they had been used to for so long on Walnut Avenue. The big difference now was that they weren't being kept in a series of tents and sheds behind a high fence, and the area was much more upscale than Walnut Avenue had been.

Another issue addressed in the article was about Angel and Starlit's lack of formal education. What was amazing, according to Joan Curry, was that tests proved that Angel functioned at the level of a high-school senior. She had been taught by Jaycee, who only had a fifth-grade education. Curry related that "Both girls are very bright." And McGregor Scott added that the girls were now being tutored in math and English for their grade equivalents.

There didn't seem to be a timetable on therapy concerning Jaycee and the girls. Joan likened it to an adopted child being introduced to her birth parents. And Schulte noted that Jaycee didn't seem to want to dwell on the past. She was more excited about what the future held for herself and her daughters.

A new revelation popped up in the article as well. Ten months after Jaycee disappeared from South Lake Tahoe, a person living in Oakley now claimed that they had seen her at a gas station in the Oakley area, not far from Walnut Avenue in the early 1990s. In fact, the girl he had seen had gotten out of vehicle and stared at a poster of Jaycee Dugard. If it was really her, she was staring at a poster of herself. A detective asked Jaycee if she recalled this incident, but she could not remember it.

CHAPTER 32

A SCATHING INDICTMENT

One revelation quickly followed another in the fall of 2009. In the early part of November, the California Department of Corrections and Rehabilitation released a report titled, "The Supervision of Parolee Phillip Garrido." It was a scathing indictment of all the missed opportunities concerning Jaycee Lee Dugard and the lax supervision of Phil Garrido.

In a cover letter at the beginning of the report, Inspector General David Shaw related, *The special report concludes that the department repeatedly failed to properly classify and supervise parolee Garrido during the decade it supervised him. Throughout the course of its supervision of Garrido, we found the department missed numerous opportunities to discover Garrido's victims, who Garrido held captive in a concealed compound at the back of his residence. We discovered that the department also failed to properly supervise and train its parole agents responsible for Garrido.*

The report was forty pages in length and started out by giving a summary of Phil Garrido's kidnapping and rape of Katie Callaway and his incarceration in federal

prison and then Nevada state prison. It noted that
Garrido had received a fifty-year sentence, but only
served eleven years in federal prison. Nevada only held
Phil for seven months and then paroled him to his
mother's house on Walnut Avenue, near Antioch. Phil
was still on federal parole, and later Nevada parole
there, until June 1999, when the supervision went over
to the state of California.

And then in a scathing aside, the special report
stated that on August 27, 2009, the day after the arrest
of Phil and Nancy Garrido, a department official actually praised the parole agents who had supervised Phil.
The special report noted that the actual supervision of
Phil Garrido had been lax to nonexistent.

Next in the report was a short timeline of the abduction of Jaycee Lee Dugard in Lake Tahoe and the incident at UC Berkeley where Phil Garrido's elaborate
deceptions began to unravel. The report went on to
tell of the initial visit by parole agents to the Garrido
home on August 25, 2009, and the subsequent details
of the Garridos the next day at the Concord Parole
Office, where the truth was finally learned about the
Garridos and Jaycee Lee Dugard.

Next in the report was a series of aerial photographs
of the neighborhood on Walnut Avenue, the Garrido
home, and the backyard, in what was termed "the concealed compound." This was followed by a lengthy
discussion of "Parole Agents' Tools for Supervising
Parolees." Among these were GPS monitoring devices,
which the registered sex offenders had to wear
around their ankles. This was because of Proposition
83 (Jessica's Law), which California voters had passed
in November 2006.

The department required Phil Garrido to start
wearing his GPS device in April 2008. Through the use
of satellite technology, the GPS device transmitted a

parolee's location, speed of movement, and direction
of travel to a receiver monitored by the department.
The department also had three levels of supervision:
high control, the most intensive level of supervision
for those with the highest risk of reoffending; mid-level
control, for parolees with average risk of reoffending;
and minimum control for those with the least risk of
reoffending.

Discussing various reports connected to Phil Garrido, the special report noted that for the 123 months
that the department had jurisdiction over Phil, the ad-
ministrator found that there were only twelve months
of satisfactory supervision. In fact, the report stated
that from the very beginning, the supervision of Phil
Garrido had been inadequate. A parole agent had not
conducted a visit of the residence where Phil and
Nancy were staying in the first month that control of
him was passed from Nevada to California. This was
something that was required by the department. In
fact, a parole officer did not visit the house until nearly
a year later. There were no visits at all to the Garrido
residence between June 2001 and July 2002; and between June 2004 and August 2005, a parole agent only
visited once.

As far back as Phil's initial contact with the California department, there had been problems. Part of
the problem stemmed from the movement of Phil
between federal parole supervision, Nevada parole
supervision, and into California parole supervision.
In the space of a few months, Phil passed from one to
another.

And through a further "screwup" at the California
department, Phil Garrido was assigned to a minimum
level of supervision rather than the high-control status
he should have had. Between November 1999 and May
2000, when he should have been supervised under a

high-control status, Phil only went to the parole office on three occasions, submitted five brief monthly reports, and made one phone call. No agent personally visited him or his residence.

It didn't even occur to the California parole agents until May 2000 that Phil Garrido was a sex offender and should be supervised at a higher level. And it was then that they began requiring Phil to take drug tests, as he should have been doing all along. And one small item popped up in the report that should have been a red flag to parole agents if they had known about it. (And there is speculation this information was never passed down from the Feds to the state of California.) A paragraph stated, *In the federal file was information regarding a federal agent's search of the soundproof recording studio that Garrido maintained in the back of his residence.* The studio was, in fact, located in the concealed compound, where Phil had raped and kept Jaycee Lee Dugard. Information from the federal agency would have alerted parole agents that Phil Garrido's yard extended beyond the backyard fence that they saw.

In January 2001, Phil's California parole agent completed a "Sex Offender Risk Assessment" to evaluate Phil's level of becoming a repeat offender. Unfortunately, based only on documents that the parole agent saw, he rated Garrido as a low-risk offender. The description that the parole agent gave of the situation: *(His) offending sexually is more opportunistic or situational than a primary deviant sexual orientation. These cases can be reasonably handled on a control service caseload.*

The special report now noted that Phil Garrido's controlling offense was clearly sexual in nature and not just opportunistic. He had kidnapped and raped Katie Callaway over a six-hour period. The special report related that Phil had shown premeditation by placing a leather strap around Katie Callaway's neck.

He had taken her on an hour-long ride to a storage shed, where he had drugs, a bed, and sex-related devices. That information was available to parole agents and should have been used to evaluate Phil's risk assessment.

The report went on to say that if Phil had been classified as a high-risk offender—as he should have been—his activities would have been watched more closely. In June 2006, the department implemented a new assessment tool, STATIC 99, which was designed to estimate the probability of sexual and violent recidivism among adult males who had been convicted of at least one crime. This tool was only used on those who were in prison and about to be paroled, rather than people like Phil Garrido who were already out on parole.

The special report added that in July 2009, just one month before Phil's arrest, a parole supervisor completing a case review on Phil requested that a STATIC 99 assessment be made of Phil. But it wasn't until September 17, 2009, three weeks after Phil's arrest, that the STATIC 99 assessment was done. This assessment correctly identified him as a high-risk offender. Of course, by that time, it was a moot point.

The report noted that on at least ten occasions, the parole supervisors had not performed the mandated reviews. In fact, between April 2001 and October 2003, no reviews were done at all. And just as bad were fifteen instances when parole supervisors completed the case reviews, but they failed to identify and correct obvious deficiencies in the manner that parole agents handled Phil's case.

Phil was supposed to have regular mental-health assessments, but this never happened from 1999 until October 2007. It was only then that a parole agent recommended that Phil see a psychologist at the Parole Outpatient Clinic.

Incredibly, on four different occasions, the California department recommended to Nevada to discharge Phil Garrido from parole altogether. These occurred in November 1999, July 2004, December 2005, and April 2008. The special report stated that California parole supervisors concurred with a parole agent's recommendation for discharge. It was Nevada that insisted upon Phil Garrido staying under parole supervision. If California's standard had been used, Phil would have been released from supervision after three years. In other words, when Phil Garrido went to UC Berkeley with his girls on August 25, 2009, Officer Ally Jacobs could not have gotten in touch with Phil's parole agent, because Phil wouldn't have had any by that point. It was only because of Nevada's insistence that Phil was still on parole in 2009 at all.

As far as GPS devices went, an ankle-type GPS device was not attached to Phil Garrido until April 2008. One of its uses was to monitor if Phil traveled more than twenty-five miles from his residence without prior approval. Even with this device on his ankle, the parole agent did not properly monitor it. In a thirty-two day period from July 23, 2009, to August 23, 2009, Phil traveled to Berkeley, Oakland, and San Francisco, well outside the twenty-five-mile range. Between April 2008 and June 2009, the GPS device proved that Phil left his residence fourteen times after curfew; something that was not allowed. In a vast understatement, the report noted, *Ignoring the alerts generated by the system defeats the purpose of this tool.*

One of the most glaring omissions about the GPS device was the fact that it alerted that on numerous occasions Phil had been going into his far backyard, where the secret compound was located. A curious parole agent might have wondered why Phil was going back there so often. One overhead photo of the

Garrido property in the report depicted red dots for
where Phil had been on one single day—April 15,
2008. The dots showed Phil as having gone into the
secret compound area at least thirty times. The report
added, *It should have led the parole agent to determine that
the boundaries of Garrido's backyard extended beyond what he
believed them to be.* Interestingly, the red dots also
showed up in Damon Robinson's backyard on at least
ten occasions that same day.

On top of all of this, there should have been alarm
bells going off, when between July 23, 2009, and
August 23, 2009, the department lost the GPS signal
from Phil's device almost every night for prolonged
periods of time. This loss of signals occurred up to
nine hours at a time. Signals could be lost because of
the structure of a person's home, but the department
also knew that offenders would sometimes mask the
GPS signal. The fact that the signal was being lost on
such a consistent basis should have sent up red flags to
the parole agent. And yet, even though the parole
agent learned about the loss of the signals, no action
on Phil was ever taken.

And then the special report got to a portion titled:
"The Department Missed Other Opportunities to Discover the Victims." In this section, it noted that various
parole agents had conducted at least sixty face-to-face
contacts with Phil Garrido at his home. Several photos
in the report showed visible utility lines, a coaxial
cable, and telephone lines running from Phil and
Nancy's home to a carport in the backyard. These utility lines then ran from the carport to the secret compound beyond an eight-foot-high wooden fence. All of
these lines should have sent out an alert to the agent,
and the report noted that parole agents had the right
to search Phil's property at any time without a warrant
or prior notification. Several agents had inspected the

main residence and backyard, but none ever looked over the wooden fence to see what might be back there. Of course, what was back there was the concealed compound in which Jaycee and her two daughters lived.

The report stated that the presence of the wires should have raised awareness that Phil might be engaged in some kind of illegal activity. Often utility wires indicated crimes such as electricity theft, marijuana cultivation, or a computer used for child pornography. Suspicions should have been raised because Phil was a known drug user in his past and a convicted rapist.

In this area of nonsupervision, the report noted that the department was not the only agency that came up short. In July 2008, a regional sex offender task force searched Phil's residence during a sweep of known sex offenders in the Antioch area. (The parole department was not part of that sweep.) During the July 2008 sweep, officers searched Phil's house and backyard, but not one of them looked over the eight-foot-high wooden fence toward the hidden compound.

On top of all of this, during a June 17, 2008, face-to-face visit with Phil, the parole agent went to Phil's house unannounced. Inside the house were Phil, Nancy, Phil's mother, and a "twelve-year-old female." The agent questioned about the girl, and Phil told the agent that the girl was his brother's daughter. The agent did not question Phil any further about this. Nor did the agent contact Phil's brother. If the agent had done so, he would have learned that Phil's brother did not have a daughter.

Not once did parole agents speak to any of Phil's neighbors. After the August 2009 arrest, commissioners for the report did speak with neighbors, and many of them referred to Phil Garrido as "weird Phil." The neighbors spoke of his strange behavior, and two of them said they had seen underage girls at Phil's home.

Another person the commissioners spoke with was apparently Dennis McQuaid, who told them that when he was five years old, he had spoken with a young blond girl on the Garrido property through a chicken wire fence. According to McQuaid, the girl had told him, "My name is Jaycee." McQuaid said that it was soon after that, Phil built his eight-foot-high wooden fence.

The report also noted that local law enforcement and emergency services had gone out to the Garrido residence on several occasions. In the years that Phil and Nancy had been there, there were at least thirty times that those types of agencies had arrived at the residence. Most of these had to do with Phil's aged and infirm mother. But on top of this list was the phone call from Erika Pratt on November 30, 2006, in which she said, "He has several tents in the yard with people living in them, and there are children there!" That report noted, *She was concerned because her neighbor has a sexual addiction.*

Another missed opportunity was in June 2002, when the local fire department responded to the Garrido residence because of a report that a juvenile had a shoulder injury that had occurred in a swimming pool. A parole agent could have learned of this report, because a juvenile should not have been in a swimming pool on the Garrido property at all. Obviously, there was a young person using a small plastic swimming pool in either the closer backyard or the secret compound.

Even as late as August 2009, parole agents were still botching their opportunities. When Phil Garrido took two girls to UC Berkeley, he was outside his twenty-five-mile limit. Also, these girls referred to Phil as their daddy, and he referred to them as his daughters. Each and every person who had ever been Phil's parole agent knew that he had no daughters. Even with all of this, the parole agent only contacted Phil Garrido on August 25, 2009, and told him to come to the agency in Concord the next day.

The special report emphasized that given Phil's violent criminal past and increasingly strange behavior, it wasn't unreasonable to speculate that the parole agent's lack of further investigation might have placed Jaycee, Angel, and Starlit in greater danger. It also might have prompted Phil Garrido to flee the area. The report noted that the parole agent clearly had concerns for the two girls, and the report added that it wasn't clear why the parole agent had not followed up on those concerns.

In addressing why there were so many failed opportunities, the special report stated that no parole agents ever got proper or adequate training for something like Jaycee's case. Agents were rushed through a ten-week program and then sent out into the field, where their caseloads were staggering. Even the parole academy instructors said that they gave their new agents "an overall picture of compliance," but never specifics about what they should be looking for in a case like this. And after the rushed ten-week course, there were no field-training programs as follow-ups. Often in police and sheriff's departments, there would be refresher courses and advance courses of training. This was not true with parole officers.

Near the end of the report, there was a list about "Parole Supervision, GPS Monitoring, Missed Opportunities and Training." The list was seventeen items long. At the very end, there was a list of recommendations. As far as parole supervision went, it was recommended that all sex offender parolees be correctly assessed for their risks to reoffend, and require parole agents to get information from other states and the federal government if those were applicable.

Also recommended was that there be a coordination with local law enforcement and public safety officials, such as in fire departments.

In response to the special report, Matthew Cate, the secretary of the California Department of Corrections and Rehabilitation, agreed with the recommendations and added, "It is regrettable that the victims in this case were not discovered sooner. We are committed to doing everything we can to improve our system so that high-risk parolees are more closely supervised."

CHAPTER 33

"ANY DAY I CAN SEE THAT MAN IN SHACKLES IS A GOOD DAY FOR ME."

Every week in 2009 seemed to bring some new development in the Jaycee Lee Dugard/Phil Garrido saga. From his jailhouse cell, Phil Garrido contacted KCRA's Walt Gray once again. This time, it was by letter. In the letter, Phil wrote with many misnomers and misspellings that Jaycee Dugard's "free speech rights" had been violated when she asked for a lawyer on August 26 at the Concord Parole Office. Phil probably meant her Miranda rights had been violated, not free speech. Phil wrote, *She has repeatedly been denied access to have an attorney present during questioning. Over and over she clearly expressed this request from beginning to the conclusion of questioning.*

Phil added that he wanted Walt Gray to contact Jaycee Lee Dugard and make sure her "civil rights" were being enforced. Phil also wanted Gray to take the letter to a "private attorney" for Jaycee's "best interest."

Phil noted that "her two children" witnessed Jaycee's request for a lawyer at the Concord Parole Office.

Walt Gray went to the jail in Placerville to see if Phil Garrido could explain himself more thoroughly about all of this. But Phil told the jail staff he would not meet with Gray, unless his attorney was present.

Susan Gellman was less than happy about Phil's latest letter, and she met with Walt Gray at the jail, after being informed by jail staff about all that was transpiring there. Gellman said that Phil was instructed not to speak to the media, and that she was going to emphasize that with her client once again. Then Gellman made a short comment that the case had a long way to go and she wanted it to play out in court, and not in the media.

About the media, Bill Clark, chief assistant district attorney in El Dorado County, told reporters that Phil Garrido now had access to television in jail and knew what was happening with the case. The unspoken word was—how much was Phil learning from the media, and then thinking about how best to finesse his defense and use the media in his plans?

The incident with Walt Gray had barely died down, when both Katie Callaway Hall and Ken Slayton went to the Placerville Courthouse to attend a hearing for Phil and Nancy Garrido. Katie and Ken sat next to each other in the gallery, and both glared at the Garridos as they were escorted to the jury box area by bailiffs.

After the hearing, Katie told reporters, "The same old fears came back, as I felt thirty-two years ago when he had me. It was intensely emotional. I just feel so intensely passionate about this. I'm going to make sure that man goes away forever this time."

One reporter asked if Phil had looked at her in the gallery, and Katie said, "He looked right at me, and I just glared back. I just wanted to say, 'Look at me! You know, I'm here!'"

Asked if she had a message for Jaycee Dugard, Katie replied, "Just be strong. Be strong. Try and remember that [Phillip Garrido] did something horribly wrong."

Asked if she wanted to meet Jaycee someday, Katie said that she did, and added, "I just want to give her a hug."

As far as Ken Slayton went, he was there with his lawyer, Gloria Allred. After the hearing, Slayton told reporters, "Hopefully, in a short period of time, I get to see Jaycee. I want her to know I am in support, and that the support will continue."

Soon there was another upheaval in the court proceedings. On November 5, Nancy Garrido's lawyer, Gilbert Maines, was ordered to a closed-door hearing with Judge Douglas Phimister. After the hearing, Maines was relieved by Judge Phimister of being Nancy's lawyer. Maines was allowed to appeal this removal, and another hearing on the matter was scheduled for November 30.

No reasons for the removal were given to the press, but rumors started bubbling to the surface as to the reason why. There were allegations that Maines had been at a local golf course and had too much to drink. On that occasion, Maines allegedly had told someone that he was going to make a lot of money on a book deal and television deals from Nancy Garrido being his client. This conversation was apparently overheard by someone else, and that person reported the comments to Judge Phimister.

Adding to the drama that month, Phil Garrido contacted KCRA television for the third time. This time, it was a letter "apologizing" for what had happened to

Jaycee Dugard. The letter read in part, *First off I would like to apologize to every human being for what has taken place. People all over the world are hearing testimony that through the spirit of Christ a mental process took place ending a sexual problem believed to be impossible.*

Susan Gellman, who was in St. Petersburg, Florida, when she learned about this latest letter from Phil, contacted KCRA by phone and said, "Mr. Garrido is expressing genuine remorse. He would like people to consider the fact that he's a changed man and his story is best told all at one time, instead of in pieces. He presents obvious issues concerning whether or not he is competent to be a defendant, and we are looking into that."

Gellman's last sentence was very important. She was hinting at the fact that Phil Garrido might not be competent enough to stand trial. One of the tenets of law for a defendant to stand trial is that they understand what is going on in a courtroom and be able to help their attorney in their defense. And yet, here was Phil Garrido, once again going against his own lawyer's wishes that he not contact anyone in the media.

A KCRA television reporter contacted UC Davis law professor Donna Shestowsky, who had a Ph.D. in psychology, about Phil Garrido's latest letter. Shestowsky said, "To me, this almost rises to the level of what psychologists would call a partial apology. It's almost like he's saying, 'I have a problem, and what I did was a problem.' But he's certainly not taking full responsibility for his actions."

El Dorado County DA Vern Pierson was having none of this "changed man" theory. He told reporters that Phil's latest letter was "eerily similar to those comments he made at his trial in the Katherine Callaway case and remarks he later made to a parole board. It

appears once again that Mr. Garrido seeks leniency
due to claims of religious transformation and alleged
personal change."

   Controversy and chaos always seemed to swirl at the
margins of the Jaycee Lee Dugard story. In November,
KCRA television learned that Shane Ryan, the director
of low-budget horror movies, such as *Amateur Porn Star
Killer,* wanted to make a movie about the case. Ryan
told KCRA that he wanted to focus on the relationship
between Jaycee Lee and Phil Garrido. A spokeswoman
for the Dugard family called the idea outrageous. The
spokeswoman declared, "It is exploitive, hurtful, and
breathtakingly unkind!"
   And the turmoil over what Nancy Garrido's lawyer,
Gilbert Maines, might have said at a local golf course
still roiled the waters all that autumn. More information was leaking out about this, and according to the
Contra Costa Times, Eduardo Bartolome, a bartender at
the Cold Springs Golf & Country Club, near Placerville,
was one person who supposedly heard this conversation by Maines. According to Bartolome, Maines had
two alcoholic drinks at the bar, and someone had reported that Maines "was discussing the case in detail."
Bartolome said, "Supposedly, Maines was talking to me
about a book deal or making money through some
kind of book or movie arrangement following the
trial." Bartolome swore, "No such conversation like
that took place."
   A fellow club member, Sam Cooper, signed a declaration that was similar to what Bartolome said, and
the declaration stated: *Mr. Maines came to the country
club to get away from all that.* (That meant anything to do
with the Garrido case.) Cooper went on to say that the
alleged conversation by Maines had not taken place.

In addition to these two individuals, Nancy Garrido also signed a declaration to the court: *I do not understand what is going on. I have a relationship with Mr. Maines and I know that I trust him.* She definitely did not want Gilbert Maines removed as her attorney.

Later in November, it seemed as if Nancy Garrido was going to get her wish. Maines filed an appeal with the California Third District Court of Appeal. After looking over the situation, the Third District Court of Appeal temporarily halted Judge Phimister's order to remove Maines as Nancy Garrido's lawyer.

Sam Cooper had some more things to say about the situation. Cooper related, "Some club members often asked about the case, and Maines said he couldn't discuss it. There are some members who are quite vocal about the fact they didn't think people like these (Nancy and Phil) deserved to be represented, and that anyone taking on their defense are of questionable ethical or moral standards."

And so whatever court proceedings that should have been moving forward in the cases against Phil and Nancy Garrido became bogged down in this morass of whether Gilbert Maines was going to stay on as Nancy's lawyer. While Katie Callaway Hall, Ken Slayton, and Gloria Allred watched from the gallery in a new hearing, they witnessed some very unhappy people in the courtroom. Nancy Garrido looked sullen as she sat next to her newly court-appointed lawyer, Stephen Tapson; while Gilbert Maines looked forlorn, sitting nearby. Susan Gellman appeared to be embarrassed for what was happening to her colleague, and even Tapson seemed to be uneasy in his new role. The whole court hearing was very brief, as Judge Douglas Phimister said that he couldn't proceed until a state appeals court ruled on the matter concerning

Gilbert Maines. The only one beyond the bar who seemed totally unconcerned by the proceedings was Phil Garrido. He just stared off into space, as usual.

Outside the courtroom after the short hearing, Katie Callaway Hall told reporters, "Looking at him, I saw the same creepy guy I saw so many years ago. I just want to make my presence known. Any day I can see that man in shackles is a good day for me."

Ken Slayton, standing next to Gloria Allred outside the courtroom, also made some statements. Slayton said, "It was a double whammy when I learned that I not only had a daughter, but that she had been kidnapped and was now free. I think they (Jaycee and her daughters) need a man in their lives, and I'm a good man."

Gilbert Maines, of course, had a few things to say as well outside the courtroom. He related, "I never get drunk or obnoxious and I never discuss the case when I'm drinking." And as to a rumor that was going around that Phil had gotten Nancy hooked on methamphetamines to make her compliant, Maines said that he didn't know the accuracy of that statement.

Between this and the next court hearing, Nancy's meth angle took on a life of its own. Apparently, numerous sources told CBS News that Phil had supplied Nancy with meth and "she was heavily into methamphetamine usage." A legal analyst for CBS News noted, "If her lawyers could establish that, not only did he have this sort of Svengali-type control over her, but he also increased that mind control with this heavy supply of drugs—maybe that cuts to her favor."

Other stories about the Garridos kept bubbling to the surface as well. Some local residents spoke of Phil taking Jaycee and the girls to the Antioch Public Library, to the beach, and to the park. And one persistent story had Phil and the girls trick-or-treating on one Halloween, with Phil dressed in a gorilla costume.

It wasn't until January 21, 2010, that the whole matter of who was going to be Nancy Garrido's attorney was settled. On that date, Judge Douglas Phimister announced that Gilbert Maines was permanently removed as Nancy's lawyer, and Stephen Tapson would represent her from that point forward. Judge Phimister noted an affidavit from Nancy to keep Maines as her lawyer, but Phimister asserted that it was his right, as a judge, to remove a lawyer if he thought that it was in her best interest. Since Nancy Garrido still had no bail amount set, Tapson asked for a bail amount, and received the figure of $20 million, which was very unlikely to be raised.

After the short hearing, one reporter asked Maines, "What did you do to warrant being replaced?"

Maines replied, "I defended my client, and I did it in public. From day one, you guys have vilified or crucified the defendant. I have the right to defend my client in any way I believe is best."

And it soon was apparent that Stephen Tapson was going to "defend" his client in the press as well. Tapson let it be known, "Nancy Garrido asked me to tell Jaycee and the kids she really misses them and loves them. She would obviously love to see them. I'm assuming the forces of evil won't allow that to happen."

To the remark about the "forces of evil," McGregor Scott, who had contact with Dugard and her children, had no comment.

CHAPTER 34

"THEY WERE VICTIMS."

It wasn't until late January 2010 that Angel and Starlit finally had birth certificates. Jaycee Dugard was listed as their mother, and Phillip Garrido as their father. The birth dates were set as being in August 1994 for Angel, and November 1997 for Starlit. Phil was forty-three when Angel was born, and Jaycee was fourteen. To try and put a different spin on her client and his actions, Susan Gellman wrote a document to Judge Douglas Phimister that the Garridos' property on Walnut Avenue was not a prison in its later years: *It was a family home with pets, a garden and activities they joined in together. Phillip Garrido had stopped sexual activities with Dugard sometime around the birth of the youngest daughter. The children were raised as the children of Nancy and Phillip Garrido and all five held themselves out to be a family.* Gellman added that they took vacations together, ran a family-operated business, and Angel and Starlit were homeschooled. Everyone had special names for each other.

And because of these contentions, Susan Gellman

now wanted Phil and Nancy Garrido to be able to visit each other while they were incarcerated because they were, after all, married to each other and part of a family. Gellman stated that Phil and Nancy needed to visit each other in jail to discuss the case. Gellman also noted that since their arrests in late August, Phil and Nancy had only seen each other during brief court appearances.

Gellman claimed that Phil and Nancy had the right, like any other married suspects, to see each other and work on their cases together. And then, in what would prove to be a more contentious area, Gellman noted that she was being denied access to Jaycee Lee Dugard and her daughters. These three were going to be witnesses for the prosecution, and under law, a defense lawyer had the right to interview prosecution witnesses.

Not only Susan Gellman was addressing the judge on this issue of spousal visits, but Stephen Tapson was as well. Tapson wrote a motion, "Notice of Motion for Order Safeguarding Prisoner's Constitutional Rights." In this motion, Tapson wrote, *The defendant (Nancy Garrido) will move for an order directing the Sheriff of El Dorado County to allow Nancy Garrido to do the following: Allow her the right to visit with her husband Phillip Craig Garrido.*

In even more flamboyant language, Tapson wrote in support of that motion, *I have prowled the bowels of the El Dorado County Jail at least 2,000 times since its opening in 1988. I believe the jail can provide visiting between two inmates without extreme budget problems or increased security risk.* Tapson added that on February 10, 2010, he contacted Lieutenant Pamela Lane, the commander of the El Dorado County Jail. Tapson asked that his client, Nancy Garrido, be allowed to visit her husband, Phillip Garrido. Tapson noted that Lieutenant Lane told him emphatically but politely that could not happen, and that he would be hearing from the jail's attorney about this.

Tapson maintained that the denial *has resulted in the inability of the defendant to effectively assist counsel in the preparation of a defense.* Tapson added that the refusal was against the United States Constitution.

Stephen Tapson's former clients generally gave him high marks. On an independent tracking service that dealt with lawyers nationwide, Tapson received five stars out of a possible five for trustworthiness, knowledge, and keeping the client informed. One review by a former client read, "Mr. Tapson took my case on as a public defender 32 years ago. I was looking at life in prison. Paying attention to details and presenting them to the jury the way he did, he saved my life." The client went on to write that Tapson had even delivered his closing arguments after his voice had given out. The client wrote, "He gave it his all."

The prosecution soon had its own document on these matters heading toward Judge Douglas Phimister's desk, titled "People's Opposition to Defense's Motion to Compel Discovery," and another document in opposition to visitation between Nancy and Phil Garrido. In the opposition for Susan Gellman to visit Jaycee Lee Dugard and her children, the prosecution argued that Phil only wanted to manipulate Jaycee some more by using his attorney as a tool.

The prosecutors used the name "Jane Doe" in lieu of "Jaycee Dugard," even though everyone in the world knew they were talking about Jaycee. In its document, the prosecution stated, *Part of the plan created by the defendants included a hidden backyard to conceal her, giving Jane Doe the name Alyssa, requiring Jane*

Doe and her daughters to run to the hidden backyard if anyone ever came to the door, and a cover story if ever questioned, that the daughters were hers and she was okay with them being around Phillip Garrido. The document added that there was a plan in place that if Phillip Garrido was arrested, Jane Doe was to request an attorney. This was so that Jane Doe could communicate with Phil through the attorney.

By that means, the prosecution contended Phil could still communicate with Jaycee secretly and plan a way to thwart justice. Jaycee might comply with his demands because she had been so brainwashed by Phil over the years.

The prosecutors also related that it was clear that Susan Gellman was "aggressively" trying to contact Jane Doe, even though Jane Doe did not want to communicate with her. The prosecution said that Jane Doe emphatically stated that she did not want any contact with the defendants or their attorneys.

The prosecution went on to say that Jane Doe wanted them to use "Marsy's Law" to protect her privacy. In part, Marsy's Law related that a person *be free from intimidation, harassment and abuse, throughout the criminal or juvenile justice process. To be reasonably protected from the defendant and persons acting on behalf of the defendant.*

The prosecution called it outlandish that the defense was trying to paint Phil, Nancy, Jaycee, and the children as a "family of five." Part of that portrait was contentions that all five had gone to the library, the zoo, and even trick-or-treating. The prosecution noted, *The defense utterly fails to recognize that Jane Doe and her children were not their "family" but were in fact captives— they were victims.* And the prosecution related that it was most likely because of the brainwashing that, after a point, Jaycee and the girls didn't even realize that they were captives and victims.

Next came a list of all the crimes that Phil Garrido had committed, and one new bit of information surfaced about his alleged kidnapping and rape of the fourteen-year-old girl in Antioch in 1972. The document stated, *At that preliminary hearing, the defense attorney informed the victim that he would make her look like a slut and a whore if she testified. The victim told the District Attorney she would not testify and charges were dropped.*

Another outrageous detail about Phil came to light as well, and this concerned Katie Callaway's contention that Phil Garrido had come to see her in Lake Tahoe after his release from prison. The document noted that on November 8, 1988, Phil was living at a halfway house in Oakland, California, after being released from federal and Nevada prisons. *Instead of keeping his distance from his victim, Katie Callaway, he purposefully drove to Nevada and contacted her at her place of work in a casino. He then told Katie, "I haven't had a drink in eleven years." She did not think he meant "drink" in the literal sense. What she thought he meant by that phrase was that he hadn't raped a woman in eleven years.*

Perhaps most interestingly of all, the document quoted several pages from journals that Jaycee had kept over the years while living in the secret compound. The contents of these journal pages were soon extensively quoted by the media.

On July 16, 1993, Jaycee had written, *I got a cat for my birthday from Phil and Nancy—they did something for me that no one else would do for me, they paid 200 dollars just so I could have my own kitten.* By this quote, the prosecution attempted to show how manipulated Jaycee had become. Jaycee had come to believe that no one else would have done something like that for her, not even her parents.

On September 5, 2003, Jaycee wrote in another journal, *I don't want to hurt him (Phil). Sometimes I think my very presence hurts him. . . . So how can I ever tell him how I want to be free. Free to come and go as I please. Free to say I have a family. I will never cause him pain if it's in my power to prevent it. FREE.* She had six more years to endure before she was truly free.

On July 5, 2004, Jaycee wrote in yet another journal, *It feels like I'm sinking. I'm afraid I want to control my life. . . . This is supposed to be my life to do with what I like . . . but once again he has taken it away. How many times is he allowed to take it away from me? I am afraid he doesn't see how the things he says makes me a prisoner. Why don't I have control of my life! I feel I can't even be sure my thoughts are my own.*

The document noted that even on August 26, 2009, while in the parole office in Concord, with real freedom so close at hand, Jaycee still stuck to the cover story that Phil Garrido had instructed her to use. It was only after a long period of questioning that she finally admitted that she was not Alyssa but Jaycee Lee Dugard.

The document also related that on January 28, 2010, Susan Gellman sent a letter to Jaycee's counsel. In part, Gellman wrote, *Mr. Garrido has asked me to convey that he does not harbor any ill will toward Jane Doe or the children and loves them very much.* Jaycee told someone in her camp of protectors that this mention of no ill will was just Phil trying to manipulate her again. Jaycee told that person, "I'm not following the plan." Then she said that if he was ever arrested, she was supposed to try and keep in touch with him through attorneys. The prosecution stated, *Defendant Garrido's control over Jane Doe was well-planned and powerful. He is still attempting to exert that control. It is time for the Court to put an end to those attempts to manipulate and control his victims and the court system.*

On the issue of visitation between Phil and Nancy, the

prosecution related that the El Dorado County Jail was going to come up with its own document as to why Phil and Nancy Garrido should not be allowed to have contact in the jail. The main reason was because of security. Already there had been numerous threats by other inmates to harm both Phil and Nancy, and the prosecution claimed that moving Phil and Nancy out of their cells would only heighten security risks at the jail.

Phillip and Nancy Garrido had another infamous inmate in their jail while they were incarcerated there. He was 58-year-old Joseph Nissensohn, and Nissensohn was facing the death penalty. In fact, Nissensohn's case would have been the "big case" that season in El Dorado County, had the Garridos not been arrested. Even ABC's *20/20* had shot some footage connected to the Nissensohn story.

Joe Nissensohn had murdered Sally Jo Tsaggaris in Washington State in May 1989, and been convicted of that murder in 1992. He received a twenty-five-years to life sentence, and was just about to be released from a Washington prison in 2008, when El Dorado County pressed charges against him for the murder of fifteen-year-old Kathy Graves of South Lake Tahoe in August 1989. And on top of that, Monterey County was adding two counts of first degree murder for the killings of teenagers Tammy Jarschke and Tanya Jones in 1981. In an unusual court move, all three cases would be going to trial in El Dorado County.

Joe Nissensohn had even sat in Judge Douglas Phimister's courtroom during his arraignment. He was so disruptive that Judge Phimister finally had to enter a plea of not guilty on Nissensohn's behalf. And then Nissensohn pulled out all the stops. Wanting to represent himself, he claimed that he was now a "corporation" and did not desire to do any business with the El Dorado County court system or State of California. In essence, he was saying that he was a product, not unlike Coca Cola, and would do business only with whom he wished to do business. His premise made up for in originality what it lacked in case law.

Even more incredibly, Joe's girlfriend at the time, who had witnessed two murders, later became a child protective services officer in Florida. Despite a drug-fueled cross-country trek with Joe in the late 1980s that included multiple crimes and murder, she had some-how managed to get hired by the Florida Child Welfare Services. And now, she was spilling the beans on Joe about the murders of Sally Jo Tsaggaris and Kathy Graves, as well as all his other illegal activities.

Yet, even with a case that involved four murders, rape, swingers clubs, prostitutes, heroin, and more, it was the Garridos' case that drew all the attention in El Dorado County. When Joe Nissensohn had his pre-liminary hearing in South Lake Tahoe, only two re-porters showed up to watch the proceedings. The gallery was empty except for them. The Garridos had completely stolen the spotlight from Joe Nissensohn.

All throughout this period, the media was starved for any scrap of news they could get about what was occurring with Jaycee and her daughters. In early Feb-ruary 2010, East Bay Fellowship senior associate pastor Mari Hanes spoke to a reporter from the *Contra Costa Times*. Hanes related that her church, located in the East Bay city of Danville, was helping Jaycee and her daughters in their present housing needs. According to the *Contra Costa Times*, Jaycee and the girls were in a secret location in a rural part of the East Bay, "within driving distance of Antioch." Hanes's church had a history of helping victims of human trafficking.

Hanes let it be known that her church was helping with the first year of rent for the family, but they were in dire need of financial support. Hanes related, "People think once your name is out there, you get paid. But unless you have attorneys to broker a deal for you, that's really not the case. The publicity in the *People* magazine article gave many the false impression that Jaycee had profited substantially from the story. But that's not the case."

Hanes added that the family received some money from the interview, but not nearly enough to pay for the housing or the long-term counseling that was going to be needed.

On February 26, 2010, in a court hearing, the issues of Susan Gellman contacting Jaycee Lee Dugard, and the possibility of Phil and Nancy Garrido contacting each other in jail, were addressed. Steve Tapson, for his part, stated that he didn't consider Jaycee to be part of the Garrido family, but Phil and Nancy definitely were, since they had been married for twenty-nine years by that point.

Judge Douglas Phimister took California law into account and declared, "Even prisoners have certain rights. I take umbrage with the sheriff's office that they should have no contact for security reasons. It is a judge who decides that. If Mr. and Mrs. Garrido were in the general population, they would have the right to make a telephone call." And then Judge Phimister ordered the jail to allow Nancy and Phil to have contact by phone with each other—two times for five minutes, in the next six weeks. And he also ordered that there would be an April 15 hearing to decide if they could have a face-to-face meeting.

On the issue of Susan Gellman contacting Jaycee Dugard—so that Gellman could plan her defense of Phil—Judge Phimister said that was going to be shelved for the time being. And it also came up that Jaycee's children, Angel and Starlit, should have their own lawyers. To that issue, Judge Phimister noted, "Sometimes teenage daughters become recalcitrant with their mothers because of a different view on dating, lipstick, and issues of importance. All I want is for the children to be able to talk to their lawyers over the evidence that involves them."

To that end, Phimister appointed a lawyer for each girl, Roger Runkle and Abigail Roseman, and said that should they be willing to talk to their lawyers, the information would be kept confidential and not shared with Phil or Nancy or their lawyers.

Another issue came up about a recent court filing by Susan Gellman that she wanted a psychiatric report on Phil Garrido. In it Gellman wrote, *The district attorney is making the very same mistake that parole authorities made concerning Mr. Garrido for many years. He is ignoring the signs of serious mental illness.* Gellman also claimed that Phil *has been hearing the voices of angels for years, is mentally ill and likely incompetent to stand trial.* With that declaration, Gellman left open the fact that somewhere down the line, she might either be using an insanity defense, or there might not be a trial at all, if it could be proven that Phil was not mentally competent to aid in his own defense.

Outside the courtroom after the hearing, Stephen Tapson told reporters, "People can be bonkers and still manipulate people, as in the case of my client. My question is, is he (Phil) crazy like a fox?" And all of this pointed to the route of defense that Tapson might take for Nancy Garrido. He hinted at the prospect that Nancy was also a victim of Phil, even though she never perceived it. Tapson also hinted at the prospect that Phil was still manipulating her. And as to the fact that Phil and Nancy could now contact each other by phone in jail, Tapson related, "Nancy is happier than whatever. She's excited."

As to where Susan Gellman now stood, in relation to the prosecutors, she let reporters know that she was offended by certain comments that the prosecution had recently made. In her opinion, the prosecution contended that Phil Garrido was now manipulating her as well. Gellman said that her relationship had deteriorated to the point with the DA's office where it could hamper her ability to defend her client.

Gellman related, "The district attorney has laudably claimed his right to champion the rights of the victim in this case. But he cannot do so while abandoning the truth for the sake of political grandstanding."

Gellman added that Phil had written five hundred pages to her while in jail about his "transformation." As to this transformation, Gellman related, "Mr. Garrido wrongly believes that Jane Doe (Jaycee) is part of his transformation. Mr. Garrido believes that he and Jane Doe had a plan to launch a Web site wherein Mr. Garrido's ability to speak to angels would be revealed to mankind. He remains confused as to why that has not happened. These are not factors indicating manipulation, but something else entirely. They indicate thinking that is delusional, but very real to Mr. Garrido."

The prosecutors, of course, thought just the opposite, and they cited Garrido's pattern of manipulation with the court system dating clear back to 1972. In that case and in the 1976 rape case of Katie Callaway, Phil had blamed drug use for his impaired reasoning. In effect, he said that because of the drugs, he had little, or no, concept about right and wrong.

Damage from this case spread out in all directions. More news reports cited the confusion and negligence within the parole offices, both in Nevada and in California. It wasn't until 2008 that any parole agent noted how strange Phil Garrido was becoming. In one report was a comment, *He is acting very strange, weird to say the least by ranting about God and loudly singing songs.*

And all during this time period, Phil pushed to be removed as a parolee. In April 2008, he wrote his parole agent declaring he should not to have to wear a GPS monitoring device around his ankle. The letter was so odd, it related that Phil would deliver a religious presentation that *will gain attention of the world leaders causing the state of Nevada a public and political crisis that will allow the state of California to release me.* Even with this very bizarre letter, the parole agent recommended the next day that Phil be discharged from oversight.

And it was related now, as well, that many times when parole agents came over to the house, Nancy Garrido would videotape their visits. Just what she was documenting, or why, did not come to light.

Around the time of these revelations to the press, a federal parole agent, Houston Antwine, apologized for the missed opportunities by his office and those of state offices in Phil Garrido's case. Antwine told KCRA television of Sacramento: "It's a crying shame that I couldn't have, or somebody couldn't have, identified this guy long before all this took place. I would tell Jaycee that I'm sorry that we did not discover this sooner."

CHAPTER 35

"IT'S BEEN A LONG HAUL."

Houston Antwine may have been sorry, but just an apology by that point was not going to be good enough for Jaycee and her family. By February 2010, Jaycee, Terry Probyn, Angel, and Starlit all were being represented in a lawsuit against the state of California. They had sent in forms to the Victim Compensation and Government Claims Board. No amount of damages was given at the time, but a box stating that the claims exceeded $25,000 was checked. And it came to light that the Dale Kinsella law firm, KWIKA, in Santa Monica would be representing Jaycee and the others. That law firm had clients such as Mike Tyson, Sean Connery, Jennifer Lopez, Julia Roberts, and other Hollywood celebrities.

Up until March 2010, there had only been still photographs of Jaycee and her newly reunited family in *People* magazine. But in the first week of March, ABC aired a home video of Jaycee, her mom, Terry, and her half sister, Shayna. The footage was shown in segments on several ABC shows, including *Good Morning America, 20/20,* and *Nightline.*

In the video, Jaycee and the others were making cookies in the kitchen at their secret location. Jaycee shook sprinkles onto the cookies, and everyone was smiling and joking. At one point, they all laughed as Shayna made a mistake on her cookie, and Shayna said, "I've never gotten to decorate a cookie before."

In another scene, Jaycee, Terry, and Shayna sat next to a fireplace with Christmas stockings hanging nearby. (Obviously, the scene had been shot before Christmas, 2009.) Terry said, "I'm Terry Probyn, and on behalf of my daughters, Jaycee and Shayna, and my two awesome granddaughters, we want to thank you for the love and support that you've given us these last few months. It is my desire to share our miracle with the world, but it has to be done on our terms.

"I feel like I need to set the record straight—we did accept financial support from an undisclosed benefactor and have no affiliation with any church. Please give us the time to heal as a family, without the prying eyes of the photographers and press. We released this video so that you can see that we're happy and well, and when we have more to share, we will. As a mother, I am pleading for our privacy in this very public story.

"It's a dream come true for me to have both my girls to be here with me. I'm so thankful for the precious moments that we have together. I had to wait an eternity for this reunion. I can hardly believe sometimes it's really here."

In yet another scene, Jaycee and Shayna were shown with horses, which was part of Jaycee's horse therapy. A reporter on the program stated that Jaycee was studying for her GED and hoped to attend college one day. Jaycee had already taken her first steps to reenter society.

She had obtained her driver's license and had obtained birth certificates for Angel and Starlit.

In the final segment, Jaycee sat on a porch in front of the house, wearing a baseball cap. She smiled and said, "Hi, I'm Jaycee. I want to thank you for your support, and I'm doing well. It's been a long haul, but I'm getting there."

A few days after the video ran, there was more news concerning the possible cases connected to Phil Garrido. The Reno Police Department had wrapped up its investigation into the kidnapping and murders of Jennifer and Charles Chia, who had been kidnapped one hundred yards from a bus stop near their home in the Lemmon Valley section of Reno. RPD lieutenant Mike Whan told reporters that investigators searched records on microfiche, contacted retired investigators, and sought other physical evidence, such as DNA. Lieutenant Whan related, "We were just looking for facts and everything came to a dead end. There was nothing (related to Phil Garrido)."

And as far as the case of seven-year-old Reno resident Monica DaSilva went, nothing new pointed to Phil Garrido, although there had been no similar case in Reno since the 1990 abduction of DaSilva from her bedroom. Whan said, "You get information where you think, 'This might be the one,' and you follow it until it goes nowhere, and then you start looking for another suspect."

Proceedings on the Garridos' case did move ahead at a slow pace. By April 20, Judge Douglas Phimister let it be known that he was going to allow Phil and

Nancy Garrido another set of phone calls to each other while in jail. There would be one allowed in May and another in June. In another decision, Judge Phimister blocked any contact from Phil and Nancy's lawyers directly to Jaycee or her children. Susan Gellman and Stephen Tapson, however, could contact Jaycee's lawyer. Judge Phimister also ordered that the district attorney's office hand over to the defense a videotape of Jaycee (still claiming to be Alyssa) talking to officers in Concord on August 26, 2009. But the defense attorneys would not receive any videotapes of Angel and Starlit.

By this time, Shawn Chapman Holley, an attorney from KWIKA in Southern California, was representing Jaycee and the girls. It was Holley's motion that Judge Phimister had granted. In the motion, Holley had stated, *Neither Jane Doe, Jane Doe 1 or Jane Doe 2 wishes to be represented by court-appointed counsel and I have advised them not to meet with Mr. Runkle or Ms. Roseman at any time. On each of my client's behalf, I hereby assert their Proposition 9 rights pursuant to Marsy's Law.*

After the brief court hearing, DA Vern Pierson told reporters, "We have an overwhelming volume of evidence to prove each and every charge against Phillip Garrido."

In response, Susan Gellman told the same reporters, "That's his take on the evidence."

As always, the Jaycee Lee Dugard story spread out in a myriad of directions. One of these directions was that a spokesperson for Jaycee said that Jaycee did not want to be contacted by her biological father, Ken Slayton. The spokesperson related, "Terry Probyn has never denied that Kenneth Slayton was the father. Rather, it was Mr. Slayton who showed no interest for the first twenty-nine years of his daughter's life. It is now Jaycee Dugard's turn to express her feelings, and she has no interest. She does not wish to see Mr. Slayton or his family at this time."

And so it went, with one court hearing or press release following another. After a brief court hearing on June 25, 2010, Nancy's lawyer, Stephen Tapson, had a few comments for the media outside the courtroom. Tapson stated, "A couple of shrinks I've talked to say that it may be beneficial for Jaycee and the kids to see Nancy before actually seeing her in the courtroom. A lot of people don't understand that Nancy loves those kids, and she loves Jaycee. This is a relationship born in evil—but at the end, it came down to a family relationship. And she honestly, truly misses her."

In July, an unprecedented settlement occurred in the lawsuit that Jaycee and her mother had filed against the state of California for all of the lapses in the parole agents' supervision of Phil Garrido. Retired San Francisco Superior Court judge Daniel Weinstein had acted as a mediator in the case, and in the end, the state of California agreed to pay Jaycee Dugard a $20 million settlement. Weinstein let it be known that the money would be placed into long-term investments. He added, "It was not an effort to make reparations for the years of abuse and incarceration or imprisonment against her will, because those are incalculable. Part of this was a prudent effort by the state to shut off liability from a catastrophic verdict."

The California State Legislature had to vote on the settlement. In the state senate, every senator voted for the bill except one, Senator Sam Aanestad. He told reporters, "Settlements involve large amounts of taxpayer money that the state legislature has absolutely no control over. These agreements are negotiated by government lawyers and judges, who are not looking out for the best interests of the California taxpayers."

In the state assembly, the vote was 74 to 2 in favor of the bill. One of those who voted against it was Assemblyman Joel Anderson. He stated if the case had gone to court, the details of the whole situation wouldn't have been hidden. "I'm more concerned about justice, and I'm more concerned about how we move forward in protecting children," he said.

Dale Kinsella, Jaycee's lawyer, would not comment on the settlement, and Terry Thornton, a state corrections spokesperson, had only a very brief statement in regard to it. Thornton said, "All I can confirm is the state and Jaycee Lee Dugard have agreed to settle any legal claims resulting from her alleged abduction by Phillip Garrido. The agreement will help them reunite with their family and obtain services and treatment that they need to overcome their ordeal in an environment that is free from unwanted press scrutiny."

Governor Arnold Schwarzenegger signed the bill into law on July 9, 2010. It was estimated that it could cost up to $7 million for a lifetime of therapy alone for Jaycee and her daughters. And it would cost about $450,000 to educate Jaycee and her daughters.

A *San Jose Mercury News* columnist, Patty Fisher, however, voiced an opinion that many others shared. Fisher wrote, *I wonder how this thirty-year-old woman, who grew up without a cell phone or designer jeans, will spend her new wealth? And will it buy her happiness?* Fisher noted that money could buy Jaycee a comfortable home and privacy. It could buy financial security for her children. But if Jaycee wanted her lost years back, money could never buy that.

One other disturbing report came out of the settlement. It was learned that Jaycee made a claim that one parole agent had actually spoken to her during the period she was confined on Walnut Avenue. And, of course, no action had been taken by that parole agent. Commenting on this, the attorney general's spokesperson, Christine Gasparac, said that there was no independent corroboration that a parole agent had seen or talked to Jaycee in the Garrido household. Gasparac added, "Ms. Dugard said she could provide no other details, such as when the contact with the parole agent had occurred. One of our lawyers said that it was a statement made by the plaintiff, and because the case was settled before litigation, they never have to prove it in court."

For many people, by August 2010, it was hard to believe that one year had elapsed since the incredible news that Jaycee Lee Dugard was alive and had been held captive for eighteen years in a secret backyard compound. The *Lake Tahoe News* reported that Terry Probyn had been scheduled to speak to the South Lake Tahoe Soroptimist Club. When Terry learned that a tabloid had just bought photos of Angel and Starlit, she canceled her luncheon date with the Soroptimist Club and would not make any statement at all on the anniversary date.

In light of this incident, FBI agent Chris Campion, El Dorado County Sheriff's lieutenant Les Lovell, and DA Vern Pierson spoke to a "no guest" Soroptimist luncheon in Lake Tahoe. In other words, only to people who had known and helped Terry Probyn over the years.

Speaking to the *Lake Tahoe News* a short time later after that event, Campion said, "In this particular case, I don't think it would have prevented them (Phil and Nancy Garrido) from getting out of the basin. It is a good idea to have the roadblock system in place. That is probably one thing we do better now. Even in 1991, the FBI was starting to do away with the old policy of waiting twenty-four to forty-eight hours for some kind of ransom note or call. And since Jaycee's abduction, the FBI has moved faster on child abduction cases." Campion noted that even in 1991, twenty FBI agents were on the scene within twenty-four hours.

As to the FBI's continuing presence with Jaycee and her family, Campion said, "We have an agent in the area where they are living now. The agent in the vicinity of the Dugards speaks to them weekly, if not more. We take the needs of the victims and witnesses very seriously, especially in these kinds of cases where there is uncharted territory. We don't know what their needs are going to be over the years. There are just a ton of things you don't think about."

Also on the one-year anniversary, a Dugard family spokesperson told Fox 40 News of Sacramento that Jaycee was doing well and making amazing progress in her therapy sessions. The spokesperson added, "Jaycee is writing weekly and working on her journal. She is great at writing. She has a talent for it and she wants to pursue it. She is also interested in starting a foundation for children victimized by men like Garrido."

Two of the Dugard family members, who wished to remain anonymous, spoke with Channel 10 News of Sacramento about Jaycee's new life. They said that Jaycee and her children had not barricaded themselves into another virtual compound. Instead, over the previous year, they had been to Old Sacramento, which was a reconstruction of how Sacramento was in the nineteenth century. And they had also been to amusement parks; and, in fact, Jaycee enjoyed taking road trips with her daughters after receiving her driver's license.

The family members also stated that Jaycee and her daughters spent a great deal of time with teachers working on their education over the previous year. And they also spent a lot of time with counselors in therapy. One family member told the reporter, "Jaycee is enjoying her freedom, happy and looking forward to the day she can put the trials of accused abductors Phillip and Nancy Garrido behind her."

In a sense, Walnut Avenue was also experiencing a period of calm and healing from the traumatic events of the previous year. A next-door neighbor of the Garridos, Helen Boyer, told a reporter that the Garrido property was filled with dry grass and weeds, and she was worried about fire danger. "We called them (the fire department) to come out and see if they would cut the lawn. It's a fire hazard. The weeds are way high."

Then Helen spoke of the years before all of the news had come out. "I never noticed anything odd in the whole eighteen years. I would have been the first to speak if I'd known anything was going on. I saw children on the property, but never guessed they were children of a kidnap victim. I thought they were friends of Phil and Nancy. They weren't out often. I think Nancy was under his thumb. She went around like a robot."

One year later, the city of Antioch was also trying to recover its image. Antioch resident Karen James Smith told Channel 10 News, "It was really sad for our city to have this." And Mayor protem Mary Rocha said, "We were all in shock. We couldn't believe it happened under our nose. I'm proud of our lush parks and well-kept waterfront business district. But the embarrassment of the Garrido case still makes me cringe, especially because it didn't happen within the city limits. I think

Antioch got a lot of blame that shouldn't have been put there."

As to the continued push by Antioch to bring Walnut Avenue and the small surrounding area into the city limits, Rocha said that many residents in that locale still fought annexation. Their reasoning was that they didn't want to pay for city services such as sidewalks, plumbing, and other infrastructure. But Rocha said that if Walnut Avenue had been part of Antioch years ago, it would have been the Antioch Police Department that went on calls to Phil Garrido's home, and not the Contra Costa County Sheriff's Office, which had done so in the past. And the Contra Costa County Sheriff's Office had a lot fewer officers to send there than the Antioch PD had. What especially would have come under scrutiny were all the sheds, tents, and other structures in the farthest corners of the Garridos' backyard. Antioch zoning would not have allowed such a ramshackle set of tents and sheds to have existed.

The California Department of Corrections and Rehabilitation also had something to say on the one-year anniversary of Jaycee's freedom. Spokesperson Terri McDonald related, "This department has enormous empathy for the victim. We understand the public's scrutiny and we stand up to it. I think that we continue to do better as we learn from the information. We want to reduce caseloads for agents." She added that learning lessons from the Garrido case took time, and it was all part of a natural progression of change and adaptation.

Closer to home, Contra Costa County sheriff Warren Rupf admitted that the case had been hard on the whole department. "There were mitigating circumstances, but there are no excuses. It was a failure." Rupf added that he was angry at not only the lapses in his own office, but in other law enforcement offices as well. "I'd like to find somebody in federal parole and shake 'em. And tell them how embarrassed I am for them that you're not only willing, but the system allows you to simply stand behind the curtain." In other words, the Contra Costa Sheriff's Office and California parole agents had all stood up and taken their lumps on the case, but no one at the federal level ever had done so, except for Parole Agent Antwine, and he was retired by that point. In fact, it had been the early release from federal prison for Phil Garrido that had set the whole set of circumstances in motion.

At least for things that had been done since the story broke in August 2009, Sheriff Rupf could point to many improvements in his office. Rupf said that a mantra at the sheriff's office was now, "Look into the backyard!" And the motto had paid off. In the previous month, a fourteen-year-old girl had been discovered in a motel room rented by a registered sex offender in Contra Costa County. Detective Greg Leonard related, "It quite possibly saved this girl's life."

GPS monitoring was being taken much more seriously, as well, by parole agents. Now they had to analyze all the dots from the GPS readings, and see just where the registered sex offender was going. The Fairfield office, which had monitored Phil Garrido, had scored a success with this in just the previous week. One of the parole agents nabbed a sex offender who had cut the GPS monitoring device off his ankle. The offender was caught as he was leaving on a bus for San Diego, over four hundred miles away.

In another case taking place in Concord, parole agents tracked down a parolee suspected in a recent auto theft. By using a laptop in one of their cars, they could pinpoint the location where the parolee was hiding out. With guns drawn, the agents stormed into a house and collared the suspect.

CHAPTER 36

"WHAT I HAVE WITNESSED HAS BEEN VERY TROUBLING."

It came as no surprise to many when Susan Gellman put before Judge Douglas Phimister a motion to halt further court proceedings on Phil Garrido until he was examined by a psychiatrist. In a hearing on that very issue on September 24, 2010, Gellman told Judge Phimister, "Mr. Garrido lacks the capacity to stand trial or enter a plea." Gellman told Phimister that she consistently had trouble in her meetings with Phil.

And even Judge Phimister was concerned about what he had observed of Phil Garrido in court. Phimister declared, "I've noticed Mr. Garrido looking away in court and not appearing to be listening to you when you were talking to him. And he would frantically scribble something on a yellow notepad when nothing important was happening. What I have witnessed has been very troubling."

With that in mind, Judge Phimister stopped all further court proceedings against Phil Garrido, including the upcoming preliminary hearing. The preliminary hearing was a means by which the prosecution would present witnesses, and Judge Phimister would decide if there was enough evidence to proceed to trial.

Also brought up during the September 24 hearing was the fact that the defense was awash in discovery material. There were now more than 150,000 pages of discovery documents that they had to wade through. Stephen Tapson told the judge, "They just gave me eight thousand more pages yesterday!"

After the short hearing on competency, Susan Gellman told reporters outside the courthouse, "When someone either wants to go to trial for crazy reasons or not go to trial for crazy reasons, that person is not competent. And that's what we're talking about. This is a fundamental fairness issue. I mean you saw him. It (the court proceedings) kind of didn't phase him."

Then Gellman added that the psychiatric evaluation wouldn't significantly delay the onset of a trial. She claimed, "We're talking about a time-out in the case. We're not talking about the case not going forward. I expect there to be a resolution. I'm not looking for this to last many, many years."

Which, of course, all depended on whether Phil was declared sane or insane by the psychiatrist. If he was deemed to be insane, there wouldn't be any trial for him for a long time to come. He would be sent to a psychiatric facility until the time he was found to be competent enough to stand trial.

DA Vern Pierson had a few comments of his own about whether Phil was competent or not. Pierson told reporters, "We think he is competent to stand trial. But we will defer to his attorney and the judge on this topic."

Katie Callaway Hall was by far more outspoken. She told reporters outside the courtroom, "I think that Phillip Garrido has shown extraordinary competency in the past in his ability to make a lot of people believe anything he wants them to believe. Everybody seems to be at his beck and call, from parole boards to federal officers. He was able to hide three human beings, hide their very existence, for how many years? That takes competence."

In light of all the problems that an open-court preliminary hearing would entail, the prosecution moved in a different direction on Phil and Nancy Garrido. They convened a grand jury, which behind closed doors found that there was enough evidence to bring them to trial. The grand jurors did this by listening to evidence presented by El Dorado County District Attorney's Office investigators Richard Pesce and Michael Franzen, and Contra Costa Sheriff's Office detective Garrett Schiro. They also heard testimony from one more very important person—Jaycee Lee Dugard.

Most of the counts in the indictment were the same as the charges put together in August 2009 against the Garridos, but there were a few new bits of information that surfaced. One occurred in Count IV wherein *Phillip Craig Garrido and Nancy Garrido did unlawfully have and accomplish an act of sexual intercourse with a person, to wit, Jane Doe, against the person's will, by means of force, violence, duress, menace and fear of immediate and unlawful bodily injury on said person.* In other words, Nancy Garrido was being indicted on rape charges, just as Phil was.

Count VI indicted Phil and Nancy on charges of *willfully, unlawfully, and lewdly did commit a lewd and lascivious act upon and with the body and certain parts and members thereof of Jane Doe, a child under the age of fourteen years, with the intent of arousing, appealing to, and gratifying the lust, passions, and sexual desires of the said defendant and the said child, by use of force, violence, duress, and menace.*

What was interesting about Counts X and XI, which

concerned the "Forcible Lewd Act Upon a Child," was the inclusion of the phrase *acts of substantial sexual conduct depicted on video produced/created by defendant Phillip Garrido*. This suggested that Phil Garrido had videotaped himself, at some point, having sex with underage Jaycee, and the videotape or tapes had later been discovered by investigators. It also brought up the possibility that Nancy Garrido had done the videotaping.

Later counts were basically the same as the previous counts, except each count covered a specific year, including 1994, 1995, 1996, and 1997. Count XVII concerned an indictment of false imprisonment and Count XVIII an indictment on possession of child pornography.

There were also special allegations of "two strikes" against Phil Garrido—one for the federal crime of kidnapping Katie Callaway, and the one for the Nevada crime of raping Katie Callaway.

Judge Phimister handed the indictments to Susan Gellman and Stephen Tapson, and then "sealed" them, which, in effect, meant that no one outside of grand jurors, the DA's office, and these two lawyers knew what had been said by witnesses who had testified at the grand jury hearing. Vern Pierson later told the media, "It was a better way to get a case to final conclusion and move it along to trial. It also protected the privacy of Jaycee Dugard and spared her family from having to take the witness stand until the trial."

Stephen Tapson didn't have much to say to reporters outside the courthouse, but one thing he did say was significant. Tapson related, "I heard from a (grand) juror that Dugard spent a full day before the panel and that her testimony brought many in attendance to tears."

One thing new that did come out was that the Bay

Area News Group reported *Phillip and Nancy Garrido raped Jaycee Dugard twice the day they abducted her from her South Lake Tahoe neighborhood, then repeatedly throughout her childhood years and Phillip Garrido recorded the sex acts on video through the early part of Dugard's first pregnancy at age 14, according to details in an 18-count indictment.* Just how much Nancy was involved in these rapes was not revealed. Nor did the Bay Area News Group go into more detail about how it was discovered that Phil had raped Jaycee twice on the very first day of her abduction.

The media wanted a lot more than just this scanty new revelation. They wanted the entire grand jury transcripts released to them. Six media companies— including the Bay Area News Group, The McClatchy Company, Associated Press, Hearst Corporation, Gannett Company, and *Los Angeles Times*—filed court papers asking Judge Douglas Phimister to unseal the grand jury transcripts through an attorney, Karl Olson, of San Francisco.

Olson argued that *no overriding interest overcomes the right of the public access to records. It is not enough for the defendants to argue that this case has received a lot of publicity, for if that were enough to seal records, all records would be sealed in every case that the public cared about.* Olson also argued that in a county of 180,000 people, sealing public records was not necessary because there was a large jury pool. The Garridos would receive a fair trial whether the records remained sealed or unsealed, according to Olson.

Phil and Nancy Garrido, however, were not the only ones who wanted the grand jury testimony to remain sealed. In an unusual agreement with the defense's position, DA Vern Pierson also wanted the grand jury testimony to remain sealed. He took up the defense claim that unsealing the testimony would harm the Garridos' right to a fair trial, and it would also violate Jaycee Dugard's privacy rights. Pierson wrote in his statement to the judge that *Jane Doe testified in detail about extremely private and violent sexual acts. If these transcripts are unsealed prior to trial, the details of the repeated rape of Jane Doe will be splashed all over the media. Jane Doe does not deserve this disrespect.* And then Pierson added, *The media is clearly entitled to access, just not yet.*

The unspoken word was that it would be most dangerous to Phil and Nancy Garrido. Several inmates had already made it known that given the chance, they would like to kill both Phil and Nancy.

Many of these issues were not resolved at the next court hearing on December 2, 2010. While the news organizations lawyer Karl Olson said that public scrutiny was vital in the judicial process, Susan Gellman countered, "The media does not care about a fair trial or privacy! They are about selling something."

Stephen Tapson was even more colorful in his language about releasing the grand jury transcripts to the media. Tapson proclaimed, "The thing oozes prejudice. Every page. It lays out what the victim went through in nitty-gritty detail. The public does not need to know that. I have examined hundreds of transcripts that vividly describe murder, rape, pillage, but nowhere in my experience have I seen a transcript that describes *evil*, as it is contained in the grand jury transcript in *People* versus *Garrido*." Then in his most flamboyant language, Tapson described the media as "sniffing, snarling, whining hounds."

In response, Judge Phimister said that he still had to wade through numerous documents on these matters. Then he chastised some of the media members present and called them irresponsible for disobeying his orders and broadcasting audio from an earlier court hearing. Phimister stated, "Just because [material] is true, doesn't always mean you can utilize it. There are cases in which photographs of pornography have been withheld from the public, for instance."

At the hearing, Judge Phimister also brought up the issue of Phil Garrido's mental state. Phimister said that he wanted another psychiatrist to examine Phil to see if he was malingering. In other words, Judge Phimister wanted a second expert opinion as to whether Phil Garrido was just "acting" crazy in court, or whether he really was too incompetent at present to aid in his own defense.

A third issue that Phimister addressed had even a more potentially important prospect for the trial and El Dorado County. Judge Phimister expressed concerns that the seventy thousand people in the jury pool of El Dorado County might not be large enough to seat twelve impartial jurors. The stories about Jaycee and the Garridos had been front and center in the consciousness of the citizens of El Dorado County since the news had broken in August 2009. If there were not enough impartial jurors, the case would eventually have a change of venue and be sent to another California county.

But the big news that week wasn't the court hearing. Instead, it had to do with a story just breaking on a Sacramento news station. Once again, CBS 13 had scooped the other media outlets. They had obtained jailhouse letters written by Nancy Garrido to a prison pen pal. The prison pen pal was a woman named Kathryn, whom Nancy had befriended while the woman had been in the El Dorado County Jail.

In part of one letter, Nancy wrote, *Phillip sends me Bible studies that I truly enjoy and bring me closer to our*

God. We have a great future in God's Kingdom. Phil and I don't have one in this world, but Kathryn, Phil and I keep our eyes fixed in God's Kingdom, there is where our future will be together.

The tone of the letter suggested Nancy had come to grips with her fate in jail and probably in a future that would never be outside of prison. She seemed almost upbeat and happy with her circumstances. In another letter to Kathryn, Nancy wrote, *Thank you for the card you made me. It's so beautiful. I'm not writing nothing in it. I'll send it to him. He'll love it. By the way, my birthday was 7/18. Turned the big 55. Hee Hee! I feel like 30. Honestly. I continue to exercise in my cell. You'll love Phillip as well. We're two peas in a pod.*

In another letter, Nancy wrote that she knew she was probably going to be convicted and spend the rest of her life at the women's prison in Chowchilla, California. Nancy wrote, *I'm happy to hear I'll be okay dokey* [sic] *there in Chowchilla. We adapt to any given situation. It's difficult at first, Kathryn. Our God gives me so much strength to endure my journey.*

When Stephen Tapson was asked if these letters were legitimate, he stated that they were. Tapson said, "My interpretation is that it's new characteristics that she found Jesus. There's no secrets on letters coming out of the jail. Correspondence written by jail inmates are copied by authorities."

Soon there were more letters by Nancy and Phil Garrido surfacing. Nancy wrote to Kathryn, *He (Phil) loves God so much.* Nancy then included a twelve-page letter she had received from Phil into the letter she sent to Kathryn. Phil began by pledging his "undying love" to Nancy. Then he addressed the situation they were in because of the kidnapping: *We understand and do not disagree with people's reactions or their feelings, as my past is pathetic and shameful to say the least. There is more to*

*all this than meets the public's eyes as we were standing up to
confront these problems and deliver a witness about how the
Lord provided a way out for me from these behaviors and
provided a powerful freedom that allowed me to love Nancy
as God intended. So powerful was the change that it ended
12 years ago. When this becomes public you will understand
I am telling the truth.*

The reference to twelve years ago tended to indicate
that he stopped having sex with Jaycee at that point.
Twelve years in the past would have made the date
around 1997 when Starlit was born.

Phil went on to write that he could add many more
details, but he wouldn't do so at present. Then in another eleven-page letter, Phil wrote, *God knows they all
love Him and has long been awaiting the day when he can
reveal a powerful and intelligently placed hidden disclosure
from within the scriptures. It will delight you and bring
great pleasure to your heart.* Here, Phil seemed to be
referencing the "book" he had written about schizophrenia. Then he added, *Christ Jesus came into the world
to save sinners, of whom I am the worst.*

Susan Gellman responded to the release of the
twelve-page letter from Phil Garrido by telling reporters, "This twelve-page letter written to another
inmate and having no connection with this case is yet
another example of the rambling thoughts of Mr. Garrido. He focuses on galaxies, powerful persuasions,
and voices of angels, showing yet again that he may not
be competent to be a defendant and make decisions
in his criminal case."

In yet another letter from Nancy to Kathryn, Nancy
wrote, *Miss Kathryn, I think I told you once about how
God's spirit is working with my husband, you never comment
on it. I'm not crazy, nutty.*

* * *

Two days before Christmas, 2010, DDA James Clinchard sent a motion to Judge Douglas Phimister declaring that the prosecution needed Dr. Charles Shaffer's report soon, because of the upcoming competency trial of Phillip Garrido. That trial was scheduled for February 28, 2011. On top of that, Judge Phimister had also appointed Dr. David Glassmire to evaluate Phil to make sure he wasn't malingering. In other words, acting crazy so that he could not be prosecuted.

Clinchard noted that Dr. Glassmire had interviewed and tested Phil on December 18, 2010, and the interview was audiotaped by jail personnel. Clinchard wrote, *Without notice to any parties, Judge Phimister met with defense counsel Gellman and a deputy district attorney not assigned to the Garrido case to discuss the jail audio taping issues. On December 20, 2010, the People requested the El Dorado County Jail turn over the audio recordings so that we could copy and discover the audio to the defense. Jail personnel refused this request.*

This was very unusual. Generally, jail personnel, who are part of a county's sheriff's office, adhere to what a district attorney's office tells them to do. But in this case, the jail staff and El Dorado County Sheriff's Office dug in their heels and refused to do so. Eventually Clinchard found out why. Judge Phimister had instructed the jail personnel to turn the audiotapes over to no one, pending the completion of Dr. Glassmire's full report.

Clinchard and DA Vern Pierson were very worried about that. If Dr. Glassmire finished his report by February 2, 2011, as he expected to do, then the prosecution team would have only twenty-six days to review the tapes. And during those twenty-six days, they would be tackling a thousand and one other issues, including seating a jury.

Clinchard argued that Judge Phimister's decision *deprives both the People and the defense their due process rights. The People are diligently preparing for the jury trial and need the opportunity to review the contents of the interview as quickly as possible to evaluate the need for any futher examination of the defendant and the need for additional expert witnesses.*

Judge Phimister wasn't going to be bulldozed by anyone, and on January 6, 2011, he made a ruling that the audiotapes weren't going to be turned over to anyone until Dr. Glassmire finished his full report. Phimister, however, was going to turn over the report of Dr. Charles Shaffer to the prosecution and defense.

On other issues that day, DDA Ed Knapp told the judge that "our fears have been confirmed" about Phil and Nancy Garrido abusing their phone privileges. Knapp said, "Sometime ago, when this subject came up, the jail was very concerned that contacts between codefendants in the same case are very problematical. They are able to conform their testimony, they are able to create false testimony in general."

Knapp said that was exactly what Phil and Nancy were doing in their brief phone calls to each other. Phil was giving Nancy instructions, and she seemed to be complying wholeheartedly with whatever Phil said. In essence, they were planning how to get their stories straight.

Judge Phimister looked into this and ruled that phone calls between Phil and Nancy would cease immediately. And Phimister also took up the issue that Susan Gellman was thinking of writing a motion that all trials be held somewhere else other than El Dorado County. The news about Jaycee Lee Dugard had been everywhere in the county since August 2009. Yet, there probably wasn't a county in California where the story hadn't been front-page news since those August days.

And then the *Sacramento Bee* had a short item not picked up by other news sources. The journalist wrote, *Susan Gellman noted that the prosecution has yet to turn over a surveillance tape from August 2009 taken at the University of California, Berkeley, where Garrido was spotted with Dugard.* If the *Sacramento Bee* was correct, not only had Angel and Starlit been with Phil on that campus in August 2009—so had Jaycee Lee Dugard. It was just one more glimpse of how much she was under Phil's power, when she could have simply walked up to anyone on campus and told them exactly who she was.

Chapter 37

A Sudden Reckoning

A court hearing was held on February 28, 2011, and Judge Phimister ruled that no grand jury transcripts were going to be released to the media. But that wasn't the big news that day. As often happened, the big news occurred outside the courtroom. In this instance, Stephen Tapson, Nancy's defense lawyer, started speaking off the cuff to the gathered reporters.

Tapson said, "For your information, Mr. and Mrs. Garrido have given full and complete statements to the Sheriff's Office in the last month or so. They've been honest with them, frankly in the hope of mercy from Mr. Garrido for Mrs. Garrido. Unfortunately, the quality of mercy is strained in El Dorado County.

"As of the moment, the current offer is two hundred forty-one years and eight months to life for Nancy Garrido. Based upon what I know of Nancy Garrido's relationship with Jaycee and the kids, after all the evil stuff—Jaycee, give me a call. I'd like to talk to you if I could.

"We[he and Jaycee] were in the same building about

a month ago, twenty feet apart, and I asked the DA, I asked Mr. Clinchard, to introduce me to her. And he said, no. So, I'm curious to know whether you think if two hundred forty-one years, eight months to life is appropriate for Nancy."

A reporter spoke up at that point and asked, "That's the offer for both of them?"

Tapson replied, "Oh, no! His is four hundred forty years to life."

Another question came in. "What did they tell the Sheriff's investigators?"

Tapson responded, "Everything they wanted to know. Except they didn't produce any missing bodies. There's no other victims."

> Reporter: "So they did admit they did the kidnapping?"
> Tapson: "Oh, yes! There's no question about it. Full confession. Obviously Nancy had nothing to do with—well, legally you can argue she had something to do with all the sex stuff. But she really wasn't involved in that. She obviously is guilty of kidnapping and a lot of other charges. But based on what happened after all this stuff started, they became the bizarre family that they were. She should at least be able to walk on the beach, probably with a walker, at some point in time before she dies."

A reporter wanted to know, "What kind of offer are you looking for, for Nancy?"

Tapson said, "Something like twenty to thirty years. Something like that. But a lot of your viewers—they're going to say, 'Ah, that lawyer! Look at that! She should be locked up forever. Blah, blah, blah.' But based upon what I know, in the relationship between Nancy and the kids and Jaycee, I don't think that length of time is appropriate."

Another reporter asked, "What was her relationship?"

Tapson replied, "She was their mother. She delivered the kids. She fed them. Took them places. I mean they had that kind of relationship—that was *like* a mother."

A reporter queried, "Was Nancy involved in the sexual . . ."

Tapson responded even before the full question was asked. "Nah. Nothing. I know, because of the law, she's an aider and abettor. That's another argument. But as far as actually being involved in any of the sexual stuff, she wasn't."

> *Reporter: "Did she grab Jaycee?"*
> *Tapson: "Of course."*
> *Reporter: "So what has she (Nancy) confessed to?"*
> *Tapson: "Kidnapping. False imprisonment."*
> *Reporter: "She grabbed Jaycee while Phil was driving?"*
> *Tapson: "Yes, yes, yes. That's a given. We're not arguing about that. So now, what's a fair settlement?"*

One reporter said, "What do you predict will happen on March 17 (the next scheduled court date).

Tapson answered, "We'll set a trial date. Mr. Garrido may or may not plead that day. I don't know. He has no expectations of getting out."

"Where were you twenty feet away from Jaycee?"

Tapson said, "The Detectives' Bureau in Placerville."

"Is Nancy prepared to go to trial?"

Tapson smiled and replied, "Her lawyer is. How's that?"

One reporter asked, "When did all of this happen?"

Tapson said, "The last month or so."

"What prompted that?"

Tapson answered, "Through their lawyers—they wanted to talk to them (Phil and Nancy). We were there (meaning himself and Susan Gellman).

A reporter asked, "What is your best case for why someday your client should walk free?"

Tapson heaved a big sigh and responded, "She had a normal life, went to Leavenworth, gets enthralled with Mr. Garrido. She never used drugs. Never was in trouble. Gets in his grasp and things go down the tubes from there. And, admittedly, she cooperated with being under his authority. Under his thumb. So, obviously, at trial, we're going to have to argue Stockholm Syndrome and Patty Hearst stuff. There's lots of psychiatric evidence to show that she was under his thumb or whatever you want to call it. Even the DA said he's (Phil's) a master manipulator. They've already conceded that point."

A reporter wanted to know, "What would there be gained by you talking to Jaycee?"

Tapson said, "I just want her opinion. Let's ask her and the kids. What do you want to happen to Nancy? And then tell the DA that."

Reporter: "What was the point of Jaycee being there in the detectives office?"
Tapson: "To see what she had to say. It was only with Nancy. Not with Phillip."
Reporter: "Did they (Jaycee and Nancy) see each other?"
Tapson: "Yep."
Reporter: "What happened?"
Tapson: "I can't talk about that."

A reporter asked, "Did they just see each other? Or did they talk to each other?"

Tapson replied, "I don't have a comment about that."

Another question was, "Does your client want to disengage her fate from that of her husband?"

Tapson answered with a small smile, "She doesn't want to disengage anything. But hopefully she will, with urging on my part."

A question came in, "How did your client react after seeing Jaycee?"

Tapson replied, "Tears."

A reporter wanted to know, "Whose idea was it to get them together?"

Tapson said, "The police and mine."

"Was it a scenario where Jaycee was listening to their statements?"

Tapson answered, "Yes."

A reporter asked if Jaycee and Nancy were twenty feet apart during the meeting. Tapson said no. He was the one who was twenty feet away. Tapson then added that Jaycee and Nancy were as far away from each other as he was from the reporter, which was about four feet. In other words, right across a table from each other.

The last question from a reporter was, "Could the two hundred forty-one years already mentioned be because that is what Jaycee wants for Nancy?"

Tapson responded, "It could very well be. But I'd like to know that."

As usual, attorneys not connected to the case gave their analysis to reporters about this latest information. A number of these attorneys spoke to KTVU television news. Joe Dane, an Orange County, California, defense lawyer, who had been a prosecutor for twelve years, weighed in on Tapson's statements. Danes said, "Before the El Dorado County DA signs off on it (a plea deal) they want to see if there is some remorse there, and to make sure they are doing their duty to the public in seeing if there are other victims."

Stephen Munketl, a Nevada City, California, defense attorney stated that the prosecution had a high visibility case with "outrageously harmful behavior" on the part of the Garridos. "One of the few things the defense has to motivate a better settlement by the prosecution is the time, trouble, and expense and stress of everybody having to go through the trial process to get the same result." One of the individuals who would have to be on the stand during a trial would be Jaycee Dugard. All of the things she had told the grand jurors in secret would now be out in the open.

Jeff Rubenstein, who was a defense lawyer, and had been a prosecutor, thought that Tapson's chances of getting a jury to reduce Nancy Garrido's sentence to twenty or thirty years only stood about a 5 percent chance of happening. But under the circumstances, Tapson didn't have many other options.

And Golden Gate University criminal law professor Nancy Rugberg said, "I could imagine if I were a prosecutor in the case, as long as I could get a satisfying lengthy sentence, I might want to suggest to the victim the best outcome would be a plea bargain rather than put her though more emotional anguish."

Just how Carl Probyn felt about all of this was expressed in remarks soon after he heard Stephen Tapson's comments. Carl stated, "I made my wife promise me that if we catch these people, that they would not cut a deal. Because the woman always says, 'I was coerced' and they always cut a deal." Carl added that he made Terry promise that the woman in this case, Nancy, would not get a plea deal. It was Nancy, after all, who had grabbed Jaycee, used a stun gun on her, and forced her into the car.

Carl related about Jaycee's and her daughters' present situation, "This is nothing like what people think it is. We're not having barbecues every Sunday and it's all back to normal."

As far as people who lived on Walnut Avenue near Antioch were concerned, they were not in favor of any kind of plea deal for Nancy Garrido. Helen Boyer told a reporter, "I don't think they should go any lighter on her. She was in on it, she helped with it, and she gets what she deserves. It's worse than murder because they wrecked that girl's life."

Johnny Unpingco was even more intransigent in his remarks. "People like that deserve the death sentence! Murder, that's something you could possibly justify in self-defense. But to actually keep someone captive and keep them in the yard as long as they did, that's sick. He ruined their lives."

If Stephen Tapson's comments to the press caused a stir on February 28, 2011, it was DA Vern Pierson who did so at another hearing on March 17, 2011. And, as usual, the fireworks were not in the courtroom, but outside. DA Pierson released a statement to the press about Tapson's remarks concerning mercy at the El Dorado County DA's Office.

Pierson began by stating that Tapson had questioned his lack of compassion for Nancy Garrido, since she confessed on her own free will at the detectives' office in January. Pierson added, "Perhaps my alleged lack of compassion comes from my awareness of many disgusting facts concerning Nancy Garrido's personal involvement in this case."

Pierson noted once again that it was Nancy Garrido who had leapt out of the vehicle to grab Jaycee off the street on June 10, 1991. And Nancy had even used a taser on the girl. Pierson then asked what kind of person would marry a convicted rapist in Leavenworth

Penitentiary and later videotape children in parks so that Phillip Garrido could watch the videos to satisfy his sexual pleasures.

And then Pierson dropped a bombshell about heretofore unknown information. "In 1993, Nancy Garrido was in the back of a van luring and videotaping a five-year-old child to bend over in front of the camera. Nancy Garrido was not an unwilling participant. She was actively videotaping a five-year-old child for the express purpose of providing her rapist husband with sexually perverse entertainment."

Pierson added that Nancy Garrido had videotaped young children even before the 1991 kidnapping of Jaycee Dugard. He summed up his statement by expressing, "I do not think Nancy Garrido deserves my compassion."

Perhaps caught off guard by this press statement, Tapson later blurted out to a news reporter, "Jeez, Vern (Pierson). I didn't know you were that pissed off at me!" And then recovering his composure, he said to another reporter, "I'm waiting for something from heaven to save us all."

Always displaying an ironic sense of humor, Tapson told one journalist, "The offer came down to one hundred forty years and eight months for Nancy. And due to my superior negotiating skills it's now one hundred eighty years to life."

Lost in all the uproar, due to Vern Pierson's revelations, were some comments by Phillip Garrido's lawyer, Susan Gellman. Gellman rarely said anything outside of the courthouse to reporters, but she did this time. Gellman related, "Let's just say for the sake of argument that nothing happened on this case. Phillip Garrido is still on parole to the state of Nevada, so he would be spending the rest of his life in prison in any event."

And then she stated a very important point. A journalist wanted to know why all of this was taking so long in pretrial motions. Gellman said that even though the outcome looked obvious to one and all, she still had to give her client the best representation possible. The law demanded that. To do otherwise could have serious consequences. An appeals court could later look at everything she did for her client, and if she came up short, the whole process would have to begin with a new lawyer for Phillip Garrido. Everything would be back to square one, and she did not want that to happen.

And so it went, with what Judge Phimister called a "glacial-like pace." Yet, he too knew as Gellman did that everything had to be beyond a later overturning of his decisions by an appeals court. So he erred on the side of caution and gave Gellman more time to gather facts about the case.

If Susan Gellman was usually tight-lipped about the case, the opposite was true of Stephen Tapson. In a very unexpected move, he commented to reporters, not about what his client Nancy Garrido was going to do at the next hearing, but what Phil Garrido was going to do. Tapson said before the April 7 hearing, "Unless some hitch develops, I'm 99 percent sure Phil will plead to the sheet and possibly be sentenced at the same time if the judge has figured out the correct number of hundreds of years." In other words, Tapson expected Phil to plead guilty to all charges and be sentenced that very same day.

Tapson said he was basing this on discussions he had heard between Gellman and DA Vern Pierson. As far as his client Nancy went, Tapson said he was not going to accept any plea deal that gave her a hundred plus year sentence. He was still holding out for a forty-year sentence.

Concerning Tapson's statements, neither Gellman nor Pierson had any comments. But Katie Callaway Hall certainly did. She told a reporter for the *Sacramento Bee,* "We all knew he was guilty, and in that sense now we can go forward and he can be sentenced and the ordeal can be over. I can put it away." As far as Nancy went, Katie said, "I have a feeling Nancy's just trying to save her own butt at this point. I don't think she's going to be thinking of Jaycee."

Tapson, as usual, made some more colorful comments about Nancy's case. He told a reporter for the *Mountain Democrat,* "I made a comment about her walking on the beach with a walker. Now it's looking more like a scooter."

If Tapson was still trying to whip up support for a more lenient sentence for Nancy, it wasn't working. At a rate of about nineteen-to-one, comments by ordinary people to the Sacramento news station Channel 13 in Sacramento were very hostile toward Nancy. One comment was, "Rot in hell, Nancy and Phillip!!!!!" Another was "Paste 'child molester' tags on their cells for all their neighbors to see." And a third person stated, "Hopefully angry prisoners have access to them and the prison guards don't do their job."

On April 7, 2011, the gallery was packed at the Placerville courthouse where Phil and Nancy were to appear, in expectation of Phil announcing that he was pleading guilty. In the background, fifteen television film crews had their large cameras up and operating. When the couple was escorted to the jury box, to await the proceedings, Phil mouthed the words, "I love you," to Nancy, who teared up at his gesture.

Proceedings began, and Judge Phimister asked how Phillip Garrido pleaded to the charges. To everyone's surprise, Susan Gellman answered for her client, "Not guilty."

As soon as the hearing was over, Stephen Tapson stepped outside to be greeted by a throng of reporters. He declared, "I'm sorry guys. I'm the one who unleashed the yellow jackets at the picnic." He added that Susan Gellman must be secretly chortling at his unfortunate earlier comments.

Gellman was not chortling. In fact, she was angrier than anyone had ever seen her after a court hearing. Gellman told the mass of reporters, "He (Tapson) shouldn't have been speaking for Phillip. Who does that? Who says those kinds of things?"

Gellman added, "We're doing our job, or at least I'm doing my job, which is to zealously advocate for my client. That's what I'm doing. Phillip will probably spend the rest of his life in prison. But that doesn't mean I roll over and play dead."

Nothing ever seemed to play out as planned when it came to the Garridos' case. Less than three weeks after pleading not guilty in court on April 7, 2011, things were brewing behind the scenes in El Dorado County. On Monday, April 25th, the DA's office contacted Stephen Tapson and Susan Gellman about a possible plea deal for Nancy Garrido. What followed was three days of intensive negotiations.

Vern Pierson made it clear to Tapson and Gellman that a plea deal for Nancy was contigent upon Phil pleading guilty to all counts and not launching any appeal about his sentence. Gellman said later, "It was pretty clear that this was the best we were going to get."

And what Phil Garrido would get in the deal was 431 years of prison time. Both Phil Garrido and Susan Gellman were already convinced that even if he went to trial, it was highly unlikely that a jury would be any more lenient with him. All he could do now was try and be part of a deal that would somehow help Nancy.

On Thursday, April 28, 2011, it appeared as if a deal was finally about to be finalized. Even Judge Phimister was taken off guard by the approach of a final decision. Phimister said, "Details were still being hammered out in the 35 minute hearing, I only had an hour myself to review the plea agreements."

What the DA's office was offering was 36 years to life for Nancy Garrido. She would be eligible for parole after 31 years, which would make her 86 years old at that point, should she live that long.

Nancy sobbed quietly as she pleaded guilty to her charges. Finally a bailiff handed her a tissue, which she clutched in her shackled hands. By comparison, Phil was composed and unemotional as he pled guilty to all his charges. In fact he even corrected Judge Phimister on one point about an aspect of his 1976 conviction for the kidnapping and rape of Katie Callaway.

All of this had happened so suddenly that only a handful of reporters were on hand for the landmark decision in the case. After the pleas were done, Vern Pierson addressed the small gathering of reporters in front of the courthouse. Pierson said that Jaycee's willingness to testify if called upon to do so allowed the DA's office to take a hard line against the Garridos. Pierson added, "Jaycee's courage and willingness to confront her abductors directly led to the defendants' plea and life sentences. She's very relieved her daughters would not have to testify."

In fact, a short statement by Jaycee was also read to the media. It stated, "I am relieved that Phillip and Nancy

Garrido have finally acknowledged their guilt and confessed to their crimes against me and my family."

Pierson also let it be known that he had asked Jaycee if she wanted to speak at the June 2nd sentencing of Phil and Nancy Garrido. As of April 28th, Pierson said he did not know the answer to his question.

Along with Jaycee, Katie Callaway Hall had a statement about the pleas of guilty by the Garridos. Katie's statement declared, "I am extremely happy that my ordeal with Phillip Garrido finally comes to a close. I know that the El Dorado District Attorneys Office is making sure that this time, Garrido will not be able to talk his way out of prison and past the parole systems."

Pierson was asked by a reporter if he thought Phil Garrido had any remorse for what he had done. Pierson replied, "Personally, no, I do not. But that is for someone else to judge."

As usual, Stephen Tapson was not at a loss for colorful statements. He said to reporters, "I told you from the get-go Nancy said just do the best you can. 'I don't want Jaycee and the kids to go through the actual trial.' Obviously you don't want to plead your client to a life sentence. But that's the best I could get and that's what she was willing to do. In her view now she has made peace with God. She wants to get on with life or what's left of it. Obviously she knows she committed a serious wrong. I believe she is genuinely sorry for what she's done."

Susan Gellman had nothing to say after the court hearing in front of the courthouse. But she did talk to a reporter from KCRA television station later. Gellman said that that Phil and Nancy asked for one more face to face meeting with each other before formal sentencing. After that they would never see each other again. Gellman related, "They seem to be at peace with that. They seem to be at peace that they will see each other at a different time." By that, they probably meant in the afterlife.

One of the lead El Dorado Sheriffs Office detectives, who was in constant contact with Jaycee and her family, didn't buy the argument that Phil and Nancy Garrido were taking a plea deal to spare Jaycee and the girls from going through a trial. This detective told a journalist after the hearing, "One thing that irritates me beyond belief is the idea that is being reported that the Garridos pled guilty because they care so much about Jaycee and the girls. That the Garridos were willing to fall on the sword to save Jaycee and the girls the torture of having to go through trial.

"None of that is true. The truth is, that the evidence we have against the Garridos that would be presented to the public if there was a trial is devastating for them. It would show the world how sick and twisted they really are. If there is no trial, the public never hears about most of the disgusting details of their crimes."

CHAPTER 38

"BEYOND HORRIBLE!"

On June 2, 2011, the El Dorado County Superior Court in Placerville was once again filled to capacity. At 9:00 A.M., the proceedings began with Phil and Nancy Garrido being escorted into the jury box, along with their lawyers. A few preliminary matters were addressed by Judge Douglas Phimister, and then both Tina Dugard, Jaycee's aunt, and Terry Probyn, Jaycee's mother, were suddenly at a lectern, ready to address the court with victim impact statements.

Both women were very emotional and filled with rage at Phil and Nancy Garrido, who sat about twenty feet away from them. While Nancy looked at the women through tears, Phil only stared at the floor. Tina Dugard spoke in part about the grief and suffering inflicted by the Garridos on her entire family. She said, "My mother died of a broken heart because of you! Jaycee was the center of her world." Tina then declared that no words that Phil or Nancy could ever say would be enough to absolve them of their guilt and depravity concerning their mistreatment of her niece.

Terry Probyn next stood before the lectern and glared at the Garridos. Terry said that on May 3, 1980, a beautiful baby was born, and she was named Jaycee. Of Jaycee, Terry said that she was a kindhearted and compassionate soul. "I lived and breathed for that baby." Whenever Jaycee had a hard time sleeping, Terry would sing the song "You Are My Sunshine" to her. The last line of that song was "Please don't take my sunshine away." And, of course, that's exactly what happened on June 10, 1991, when Jaycee was eleven years old.

Terry said that her world was turned upside down, and she ranted, raved, cursed, and thought she would go insane. She wondered if Jaycee was frightened, cold, and hungry. She also wondered how God had allowed such evil to occur.

Turning directly to Nancy Garrido, Terry declared, "It was you, Nancy, who took her. I hate you both! I'm sickened that she had to suffer because of you!" Terry added that Jaycee would be ashamed to think that Nancy ever loved her.

Regarding Phil, Terry said that he was self-serving and despicable. Then she said that her energy from now on would be spent helping any mother and father who had a child missing. It would be her quest for the rest of her days. As for Angel and Starlit, Terry said, "They know what you did to their mother. They realize your backyard was a prison and understand your filthy, despicable secret. They are aware that they have been deceived, and I am here to tell you that there is no love lost."

Additionally, Terry read a short statement from Shayna. Because of the Garridos and their actions, Shayna had been forced to miss sharing birthdays, proms, parties, and family events with Jaycee.

Shayna's statement declared: *I hope you live a very long life in a cold dark place. You will slowly rot in prison. You'll never be able to manipulate anyone again. If you spent all of eternity in hell, it would not be enough. There is no salvation for you!*

Then Terry read from a statement prepared by Jaycee. Her daughter began by saying why she chose not to be in court: *I have chosen my mom today because I refuse to waste another second of my life in your presence.* Then Jaycee stated that Phillip was wrong in all his beliefs, and that what he and Nancy did was "reprehensible." Jaycee stated that they always justified what they did; but in the end, it was always someone else who suffered because they could not control themselves.

As for Nancy specifically, Jaycee wrote that there was no excuse for her actions. What she did was to *trick young girls for his evil pleasure.* Jaycee declared that no God would ever condone her actions. As for Phil: *Words were your tools of choice, and you wielded them with brutal force.* Then she wrote, *I hated every second of every day of eighteen years because of you and the sexual perversion you forced on me.*

Jaycee added that they could both save their empty words about how sorry they were. She hoped they both spent as many sleepless nights as she had. She related that she was angry because they had stolen her life and the lives of her family and friends: *I have wonderful friends and family around me now. Something you can never take away from me again. You do not matter anymore.*

Before sentencing, Nancy Garrido had a chance to speak. She declined, and instead had lawyer Stephen Tapson read a short prepared statement. In a low voice, he read about Nancy's humiliation and sorrow about what had occurred. In part, Nancy stated, *Being sorry is not enough. Words cannot express my remorse for what I did. I stole her childhood. When I walk by a mirror, I hate what I see.*

Nancy Garrido's written words mainly fell on deaf ears. Judge Phimister sentenced her to the full extent of the law, which came to thirty-six years of prison time. Phimister also denied a motion by Tapson that Nancy be allowed one more visit with Phil, before being sent to prison. Members of the El Dorado County Sheriff's Office escorted Nancy out of the court. As she was exiting, she mouthed some words to Phil. Some in the gallery thought she was saying, "I love you."

Phil Garrido did not speak on his own behalf, either. Instead, Susan Gellman, his lawyer, read from a short prepared statement. She said, "'He had accepted responsibility for his actions and he has done this without any expectation of leniency. He has done this because he wanted to spare everyone, especially Miss Dugard and her children, a trial.'"

Despite this supposed contrition, Judge Phimister saved his angriest words for Phil Garrido. Phimister declared, "Basically what you did, you took a human being and turned them into chattel. A piece of furniture, to be used at your whim. You reinvented slavery. I think Mr. Garrido qualifies as a poster child of a sexual predator. What you've done to this child is beyond horrible!"

With those words, and many more about Phil's depravity and his manipulation of the court system and the parole system over the previous years, Judge Phimister sentenced him to 431 years.

* * *

When the sentencing was over, events ended in full circle. UC Berkeley officer Ally Jacobs had been in the gallery watching all that occurred. On a grassy area outside the courthouse, she faced a battery of microphones and reporters. Modest, as always, she repeated that she just had been doing her job in August 2009. But, in reality, it had been much more than that, as far as she and Lisa Campbell were concerned. Their actions changed the lives of many, many people forever.

And as so often happened, outside of the actual courtroom, there was one last dramatic event. On the afternoon of June 2, Judge Douglas Phimister released major portions of the grand jury transcripts from when Jaycee Dugard had testified. At last, here, in Jaycee Lee Dugard's own words, was a clear look at what had occurred during the kidnapping and through her years of captivity.

On September 21, 2010, during sworn testimony, DA Vern Pierson asked Jaycee specifically about her memory of the morning of June 10, 1991. To his questions, Jaycee replied, "I made breakfast and left the house. I think my stepdad, Carl, was in the garage. I [began] walking to the bus stop. It's up the hill, [about] a ten-minute walk. I called to Carl 'I'm leaving,' and not halfway [crossed the street] because Carl taught me to face the oncoming traffic.

"There's a bend in the hill that bends up to the bus stop. And I got halfway there, and this car comes up behind me. I didn't think it was weird at the time, but it kind of pulled in close to me. I thought he was going to ask for directions, because he started to say something. And all of a sudden, his hand shoots out of the car window, and I feel a shock. And I stumble back into the bushes. I'm sitting down in the bushes, trying to back away, but I feel like my whole body wouldn't work. It was tingly and nothing worked."

(Obviously, this was different from Carl's recollection
that the woman passenger had jumped out, Tasered
Jaycee, and dragged her, screaming, into the vehicle.)

Jaycee continued, "All of a sudden, I'm in the car,
and there's something on top of me. And I feel like
there's pressure on me. Like a body. Legs. But there was
something on top of me, too, like a blanket, because it
was really hot. [I was] on the floorboard, facedown. I
remember the car pulling away, and I did lose control
of my bladder. I felt embarrassed. My limbs felt tingly
still, and just everything was jumbled."

Asked about a second person, Jaycee said, "There
had to be, because I could feel the pressure. I could feel
legs moving, switching around. I could hear a voice
some time later. The person that took me [asked] later,
'Do you want something to drink?' And I heard voices
in the front, and the man said, 'I can't believe we got
away with it,' and he started laughing.

"And then some mumbling. It didn't sound manly,
so my instinct was that it was a woman. [Being in the
car] seemed like forever. It was really hot and there
was still something on top of me. It was kind of like I
was blacking out."

Pierson asked about what happened when the vehicle finally stopped. Jaycee said, "I could hear the car
stop. The door slammed shut and, like, [a] squeaking
of a gate or something. He put the blanket back over
me, and he said be really quiet because there were
dogs patrolling the area. He said he had Dobermans,
and that if I was to run, or try to do anything, they
would come after me.

"He walked me . . . I couldn't tell where we were. . . ."
(Then the next two pages went blank. Judge Phimister ordered this blackout whenever passages of sexual
molestation occurred.)

When the transcript picked up again, Pierson

asked, "Were you afraid of him from the moment this all started?"

Jaycee replied, "I was very scared. I didn't know who he was. I didn't know why he was doing this. I just wanted to go home. I think in the bathroom I kept telling him that. I told him, 'If you're holding me for ransom, my family doesn't have a lot of money.' I didn't know his purpose. I'd heard about kidnapping before. They were usually for money."

Jaycee was shown two photos of Phil Garrido. She said, "That's the man who took me." Then she continued, "He didn't say much in the beginning. Very quiet, just telling me what to do. About the dogs, [he told me] they were very territorial, and if they found anybody on their property that they didn't know, they would attack." Jaycee also related that in this early period, she never saw the supposed woman, who had also been in the car.

Of the early experience there, Jaycee related, "I was sitting on the couch for a while, petting the cats, and he went upstairs. Then he came back down and he said that we were going to take a little walk to the back[yard]. And I asked him, 'When can I go home?' My mom was going to be worried. But he didn't say anything. He just said, 'This is what we're going to do.' And he put the blanket back on me and said that we were going to walk, and that he would lead the way.

"We walked. I could feel . . . I didn't have any shoes on. I didn't have anything on but the towel. So I could feel grass. And then later it turned to, like, cement or something. And then we were standing in front of something. You know when something is near. I could hear a lock turn, like a click, and a door open, and then I'm ushered into . . . I feel a carpet. I'm ushered into what felt like the back [of a room].

"I didn't see the first part [of the room], but

music . . ." And then the transcript stopped again for four pages, because Phil Garrido was raping Jaycee at that point. When it began again, Jaycee continued for a short time describing the layout of the yard and the house, as she knew it. This short section was interrupted again by two missing pages, in which more sexual molestation and rape occurred.

Pierson asked Jaycee about Phil's stun gun. Jaycee said it had a "zappy" sound. "He would have it on a table, and when I didn't want to do something he wanted me to do, he would turn it on and say something like, 'You don't want it to happen again. You should be good.' I didn't want it to happen again, so I was good. I tried to do what he wanted me to do, even though I didn't like it."

More blank pages followed, concerning what Phil Garrido did to Jaycee, when she was "good" to him. This went on weekly for three years, according to Jaycee. Phil would call their sexual episodes, his "runs." She was isolated and alone in a room she called the "studio room" for a year or more. She didn't know how long. She recalled, "He did bring me a cat. It wasn't very happy in that room, I guess, because it would pee everywhere. He started smelling it, and he took it away."

It was after this period that Jaycee first recalled seeing Nancy at the house. She didn't know how many months after she was first brought there that this occurred. Phil referred to Nancy as his wife, and Jaycee remembered, "Nancy started coming in and feeding me. I was basically living in a room. The blue one. I had a pallet on the floor, and they were living on a pullout couch. Basically, we were all sleeping in the same room. We watched TV together. I didn't feel as lonely anymore. For the first year, I was by myself mostly.

"Things changed. He moved me in next door to

where they were sleeping. And after the run (sex), he would go get food, and we'd sit up and watch TV and movies and stuff. Eventually Nancy started getting me clothes. There was a time that Phil, all of a sudden, wasn't showing up." (This was when he was arrested in 1993 for a parole violation.) "Nancy would come in and bring me food, and we would watch TV together. And I remember asking her, 'Where's Phil?' And she said that he was on this island for a little vacation or something. It was nice because I didn't have sex or runs or anything. I think it lasted about a month. We would eat dinner together and watch TV, but usually she would just lock the door and leave. It had iron doors. Iron gate."

Jaycee later learned that Phil actually had been arrested because, she testified, "he came back with an ankle bracelet. By then, I was watching morning shows, [which] would give the date. So I had a better idea of time. After Phil came back from prison, the runs were less often." Jaycee thought they occurred about once a month. "By that time, I think Nancy was smoking crank. And sometimes she would tell me, 'I'll take this run for you.'" (This meant Nancy would have sex with Phil instead of Jaycee.)

Jaycee recalled her first child, Angel, being born on August 18, 1994. She also recalled Phil saying that "he was eventually going to stop having sex with me, and he was really trying to change and wanted us all to be a family. He took the wall out from the studio room because we lived over there for a little bit. He was always switching us back and forth. And during the runs situation, he started to listen to the walls and he bought bionic ears. He said he heard voices and stuff. I could never hear anything, but he said he heard a lot of voices and he had to make sure the cops weren't out there or something. He was getting paranoid."

Jaycee noted, "It seemed like everything changed when she (Angel) was born. Phil made a fence in the back, just a small portion, and I could go out there with the baby. He bought a little swing set and stuff."

Pierson asked Jaycee if she felt like Phil Garrido was still controlling her life. She answered, "Yeah. I didn't know where to go. Then I had a baby, and I just wanted it to be okay. I don't know if I was afraid that he would kill me, or something. He would get mad sometimes, but I don't think I was afraid for my life. I just felt like there was no other place for me."

About the so-called runs, she said they were less frequent, and "Nancy would take care of the baby in another building. These runs only lasted for maybe the night, and then it was over. In the beginning, Phil said I was helping him. That he had a sex problem and he got me so that he wouldn't have to do this to anybody else. So I was helping him."

Jaycee said that her second child, Starlit, was born on November 13, 1997. Jaycee recounted that after she and Phil knew she was pregnant for the second time, the runs stopped altogether. It was also around this time that Jaycee agreed to call Nancy "Mom." She recalled, "He (Phil) said I should pick a name that I wanted to be called. Before that, he'd been calling me 'Snoopy.' So I picked the name 'Alyssa.'"

"He started his printing business and I started working there. We had a lot more freedom outside. The kids could go play out there, and we had a pool, one of the stand-up ones aboveground. I had my own tent. It was really nice to have my own room and tent space. We just started acting like a family, and we would celebrate their birthdays together. Just trying to be normal."

Pierson showed Jaycee some handwritten notes that she had kept while confined. He asked her to explain about them. She said, "It's just like a journal that I kept. I didn't want to write a lot because I was afraid he would find it and be mad. But I didn't totally love the situation that we were in. So I kind of kept it hidden and didn't write that much. When I did, it was usually because I was feeling strong feelings about being trapped and not having a life and just wanting to be free. Free to come and go as I pleased."

After a short break, Pierson showed Jaycee a note that she had written and asked, "Among other things, you indicated that you sometimes wanted to run away and essentially get away from the situation that you were in." Jaycee said that was true. Pierson continued, "On the second page, you indicated that you would never leave them, that you were a coward. Did you ever attempt to escape from the situation?"

Jaycee responded, "No." When asked why, she replied, "In the beginning, I was scared. I didn't know what I would do. I was afraid of, I guess, what Phillip would do. I forgot to mention it before. I don't know if I should mention it. . . ." And then there were two missing pages that obviously concerned sexual abuse and possibly threats by Phil. The text picked up again by Jaycee relating, "He was so sorry for what he did. He said, 'I can't believe I did it.'"

Later she made reference to her compound: "It was just very confining. We went places later on as a family, but never by myself. And I wanted him to teach me how to drive and stuff. And that never came. I didn't know what to do. I couldn't leave. I had the girls. I didn't know where to go, what I would do for money or anything."

Pierson showed her a note she had written on March 28, 2006, and asked Jaycee about it. She said, "I wanted to see my mom. What I always wanted to do.

When the girls first went out, they would duck in the car and not be seen by the neighbors. That was in the beginning.

"I just didn't want to make him mad. He would go through . . . not physically violent, but just really mad. Like, we had the printing business, and he would shut it down, and then we wouldn't make any money. I tried to go with the flow, that kind of thing."

About Nancy, Jaycee recalled, "When she was coming in [the room], she would bring me things. She said that she couldn't stay long because she would always start crying and tell me how sorry she was, and she couldn't believe he did it. It was very hard for her to come in and see me.

"I would tell her how lonely I was and wished she would stay longer and talk to me." Jaycee added that Nancy was never present during the sexual runs, but that she was aware of what was happening. Jaycee added, "Later, when I had the baby [Angel], she would say, 'Oh, I'll take this run, so you can spend time with the baby.'"

Once again, when asked by Pierson why she never tried to escape, Jaycee said, "I felt like I didn't have anywhere else to go. I knew my stepdad . . . I felt like he didn't like me. They would be happier without my being at home. He would always call them the 'Three Musketeers'—him, my mom, and his daughter (Shayna). And I was helping someone (Phil), even though it was in a really sick and perverted way. Helping him so that it wouldn't happen to anybody else. He said he needed help with his sexual problem, and that I was helping him. He didn't say that he would take somebody else, but the impression I got was that I was helping prevent something."

Pierson asked about Phil videotaping the runs (the

sexual abuse episodes). Jaycee said that he didn't videotape each one, but that he might have done so with her five to ten times. Jaycee thought the last time this happened was right before Angel was born. And then Jaycee added, "I know that Nancy used to talk about her hating summers because he would have her go out and videotape kids in the . . ." (Two pages were then blanked out.)

When Jaycee's testimony continued, she related that after her release from captivity she had watched, along with a detective, some videos Phil had made. She agreed that she was depicted in the videos.

Regarding these videos, Garrett Schiro, a deputy sheriff for the Contra Costa County Sheriff's Office, later testified to the grand jury. He had been involved in the search on the Garridos' property on August 29, 2009. When Schiro started removing trash from one corner of the lot, he discovered a large black trash bag filled with VHS and eight-millimeter tapes. There were seventy-five or more such tapes. Some sort of "sticky substance" had "melted them together." Schiro set the bag aside so that forensic technicians could take a look at the tapes later.

VHS videotapes were sent to Richard Pesce, who was an El Dorado County District Attorney's Office investigator. He testified that he went down to Aerospace NASA in the Los Angeles area to try and restore what was on the videotapes.

The tapes had been partially destroyed by a chemical that "melted" the plastic housing and encased the actual videotape. By a very tedious and time-consuming process, using various techniques, Pesce was able to "unspool the tapes and put them into new housing so that the contents could be watched."

Pesce and his team were able to recover about 60

percent of the images videotaped on the original tape. And then pages 125 through 140 were blanked out by orders of Judge Phimister. These pages included material concerning what had been found by investigators on the videotapes that were made by the Garridos.

By page 141, a glimpse of what had occurred on the videotapes could be ascertained. Pesce said in direct testimony, "Crotch level of this little girl, and the camera was stationary. And the little girl noticed the camera was recording. She asked Nancy about it. And Nancy deflected and said, 'I don't know anything about a camera.'

"And when the girl's father appeared in the scene, Nancy casually draped a jacket over the camera so the dad wouldn't see the camera recording his daughter. In another scene, Phil and Nancy went to a park and found a spot where children were playing in the background in a play structure. Phil gave Nancy some instructions on how to use the videotape camera and how to pretend to film him while, in fact, filming the children in the background. The scene continues, Phil plays the guitar, sings a couple of songs, while Nancy is shooting past him on high zoom at the young children playing in the park."

Referencing another tape, Pesce noted, he had shown it to Jaycee and asked her about what sounded like another man's voice on the audio portion—in other words, different from Phil's voice. Jaycee told Pesce, "That's the way he talked. He used multiple voices and things like that." When asked by a grand juror if Phil Garrido had ever sold any of these tapes or passed them around, Pesce said they never found any evidence of that.

And then Pierson got to the point of the events of

August 26, 2009, and asked Jaycee to tell about what had occurred. She said, "His parole officer came to the house. I was scared. I didn't know what was going to happen. Phil said everything was going to be okay. He said he just needed to set the record straight. He never thought he was doing anything wrong.

"I said to him, 'Well, what do you want me to say?'" (Jaycee meant when she met with the parole officer at the station.) "He said, 'Just stick to the plan. And if they ask you any questions, just say you need an attorney. You just need to tell them that you're the girls' mother and you give me permission to take them around.' He was trying to get his church going, God's Desire."

Jaycee basically reiterated what already had been written about in the parole officer's report, but with a few major differences. One was that the parole officer came out to the car when she had been sent there by him after the initial meeting in the parole office, and Jaycee said that he called her "a liar."

She related, "He said I wasn't their mother. They were his (Phil's) brother's kids. They were going to call Child Protective Services, and I said, 'You can't take them away!'"

And then there was a key point about how and when Jaycee finally let an officer know that she was not Alyssa. This also differed from the parole officer's report. Jaycee testified, "An officer came in. Melanie. A female officer. The males were really scary. They thought I was a runaway. And they said they were going to arrest me, take me downtown, and find out who I really was.

"And Melanie came in and said that Phillip confessed and said that he had taken [me], and I started crying. She said, 'You need to tell me your name.'

And I said that I can't, because I hadn't said my name in eighteen years. And—"

Pierson interrupted her and asked, "Did she have you write it down?"

Jaycee replied, "I wrote it down. And then I wrote down my mom's name (*Terry Probyn*)."

It was those few written words that were the keys to unlocking Jaycee Lee Dugard's prison doors at last.

END NOTE

Even after the sentencing against Phillip and Nancy Garrido, for many the damage had already been done. When Phil Garrido kidnapped Jaycee Lee Dugard on June 10, 1991, it was like a large rock being thrown into a still pond. The shock waves spread out in all directions. Jaycee, her family, South Lake Tahoe, law enforcement officers, judicial officials and ordinary citizens were all affected to some degree. None more so than Jaycee and her daughters.

And all of it could be traced back to one individual: Phillip Garrido. In a very real sense, it was because he refused to keep the worst of his nature in check. Drug use only fueled his refusal to take responsibility for his actions. The use of LSD along with his erratic and narcissistic nature was a lethal combination. He readily admitted to being a spoiled child, and from the late 1960s onward, he acted upon his worst impulses.

Only when he was caught did Garrido pretend to mend his ways. Phil was good at that—convincing authorities in the judicial system and parole boards that he was a good candidate for release. Always a model prisoner, Phil bided his time until he was released.

And then, once again, he placed no restrictions upon himself when it came to doing what he desired, which included kidnapping and rape.

In many ways, Jaycee's case was not unlike a Thomas Hardy novel, where incidents that began as such small factors turned into a major tragedy. If there had been a roadblock on the highways out of the Tahoe Basin within the first crucial minutes after the kidnapping, none of the years of agony would have taken place. If Phillip Garrido's 1976 kidnapping and rape case had been looked at more closely by law enforcement in the summer of 1991, there may have been an inspection of his Walnut Avenue residence that year. If the Nevada parole board had factored in Phil's major drug bust of 1972, they may not have voted 3–2 to release him from the Nevada prison when they did. If Nancy Garrido had released Jaycee in 1993, when Phil went back to prison for six weeks, sixteen more years of captivity for Jaycee would have been avoided.

But as in Churchill's words, "the terrible ifs" accumulated, and freedom for Jaycee and her daughters had to wait until two vigilant women at UC Berkeley felt that something was wrong with Phil Garrido and the two girls who accompanied him to Sproul Hall on August 25, 2009. At least then, there was a chance for a new beginning for Jaycee, Angel, and Starlit.

There was one silver lining to all of this. Because of changes and improvements in the way sex offenders were monitored after all the news about Jaycee came out, a fourteen-year-old Concord girl was saved from a similar fate. In a very real sense, that girl owed her life and freedom to Jaycee. Without Jaycee, that girl most likely would have ended up raped and confined, or more likely dead.

Jaycee had endured what no one should have had

to endure. And yet she did it with such unbelievable dignity and grace, as to become the remarkable young woman that she is. Filled with compassion, strength, and an indomitable will—Jaycee became the daughter that any mother would be proud to call her own. She became the mother who any daughter would look up to and announce with pride that Jaycee was her Mom.